Hegelian-Lacanian Variations on Late Modernity

The current rise in new religions and the growing popularity of New Ageism is concomitant with an increasingly anti-philosophical sentiment marking our contemporary situation. More specifically, it is philosophical and psychoanalytic reason that has lost standing, faced with the triumph of post-secular "spirituality". Combatting this trend, this treatise develops a theoretical apparatus based on Hegelian speculative reason and Lacanian psychoanalysis.

With the aid of this theoretical apparatus, the book argues how certain conceptual pairs appear opposed through an operation of misrecognition christened, following Hegel, as "diremption". The failure to reckon with identities-in-difference relegates the subject to more vicious contradictions that define central aspects of our contemporary predicament. The repeated thesis of the treatise is that the deadlocks marking our contemporary situation require renewed engagement with dialectical thinking beyond the impasses of common understanding. Only by embarking on this philosophical-psychoanalytic "path of despair" (Hegel) will we stand a chance of achieving "joyful wisdom" (Nietzsche).

Developing a unique dialectical theory based on readings of Hegel, Lacan and Žižek, in order to address various philosophical and psychoanalytic questions, this book will be of great interest to anyone interested in German idealism and/or psychoanalytic theory.

Alireza Taheri provides psychoanalytic psychotherapy in a private practice in Toronto where he is also actively involved in teaching Lacanian theory at the Toronto Psychoanalytic Institute and Society. Alireza is a permanent faculty member of HamAva Psychoanalytic Institute in Tehran (Iran) where he teaches psychoanalytic theory and practice. He is also engaged in writing articles on philosophy and psychoanalysis and is presently the editor-in-chief and book review editor of *Psychoanalytic Discourse* (an independent international journal for the clinical, theoretical and cultural discussion of psychoanalysis).

Hegelian-Lacanian Variations on Late Modernity

Spectre of Madness

Alireza Taheri

Routledge
Taylor & Francis Group

LONDON AND NEW YORK

First published 2021
by Routledge
2 Park Square, Milton Park, Abingdon, Oxon OX14 4RN

and by Routledge
52 Vanderbilt Avenue, New York, NY 10017

Routledge is an imprint of the Taylor & Francis Group, an informa business

© 2021 Alireza Taheri

British Library Cataloguing-in-Publication Data
A catalogue record for this book is available from the British Library

Library of Congress Cataloging-in-Publication Data
Names: Taheri, Alireza, 1976– author.
Title: Hegelian-Lacanian variations on late modernity : spectre of madness / Alireza Taheri.
Description: New York: Routledge, 2020. |
Includes bibliographical references and index. | Summary: "The current rise in new religions and
the growing popularity of New Ageism is concomitant with an increasingly anti-philosophical
sentiment marking our contemporary situation. More specifically, it is philosophical and
psychoanalytic reason that has lost standing
faced with the triumph of post-secular "spirituality". Combatting this trend, this treatise develops
a theoretical apparatus based on Hegelian speculative reason and Lacanian psychoanalysis.
With the aid of this theoretical apparatus, the book argues how certain apparent contraries appear
opposed through an operation of misrecognition christened, following Hegel, as "diremption".
The failure to reckon with identities-in-difference relegates the subject to more vicious
contradictions that define central aspects of our contemporary predicament. The repeated thesis
of the treatise is that the deadlocks marking our contemporary situation require renewed
engagement with dialectical thinking beyond the impasses of common understanding. Only by
embarking on this philosophical-psychoanalytic "path of despair" (Hegel) will we stand a chance
of achieving "joyful wisdom" (Nietzsche). Developing a unique dialectical theory based on readings
of Hegel, Lacan and Zizek, in order to address various philosophical and psychoanalytic questions,
this book will be of great interest to anyone interested in German idealism and/or
psychoanalytic theory"– Provided by publisher.
Identifiers: LCCN 2020032308 (print) | LCCN 2020032309 (ebook) |
ISBN 9780367523077 (paperback) | ISBN 9780367523084 (hardback) |
ISBN 9781003057390 (ebook)
Subjects: LCSH: New Age persons. | Dialectical theology. | Reason. |
Psychoanalysis–Philosophy. | Hegel, Georg Wilhelm Friedrich, 1770-1831. |
Lacan, Jacques, 1901-1981.
Classification: LCC BP605.N48 T34 2020 (print) |
LCC BP605.N48 (ebook) | DDC 190–dc23
LC record available at https://lccn.loc.gov/2020032308
LC ebook record available at https://lccn.loc.gov/2020032309

ISBN: 978-0-367-52308-4 (hbk)
ISBN: 978-0-367-52307-7 (pbk)
ISBN: 978-1-003-05739-0 (ebk)

Typeset in Bembo
by Newgen Publishing UK

To the memory of my mother, Pari.

Contents

Acknowledgements

Firstly, my deepest thanks go to Donald Carveth who took the time to read my proposal and encourage me to write. I would also like to express my appreciation for the time Adrian Johnston, Sergio Benvenuto and Slavoj Žižek took to read and endorse my work. Many thanks to Hannah Wright and Kate Hawes from Routledge for all the effort they put into realizing the publication of my book. The many conversations I had with Joël Legault, Zabih Yaqeen, and Maziar Raz over the years enabled the dialectical shift on the Moebius strip from philosophic despair to joyful wisdom. My sisters (Sharzad and Mojan) have also been a source of support and love throughout this time. Most importantly, the love and care of my father (Siavash Taheri) and the many great conversations and exchanges we had over the years granted me the sobriety of spirit necessary for philosophic thought. Finally, the memory of my mother was the source of constant inspiration through every patient step of the conceptual labour involved in shaping this treatise. I dedicate this work to her.

Introduction

The paradox of self-reflection

… beginning where contraries are stringently opposed and where in their unyielding antagonism each element falls prey to *conceptual narcissistic suicidal aggression* by which inner contradiction transpires, through a process of oppositional determination, in the disparaged mode of a struggle of pure prestige with the unduly expelled other. The culprit here is the triumph of common understanding over speculative reason concomitant with the demise of dialectical thought (a pleonasm *par excellence*). Dialectical reason is not, to echo Žižek, this book's "topic" but is, rather, performed in the very form of its exposition. Thus, the head and tail of this speculative serpent meet to achieve the proverbial squaring of the circle.[1] If neurosis is the index of self-incarceration, we must wonder whether a book that spirals around itself, thereby mimicking the circularity of the repetition compulsion, is not the height of neurotic self-enclosure. Though this remains probable, one must not forget the *speculative* verity that only an exorbitant neurosis can lead the way out of neurosis. Every revolution paradoxically brings forth the new through the repetition of an older form. The book's self-revolving form thus embodies for us the unexpected identity-in-difference of the innovative and the timeworn.[2] This treatise rejects the usual format of segregation into chapters and eschews the form of the aphorism, espousing instead the musical practice of *variations on a theme*.[3]

If, as François Balmès (2007) argued, for every statement made by Lacan one can also find the opposite claim, I argue, it is because apparently opposed pairs conceal deep affinities that common understanding cannot fathom. Throughout this enquiry, I show how apparent contraries such as truth and lie, religiosity and atheism, as well as good and evil (to name a few) appear opposed through an operation of misrecognition I have christened, following Hegel, as "diremption".[4] I argue that the failure to reckon with identities-in-difference relegates the subject to deeper contradictions that define central aspects of our contemporary predicament. I use the word "paradox" to denote the unexpected identity of seemingly opposed elements as it literally evokes the idea of something beyond the grasp of ordinary doxa. By contrast, I reserve the term "contradiction" for the consequence of the diremption of the identity-in-difference in question. Where the former denotes a dynamic interrelation enriching both elements of the identity-in-difference, the latter signifies an insuperable impasse of thought. In contradiction, the opposed terms are mistakenly perceived as external to each other, while in paradox the alleged contraries are perceived as mutually implicated. Borrowing Kantian vocabulary, one may speak of "noumenal" unity obfuscated by "phenomenal" opposition. However, the opposition between the noumenal and the phenomenal also collapses as it can only perdure under the spell of diremption. By insisting on the identity-in-difference of noumena and phenomena we are repeating Žižek's move from epistemology to ontology, namely the move from Kant to Hegel. The unknowability of the world is henceforth not a consequence of human limitation but, rather, of the essentially "not-all" or incomplete-inconsistent character of the world itself: "*the limitation of phenomena is not external but internal,* in other words … the field of phenomena is *in itself* never 'all', complete, a consistent Whole" (Žižek, 2012a, 283). There is thus only a phenomenal realm and the noumenal is nothing other than phenomenon's non-self-identity; or as Žižek puts it, "there is no need for any positive transcendent domain of noumenal entities which limit phenomena from outside – phenomena with their inconsistencies, their self-limitations, are 'all there is.'" (ibid, 283). We may import this argument to the other aforementioned contraries: religiosity's non-self-identity makes it identical to atheism, truth's non-self-identity equates it with fiction and lie, the good's non-self-identity likens it to evil.

For Kant, reason must capitulate before metaphysical questions as these yield antinomies of thought, namely contradictory answers incommensurable with the principle of non-contradiction. Hegel agrees that reason encounters contradiction when probing foundational questions such as the spatial and temporal limits of the universe, the existence of an indivisible substance, the possibility of free will and the existence of God. However, Hegel takes this epistemological fact (the arising of antinomy) as an ontological clue. Hegel's response to Kant is that reason encounters contradiction because nature is *in-itself* contradictory or, in Lacanian parlance, *not-all.* According to Hegel, Kant wants "to remove contradiction from [the world] and then to transfer the contradiction to spirit, to reason, where it is allowed to remain unresolved" (Hegel, 1969, 237). For Hegel, the "world … is never and nowhere without contradiction" (ibid, 238). Thus, reason, far from entangling thought into an unnecessary quagmire, points in the right direction, namely the truth regarding contradiction. For Hegel, the antinomies of pure reason provide, therefore, a correct reflection of the contradictions of the natural world rather than testify to the follies of the mind. Kant aptly recognizes the ineluctability of contradiction but misses the final step which consists of taking these as *real* attributes of nature rather than shortcomings of reason. Insofar as Kant wants to hold on to a noumenal realm free of contradiction, we would say that his thinking is diremptive of the ontological paradoxes of nature. This diremption leads his philosophy into the contradiction of depending on a noumenal beyond which he cannot think.[5] The move from Kant's divided ontology of noumena and phenomena to Hegel's ontology of immanence necessarily takes us to another central theme of Hegelian dialectics, that of the identity of contraries. If we restrict ontology to the singular plane of phenomena, the latter must be envisioned as non-self-identical or, what comes to the same, as identical to its Other. Two principal interrelated philosophical ideas stand out in the transition from Kant to Hegel. The first concerns the abolition of ontological dualism for the sake of immanence, while the second involves the assertion of the unity of contraries. By absolving the realm of noumena and thereby reinstating the gap that allegedly separated noumena from phenomena as a fissure within phenomena itself, Hegel confirms both of these central philosophical postulates. If there is only one ontological plane (the first thesis regarding immanence), it is because noumena and phenomena form a dialectical unity of contraries (the second thesis).

This manner of conceptualizing the transition from Kant to Hegel echoes with the psychoanalytic concept of *structural impossibility*. For Lacan, the impossibility of enjoyment (castration) is not the result of an interdiction. Lacan is not as ardent a theorist of the law as he may appear. Impossibility is not tied to the imposition of a specific agent or socio-cultural norm. For Lacan, it is language itself that introduces an inevitable and therefore *structural* loss in the living body. In technical parlance, it is the incidence of the "master signifier" that determines castration. The limitation of enjoyment and the impossibility to find again the lost object are not the consequences of the paternal law but are, rather, imposed on human beings simply from the fact of speaking. My contention is that this Lacanian conceptualization of castration as *structural* is best grasped in light of the move from Kant to Hegel. Rather than view symbolic castration in terms of "an unconditional obedience of moral Law" (Copjec, 1996), I contend that it is best understood in light of the Hegelian conception of the unity of contraries. Symbolic castration represents an ideal point where the subject is reconciled with the identity of contraries and is no longer captive to the illusion of their opposition.[6] The difficulty of symbolic castration is not simply that one knows what it involves but refuses to accept it. Beyond the emotional difficulties such as the pain of loss, symbolic castration represents a challenge to ordinary cognition: how can two things that seem stringently opposed constitute a deeper identity? Kant's limitation on reason paradoxically attests to a refusal of castration insofar as it goes hand in hand with the stubborn insistence on non-contradictoriness. For Hegel, all things are contradictory in themselves though consciousness of such inner division will vary depending on the entity. While inanimate nature knows nothing of contradiction, finite living nature (e.g. animal life)[7] endures it in the form of pain.[8] Finally, humans represent the pinnacle of the consciousness of contradiction; awareness of this inner division is the cause of infinite anguish.[9] Things only evolve and develop at all because of the inner division that forbids stasis. Contradiction, for Hegel, is the origin of self-movement and hence also the source from where novelty is born.[10] The human, through its anguish, is the creature most attuned to grasping its own paradoxical nature as well as that of the world. In other words, the human is best equipped with fathoming castration.

Prior to Hegel, Lebrun explains, we had the "ontology of juxtaposition" where properties are simply juxtaposed rather than united.[11] In this community of properties we have *diversity* rather than *opposition*. There is union *and* difference here but no union *in* difference. As Lebrun's Hegel would say, the moments of similitude and dissemblance fall outside of each other (Lebrun, 1972, 272). Lebrun attributes to Kant the ontology of "real opposition" which, unlike the community of juxtaposed properties, does not put forward a simple indifferent diversity. Each term of a real opposition is determined in relation to its other (ibid, 290). However, the problem is that neither term of a given opposition is ever thought in-itself. Kant's ontology of real opposition is based on what Hegel calls the operation of "external reflection" through which the two terms of an opposition acquire their signification through contrast with one another. Self-reflection, by contrast, is the operation through which each term is considered in-itself and, moreover, through which this consideration leads to a passage into its Other via a process of *self-undermining*. Self-reflection leads to each term's suppression and passage into its Other. Contradiction is now inscribed in the texture of concepts; it is not the effect simply of their bad handling (ibid, 297). Where external reflection compares opposites in order to arrive at a relative determination of each term, self-reflection is the process by which an element reaches its Other by undermining itself from within. Thus, external reflection highlights a term's difference from its Other while self-reflection points to its inner division. Concepts conceived by external reflection exclude their contrary.[12]

For Hegel, the move to the Other is more than mere loss or perdition (ibid, 299). It is paradoxically by evacuating itself out into its Other that a given concept becomes what it is (to borrow a Nietzschean idiom). Self-reflection, or sublation as Hegel also calls it, involves an element's entry into unity with its Other. For Hegel, something is "sublated only in so far as it has entered into unity with its opposite" (Hegel, 1969, 107). This move elevates the given element to its *notion* and sums up, for us, the whole paradoxical nature of self-reflection; identity can only be reached through the positing of contradiction. Non-Hegelian conceptions of opposition lead to the phenomenology of "narcissistic suicidal aggression" where the subject does not see that it is "precisely the *kakon* of his own being that [he/she] tries to get at in the object that he strikes" (Lacan, 2006, 143). Quipping Lacan, we could say that my argument is based on the following maxim: what is not recognized in its paradoxical identity-in-difference with its Other returns in the guise of the impasse of a contradiction. The move from the ontology of juxtaposition to Kantian external reflection and, finally, to Hegelian self-reflection requires therefore the ascent (or shall I say *descent* and thereby remain equal to Biblical wisdom?) to castration.

Though my argument is centrally based on the Hegelian insight concerning the coincidence of contraries, I maintain, as aforesaid, a distinction between contradiction and paradox such that the former is given a negative valence while the latter connotes the highest achievement of speculative reason. I am thus sympathetic to the negative valence the Marxist tradition grants the notion of contradiction, while agreeing with Hegel that paradox (what he calls contradiction) is ineradicable. Hegel's *Phenomenology of Spirit* and *Science of Logic* trace the movement by which the resolution of one contradiction indelibly leads to another contradiction that is more difficult to resolve than the previous. Hegel resolves contradictions only to bring to the fore progressively more stubborn ones.[13] The absolute, for Hegel, denotes the achievement of the highest contradiction without resolution. It testifies to contradiction that has become internalized such that it no longer manifests as external opposition. In Lacanian parlance, the absolute designates the moment narcissistic suicidal aggression (the specular imaginary) is maximally obliterated such that internal division is assumed rather than projected. The aim of this treatise consists of presenting a number of speculative propositions stating paradoxical identities-in-difference that cannot be resolved. I thus begin somewhere akin to the Hegelian absolute.[14] Though it is conceded that Hegel ends with the absolute idea (the title of the concluding chapter of *Science of Logic*), it is also common wisdom to add the proviso that the absolute was always implicitly there from the beginning.[15] Moreover, my treatise engages with the contradictions that result from the diremptions of the understanding. Here, contradiction takes on the negative sense of an internal division that is heeded as external opposition. Dialectical advance moves towards paradox (to sustain contradiction as inner division) while dialectical regression (diremption) moves towards the apprehension of contradiction as opposition to an imagined enemy. In Hegel's own theoretical edifice, contradiction has a positive and negative valence. The contradictions of finite nature are, for Hegel, "low" contradictions insofar as they assail entities form the outside. Ignorant of its own division, finite nature remains at the mercy of external opposition. Contradiction gains a positive valence as spirit no longer misperceives it as an ailment attacking it from without. As contradiction is internalized and the weight of projection (to borrow a post-Freudian idiom) is reduced, I speak of paradox. Contradiction results from the understanding's will to eliminate another (dialectically more evolved/internalized) contradiction. Paradox, by contrast, results from reason's ability to reckon with contradiction. My distinction between paradox and contradiction is implicit in Hegel's claim that when concepts are severed from their contrary, thought gets "entangled in unreconciled, unresolved, absolute contradiction" (Hegel, 1969, 139) where the word "absolute" clearly does not carry its usual positive connotation. For Hegel, "*Speculative thinking* consists solely in the fact that thought holds fast contradiction, and in it, its own self, but does not allow itself to be dominated by it as in ordinary thinking, where its determinations are resolved by contradiction only into other determinations or nothing" (ibid, 440–441). The abolition of contradictoriness paradoxically leads to contradiction; we move from contradiction acknowledged as belonging to the concept, to contradiction experienced externally as an alien force "that dominates it and resolves it into nothing".

Notes

1 Much like *Finnegans Wake* where the circularity of "narration" overlaps with the square shape of the book thereby achieving a truly dialectical feat, squaring the circle.

2 The idea that novelty arises out of repetition is a paradox captured by many thinkers from Nietzsche's *eternal return* to Deleuze's *difference and repetition* and Lacan's idea that love is at once "the sign ... that one is changing reasons ... one changes discourses" as well as the source of a repetitive (*encore*) demand.

3 Was Nietzsche not one thousand times right when he advocated that, as philosophers, "our thoughts ... grow from us with the same inevitability as fruits borne on the tree – all related and referring to one another and a testimonial to one will, one health, one earth, one sun" (Nietzsche, 1998). I chose the *theme and variation* model to keep thought within a singular source of inspiration. Adorno's *Negative Dialectics* – also following a model based on music – "will become one infinite variation in which everything is recapitulated at every moment" (Jameson, 2007, 62).

4 As Bernstein (2002, 63) comments, the "theme of diremption – self-diremption as internal cleavage – reverberates throughout Hegel's philosophy". I consider "diremption" in terms of a separation from self (a refusal of castration and the unconscious) resulting from common understanding's inability to fathom the paradox of identity-in-difference. Thus, diremption and the understanding are commensurate insofar as the latter is taken as "as separating and remaining fixed in its separations" (Hegel, 1969, 45).

5 Kant "constructs a realm external to the understanding that it has no knowledge of and yet depends on" (McGowan, 2019, 68).

6 Like Hegel, psychoanalysis embraces paradox. Leclaire argues that the function of the subject is *contradiction itself*. He reminds us that, for Freud, the principle of non-contradiction does not hold in the unconscious (Leclaire, 1968, 137). The expletive "ne" (the marker of the subject in language) leaves an unresolved ambiguity that reflects, according to Lacan, a central characteristic of subjectivity. Recent efforts at bridging neuroscience and psychoanalysis speak of the paradox of neuroplasticity. Ansermet argues that "experience leaves a trace in neuronal network", a process he describes as a "universal mechanism that makes you unique" because the trace is contingent. Secondly, "the trace will be re-associated with other traces creating new traces which are in discontinuity with the experience". This is "the root of freedom". Thirdly, the "ever-changing brain" introduces "the unpredictability of becoming". In short, under the rubrics of *uniqueness*, *discontinuity* and *unpredictability*, Ansermet highlights the paradox by which *universal* experience gives way to *singular* freedom (interview retrieved on February 21, 2018 from: https://m.youtube.com/watch?v=fqNkMQZT-3g).

7 Something is "alive only in so far as it contains contradiction within it, and moreover is this power to hold and endure the contradiction within it" (Hegel, 1969, 440).

8 "It is said that contradiction cannot be thought; but in the pain of the living being it is even an actual, concrete existence" (Hegel quoted in McGowan, 2019, 35).

9 For Hegel, humans "are inwardly conscious that in their innermost being they are a contradiction, and have therefore an infinite *anguish* concerning themselves" (Hegel quoted in Bernstein, 2002, 66).

10 Hegel thus famously argues that "it shows an excessive tenderness for the world to remove contradiction from it" (Hegel, 1969, 237). Contradiction permeates all things as "nothing, either in heaven or on earth ... exhibits the abstract 'either-or'

as it is maintained by the understanding" (Hegel, 1991, 187). Hegel's philosophical precursor here is Heraclitus who made licit the union of contraries (Lebrun, 1972, 267).

11 I rely on the sixth chapter of Lebrun's *La patience du concept* entitled "La négation de la négation" where he discusses the ways contradiction has been (mis)-conceptualized in the history of philosophy.

12 Since the exclusion of the contrary is tantamount to the loss of self, Hegel also refers to external reflection as "self-alienated reflection" (de Boer, 2010, 354).

13 The contradiction of God on the cross is the hardest to resolve (McGowan, 2019, 19).

14 I begin with the absolute because this treatise is principally concerned with human infinite spirit (psychoanalysis) rather than finite nature (general ontology).

15 Regarding the "True", Hegel says that it is "the process of its own becoming, the circle that presupposes its end as its goal, having its end also as its beginning" (Hegel, 1977, 10).

Variation 1   The diremptive remains

Under the rubric of "diremptive remains", I reflect on the paradoxical dialectical unity of diremption and self-reflection. Every self-reflective act of self-evacuating kenosis[1] harbours a diremptive shadow. In *Science of Logic* Hegel delights in the fact that,

> "To sublate" has a twofold meaning in the language: on the one hand it means to preserve, to maintain, and equally it also means to cause to cease, to put an end to ... It is a delight to speculative thought to find in the language words which have in themselves a speculative meaning; the German language has a number of such.
>
> (Hegel, 1969, 107)

The twofold paradoxical meaning of "sublate" points to the necessity that every sublation carries with it a diremptive remain. Interestingly the verb "to dirempt" does not contain its opposite meaning; it is thus itself diremptive. The sublation of an element into its Other is never complete as something always remains testifying to the fact that even the most thorough sublation is always partial. A minimal diremption is a *structural necessity* of the dialectical process; otherwise we would be relegated to the "night in which all cows are black" (Hegel, 1977, 9). The diremptive remains, insofar as they resist philosophical *speculation*, are akin to the object *a* which is "negativized" from the *specular* image. The object *a* is the diremptive remain that hinders the identity of opposites and yet it is also that which makes that identity possible. The object *a* is a *diremptive-speculative* remain.[2] Likewise, the diremptive remain makes sublation possible, precisely and paradoxically by virtue of the limitation it imposes on it. Like Hegelian "Spirit", it is the "bone" that is at once "the condition of possibility and the condition of impossibility of the dialectical process" (Žižek, 2015, 32). It provides resistance to the dialectical process and is yet also its motor. Psychoanalysis deals precisely with those remnants that philosophy prefers to repress.[3] More generally, the remnants of the self-reflective process are what the psychoanalytic *clinic* testifies to most faithfully and what, by contrast, the purity of *theory* ignores.

Once we reach a conception of difference that first passes through the experience of identity which it then relinquishes through the choice of a diremptive remain then, and only then, do we accomplish an ethical and/or aesthetic position which, despite marking its difference from its Other, recognizes the Other as its neighbour. Sublation posits the *essential unity* of a concept with its contrary (a unity that both disturbs and consolidates its identity) while the diremptive remain testifies to the ineradicable *opposition* that resists (and yet also makes possible) the self-reflective process.[4] Speculation emphasizes identity-in-difference and the unity of opposites. This position, though laudable for freeing the mind from the impasses of common understanding, risks leading to inaction. The *decision* for a diremptive remain frees us from the stasis of identity-in-difference. Karin de Boer insightfully distinguishes between the "essential unity" of contraries and their "prevailing opposition" (de Boer, 2010, 363). While the former designates the speculative identity of contraries in the concept, the latter refers to the *actual* determination of the opposed pairs in time and space. According to de Boer, there is always a gap between the speculative identity of the elements and the opposed manner they *actually* transpire in the world, and, moreover, this gap accounts for movement and change (ibid, 365). The speculative identity of contraries is akin to the quantum *superposition of states* and the actual determination to *the collapse of the wave function.*[5] What I call *deciding* for a diremptive remain is akin to collapsing the wave-function and thereby partially annulling the speculative superposition of states. This ethical-aesthetic moment marks the choice for one element over its Other without, however, reverting to blind diremption. The importance of the diremptive remain consists in that one cannot simply equate all things insofar as opposed pairs retain their difference in actuality despite their essential unity. Otherwise it would make no difference if one lies or tells the truth:

> Just as to talk of the *unity* of subject and object, of finite and infinite, of being and thought, etc. is inept, since object and subject, etc. signify what they are *outside* of their unity, and since in their unity they are not meant to be what their expression says they are, just so the false is no longer *qua false*, a moment of truth.
>
> (Hegel, 1977, 23)

Cast in Heideggerian parlance, at an ontological level, opposites unite such that each element reaches the dignity of its notion through a paradoxical kenosis into its Other. Ontically, however, an ethical-aesthetic[6] remainder forces one to choose one element over its Other. This ethical–aesthetic-ontical remainder disrupts and organizes the domain of speculation.

The coincidence of contraries leads to increased harmony between previously falsely opposed terms insofar as, *post-speculation*, each term recognizes itself in the Other; the Other becomes *my* Other. In full-fledged diremption, prior to sublation, conflict is reducible to Lacan's *narcissistic suicidal aggression*, Hegel's *battle of pure prestige* and Freud's *narcissism of small differences*. The "enemy" is a mere reflection of a disavowed part of the self. By contrast, conflict that occurs post-sublation involves two terms, which, having recognized their respective internal divisions, do not split off an undesired aspect ("moment") on the Other. Any conflict that may exist concerns actual rather than the imagined differences.[7] Such conflict can be contained within the medium of speech without spilling into a shouting match. In *L'envers de la dialectique. Hegel à la lumière de Nietzsche*, Lebrun puts forward a Nietzschean critique of Hegel arguing that for the latter there is conflict only insofar as one fights with one's shadow (Lebrun, 2004, 113). Lebrun lauds Nietzsche for keeping contraries opposed rather than reconciling them through speculation. However, the idea of diremptive remains shows that conflict may subsist even after the specu- lative identity-in-difference of falsely opposed terms has been established. It is not necessary, as Lebrun's Nietzsche imagines, to keep contraries opposed in order to maintain the possibility of conflict. By first subjecting opposed terms to the operation of self-reflection, one can better guarantee that conflict involves *difference* rather than *narcissistic* strife. With this Nietzschean critique, Lebrun feels that he has unearthed the hidden *moral* core of Hegel's dialectic in its alleged evasion of conflict. Nietzsche, as the great celebrator of war, is thus presented as the welcome antipode and antidote. But this is to misun- derstand both thinkers. Nietzsche does not keep the contraries apart prior to self-reflection. If he celebrates conflict it is, I believe, only insofar as the conflict stages a battle between different terms – a difference properly established after self-reflection. It is the Nietzschean slave who cannot accomplish self-reflection and is thus drowned in a *ressentiment* that is the mere obverse of his/her self- disrespect. When the Nietzschean master goes to war it is not him/herself that he battles but precisely the Other recognized as Other through self-reflection. One is more loyal to the essence of Nietzsche's thought by recognizing him as a thinker of the diremptive remain rather than as one insouciant of the dialectical process. Lebrun's oversight is symptomatically betrayed in the title of the work (*The Inverse of the Dialectic*). A more fitting title – one that would better heed to the intricacies of both Nietzsche and Hegel's thought – would have been *The Remainder of the Dialectic*. The intelligence of the Nietzschean master consists of engaging in conflicts against the Other as perceived through the clarity of the *speculative* rather than the murky spectacles of the *specular*. Narcissistic discord that cannot discern between self and Other is the folly of the slave incapable of self-reflection and the subsequent decision for a diremptive remain.[8] Hegel's work (akin to psychoanalytic treatment) is to diminish as much as possible the reign of the imaginary (the misrecognition of internal division as external opposition) so that the Other can be rightly ascertained as Other, rather than the mere shadow of the self. This is not to abolish conflict in favour of harmony but, rather, to create the possibility of a bearable conflict. I thus also part ways with Žižek's (2009b, ix) rather one-sided critique of dialogue. Though there is truth to Lacan's indictment according to which all dialogue is the exchange of two monologues, this should not entail that we relinquish all discussion. The properly Hegelian view is that a *reason*able interchange can be maintained if the parties involved have sufficiently submitted themselves to self-reflection. This is particularly important today with respect to the question of sexual identity-in-difference, where discussions around gender and sexuality often take the regressive form of a puerile battle of the sexes.[9] Men's movements cast their own frustrated masculinity on the figure of woman while certain feminists hold an allegedly wicked patriarchal order responsible for all the weight of castration. In both cases, the failure of each sex to constitute itself through its paradoxical kenosis in the Other is blindly played out as an external conflict with an Other that is increasingly little more than a reflection of one's self.

It is arguably the case that the diremptive remains divide in accordance to the sacred-profane identity-in-difference. One of two diremptive remains generally falls on the side of sacralization while the other pertains to profanation. Thus, the particular identity-in-difference positing the unity of the sacred and the profane provides the general content for the others; a diremptive remain will thus either choose the sacred or the profane as the determining tendency of its *content*. As to *form*, however, the identity-in-difference of the feminine and the masculine will provide the general prototype. Sexual difference provides the form of difference *tout court*.[10] Let us recall for a moment Lacan's formulae of sexuation:

- Masculine sexuation:

  - For All x PHI x.
  - There is One x Not PHI x.

- Feminine sexuation:

  - There is no X Not PHI x.
  - Not All x PHI x.

Masculinity arguably hinges on a profanation that occurs against the background of the sacred while femininity hinges on a profanation that permeates the sacred realm. Masculinity is marked by profane *exceptions* – the obscene primal father representing its most overt form – while the feminine lacks a profane *exception* insofar as it is *constitutively* profane. Linking the perverse and the profane we may argue, following Benvenuto (2016), that the feminine is constitutively perverse-profane while masculinity, essentially on the side of the non-perverse (sacred) is, instead, plagued by "attacks of femininity" (ibid) or "attacks of profanity". Thus, our initial division of form and content (the product of the understanding's labour) now reveals itself as a moment to be surpassed. By providing the form of difference in general, sexual difference also determines the content (sacred and profane). With this we may posit the primacy of the feminine and argue that the masculine is a defence against the feminine. The feminine position is marked by greater anxiety, insofar as "'male anxiety' stops at castration anxiety" (Zupančič, 2017, 56). According to Lacan, Zupančič explains, "the feminine position is closest to subjectivity in its pure state". For this reason it is more prone to the "radical ontological anxiety" that is "the *prerogative of subjectivity as such*" (ibid, 56). With this we can appreciate why the masculine would want to defend against femininity. Hysteria, for instance, provides a rather expedient defence, as the hysteric's *belle indifférence* amply testifies. The feminine is less diremptive of the identity–in–difference of femininity and masculinity. The masculine insists more fervently on an alleged abyssal difference from the feminine, something Adler diagnosed as the "masculine protest" and Freud (1937) christened as the "repudiation of femininity". The feminine thus better recognizes that femininity and masculinity are brethren or, shall I say, sisters. The masculine is on the side of semblance while the feminine is on the side of the real.[11]

The separation of the diremptive remains into a profane and a sacred element means that the unity of contraries does not always imply symmetry. Generally, the profane term represents the Other for both. This is exemplarily so in the case of the masculine-feminine identity-in-difference where the feminine stands in the place of the Other for both male and female positions. This insight marks male and female homosexuality as radically opposed; where the former involves two subjects seeking the *same*, the latter involves two subjects seeking *difference*.[12] St. Paul and Judas are arguably the respective representatives of the alternative sacred/same and profane/Other diremptive remains. This means that Judas better renders the truth of the Christian message – precisely insofar as he is Other. The Christian message is, after all, ultimately an *atheistic* message and the incarnation and the crucifixion mark the moments where God, according to Žižek's formulation, profanes Himself, i.e. becomes Other to Himself.

Notes

1 Kenosis refers to the process by which a term empties itself out into its Other in order paradoxically to reach itself.

2 Žižek underlines this paradoxical function of the object: "In this element (baptized by Lacan the *objet a*), opposites immediately coincide … it is simultaneously a particular idiosyncratic object which disturbs the frame of reality … and the frame itself through which we perceive reality" (Žižek, 2015, 109).

3 Žižek holds that psychoanalysis deals with what philosophy brushes aside. In our terms, psychoanalysis obstructs and inspires philosophy at once.

4 In the context of bringing psychoanalysis and Hegel together, the word "resist" is simply irresistible. The resistance to the speculative process provided by the diremptive remain is akin to resistance to psychoanalysis. Both are, at once, an obstacle and a condition. Psychoanalysis without resistance disparages to a facile exchange scarcely distinguishable from leisurely afternoon tea.

5 Žižek's interest in quantum physics finds its source in the paradoxes it brings to light. Lacan also refers to the paradoxes of quantum mechanics as a means of elucidating something of subjectivity (cf. Lacan, 2007, 103–104).

6 The aesthetic diremptive remain is none other than *taste*.

7 McGowan (2019) distinguishes between *difference* and *contradiction*. Where the latter designates internal division, the former represents the obfuscation of division by falsely presenting it as the difference between two terms. The fascist, for instance, is preoccupied by his/her alleged difference from the Jew rather than his/her own internal contradiction.

8 That self-reflection is operative in Nietzsche is well attested to in the first essay of *On the Genealogy of Morality* where he explicitly states that we are all made up of slave and master traits.

9 The last American elections boil down to a pipi-caca kindergarten variety of the battle of the sexes.

10 "Their homeland [that of the masculine and the feminine positions] is one and the same: yet this oneness and sameness is the oneness and sameness of pure difference" (Zupančič, 2017, 61). The idea of two elements sharing a homeland and, furthermore, that this similitude founds the basis of absolute difference provides a succinct formulation of the way identity-in-difference is conceptualized throughout this treatise.

11 Zupančič argues that masculinity hinges on belief, while femininity rests on pretence. Belief opens the space of the sacred, while pretence hinges on a prior disbelief – one feigns because one does not believe.

12 Bruno (2010) remarks that female homosexuality involves the relation of Other to Other rather than same to same.

Variation 2   The triumph of dialectical "lower" terms

Following an insight from Karin de Boer regarding the *asymmetry* of the unity of contraries we can translate the idea that one element (the profane-feminine-Other) has primacy over another into more rigorous Hegelian theorization. De Boer argues that only one of the two contradictory elements "constitutes the true principle of its contrary determinations" (de Boer, 2010, 369). Hegel makes this point specifically regarding the dialectical unity of infinitude and finitude where the former has primacy over the latter.[1] There is thus an asymmetry between the two elements of an opposition and, I would add, this asymmetry, when viewed from the standpoint of the understanding, is interpreted as *hierarchy*. For instance, the man–woman opposition, viewed from the perspective of the understanding, may lead to a misogynistic conception by which man is "above" woman. Indeed, the moment of the discovery of sexual difference when the child perceives the mother's privation of the penis, can lead to misogynistic contempt. Much of psychoanalytic treatment consists of correcting this one-sided perspective. According to psychoanalytic reason the "lower" term reveals itself as the symptom (or "truth") of the alleged "higher" term. Thus, woman is a symptom of man and thereby stands for his truth while children play this part for their parents and the psychoanalyst (the quintessential Other) for his/her patients. The symptom is a diremptive remain, an index of *asymmetry*. It testifies to an encroachment; the element that occupies this position is felt to impinge upon the imagined self-identity of the "higher" term. Men are thus wont to feel persecuted and suffocated by their wives, parents feel that their children drive them mad while analysands feel pained by the analysts and secretly long for the end of treatment. The symptom provides a minimal exteriorization of internal division as outward opposition.

Given this asymmetry, the "higher" term faces the ethical decision of accepting or rejecting incorporation with the "lower" term. The "higher" term is now challenged with the task of recognizing in the Other its own truth and symptom rather than retaining the conceit of its superiority. If the "higher" term resists-dirempts incorporation out of fear or conceit, an unexpected *triumph of the "lower" term* occurs. In this case, both terms dwindle into an excessive form of the "lower"-profane element[2] leading to tremendous suffering. At times, a nefarious contradiction occurs by which the "lower" term triumphs *arrogantly* (with *the spirit of revenge* fed by *ressentiment*) in the very oppression of the "lower" by the "higher". Nietzsche's *slave revolt in morality* points precisely to this inversion by which the "lower" term, the slave of yesteryear, seizes power and oppresses the former noble master with unparalleled rancor. The *revaluation of values* occurs when the angry dirempted symptom finally becomes the creator of value. We may christen the symptom that returns after suffering the blows of the "higher" term's snubbing diremption as *hyper-symptom*.

For Freud, the psychoanalytic symptom is a compromise formation between the law ("higher" term) and the unconscious wish ("lower" term) that inexorably veers towards the fulfilment of the latter to the detriment of the former. The very effort to resist one's wish (one's *jouissance*) becomes the very locus of the satisfaction of that self-same wish. Resistance is co-opted by the wish for the sake of its satisfaction. Nietzsche (1998), with the signature prescience of the genius of his nostrils, had already sniffed out a similar mechanism in the manner that the ascetic ideal becomes co-opted as the principal means to lascivious *jouissance* – the ascetic ideal thus becomes hyper-symptom of humankind. In like manner, the conceptual oppositions put forward here veer towards the "lower" term of the opposition when the "higher" term dirempts its truth as incarnated by the "lower" term. For instance, in the opposition of truth and lies, everything slowly veers towards the dominance of lies, which, despite being the "lower" or profane element of the opposition provides the truth of the "higher" term. Cast aphoristically, the lie provides the truth of truth. This is a profound psychoanalytic insight rendered eloquently by Lacan: "there is no truth that, in passing through awareness, does not lie" (Lacan, 1977).

It is likewise with the inhuman treatment of criminals. Here the good functions as a "higher" term which, in refusing to recognize its symptom-truth in evil, degenerates all the more into savage evil. The good's domination of evil thus becomes an even graver instance of evil than the evil it sought to tame.[3] Likewise, love that ignores its symptom in hate is an idealizing love more violent than hate itself. Similarly, love that dirempts its foundation in lack disparages to bourgeois love, a form of legalized prostitution, as Žižek would say. It is likewise with the innocence-guilt dichotomy. We are innocent because Jesus died for our sins. Yet we must not forget that Jesus' guilt is a symptom of our innocence (dare we say that God is a symptom of man?); his guilt is the truth of our innocence, which is, by virtue of that fact, a compromised innocence (the only possible kind). Failing to recognize this, our innocence becomes the *conceit of innocence* and the height of the most heinous guilt: what is the guilt of lost innocence in comparison to the guilt of the conceit of innocence? Of course, the greatest instance of such hyper-guilt posturing as innocence consists of all the myriad systemic forms of violence that permeate the space of late modern capitalism; in comparison to that the robbing of a bank is, indeed, mere child's play. Similarly, beauty that resists its dialectical unity with ugliness becomes mere kitsch, the quintessence of ugliness. Wealth that refuses its kinship with poverty is the height of all paucity; something that Biblical wisdom knew well when it counseled that "it is easier for a camel to go through the eye of a needle than for a rich man to enter the kingdom of God". Likewise, Lacan (2001b) warned that the rich man is impotent and cannot love. For Lacan, great dialectician that he is, to give *what one does not have* is the crowning pinnacle of wealth. Sanity that dirempts madness is paradoxically the height of madness. Finally, freedom that dirempts its ties to dependence risks falling into empty wantonness. One may even argue that it is generally the pretence to "freedom" and "autonomy" that seduces the "higher" term to imagine a life untainted by the blemish of the "lower" term. The reign of the "lower" term (the symptom) is at once farcical and catastrophic. We live in comical times with the proviso that the comical represents the height of the tragic. For this reason, Žižek is the philosopher most contemporary of our time; he is a jester-philosopher to be taken with utmost earnestness.

The "lower" term, the symptom-truth of the "higher" term, also stands for universality while the "higher" term stands for particularity. By refusing its identity-in-difference with its Other, the "higher" term defines its identity in opposition to this Other. The "higher" term thus places the Other "as the universal against which [its] identity must define itself" (McGowan, 2019, 194). This insight has its psychoanalytic counterpart in the idea that the abject and destitute provides the universal truth of humankind once semblances are finally cast aside. The aim of psychoanalytic treatment is to re-appropriate as one's own the abjection cast out through diremptive self-conceit. Thus, woman stands for the universality of castration (anatomy serves as destiny in this regard) that man, ensnared by the illusion of his masturbatory autonomy,[4] pretends to escape. The child's helplessness, falsely opposed to the pretence of adult self-sufficiency, also belongs here. Likewise, guilt, evil, hate, lies, ugliness and servitude are some of the many exemplars that provide the ineradicable stain of human destitution which the semblances of the conceit of innocence, moralistic good, idealized love, pedantic truth, artificial beauty, idle freedom, boring sanity and vacuous wealth try to obfuscate. The symptomatic "lower" terms are the torsion in the Moebius strip that our never ceasing Ptolemaic conceit tries to iron out in vain. Fear is always *fear of the dialectical "lower" term* and, therefore, in fearing it one becomes it.[5] The rejection of the dialectical "lower" term reduces the "higher" term to a degenerated and farcical version of the "lower" term and infuses anger in the "lower" term, which eventually rises up with the will and *ressentiment* to wage a veritably daunting slave revolt.[6]

Notes

1 Our decision to map this on Lacan's (1998) formulae of sexual difference is validated by the fact that Lacan designates masculinity as finite and femininity as infinite.

2 I have cursorily equated the "lower" and the profane term of an opposition. Though this overlap may often hold, it may be wiser not to raise it to a universal truth without exceptions.

3 We enter Nietzsche's dialectical paradigm of a radical *revaluation of all values* that recognizes in moralistic "good" an evil greater than evil itself.

4 The penis is an ellipse that thinks it's a circle. To truly subsist it needs the two centres of man and woman. However, in its delusion of self-sufficiency it sees only itself.

5 The psychotic "push-to-Woman" is inseparable from the fear of the feminine.

6 At the risk of anthropomorphism (no sin among we Hegelians), one could frame the massive changes in the climate as the "lower" term ("Nature") taking vengeance on humanity's diremption of its belonging to it. Nature is today our most angry hyper-symptom and Sodom and Gomorrah (or shall I say "corona") lurk not far away!

Variation 3 Speculative topology

Lacanian topology is the contemporary heir to speculative philosophy. Interestingly, the word "speculative" with its explicit reference to mirrors already points in the direction of topological rather than temporal thought. Lacan's Moebius strip, the torus and the Klein bottle all stage paradoxes for the common understanding (e.g. an object that has its centre of gravity outside itself, a surface with only one side). The move to topology is altogether different from Lacan's notion of the "imaginary" and Hegel's "picture" or representational thinking. For Hegel, the limitation of picture thinking consists of the fact that reflection cannot keep firm the unity of the object. By contrast, to

> think speculatively means to resolve anything real into its parts and to oppose these to each other in such a way that the distinctions are set in opposition in accordance with the characteristics of thought and the object is apprehended as the unity of the two.
>
> (Hegel, 1970, 147)

Hegel holds that "the object is one, although it has characteristics which are distinguished from it, and it is speculative thought which first gets a grasp of the unity in this very antithesis as such" (ibid, 147). Only a paradoxical topology, beyond the limitations of temporal thinking, can grasp the object in its inherent contradictions. Inasmuch as the term *picture thinking* points to the visual, we may surmise that Hegel's critique also involves a critique of the spatial. As a result, Lacan's move to topological thinking must be seen as a corrective to both spatial and temporal thought (two aspects of picture thinking). The Lacanian equivalent of "picture thought" is the imaginary, the lure of the mirror image where the object *a* is "negativized". The mirror image cannot grasp the subject in his/her dialectical unity (i.e. a true unity that includes all contradictions). Interestingly, however, the mirror image nevertheless points towards dialectical-paradoxical unity in that the image shows the subject in inverted form (the left and right sides are switched).[1] We could say, quipping Lacan himself, that *the mirror returns the subject's image in an inverted form.*[2]

For Hegel, "space and time are the primal forms of ideology" insofar as their form "permits us to see difference in the place of contradiction" (McGowan,

2019, 117). An inherent limitation of representational thought is that it depicts contradiction in such a way that "the contradictory is held *external to itself*, next to and after itself" (Hegel quoted in ibid, 118). Time and space are ideological categories insofar as they dirempt the paradoxical unity of an entity by falsely dividing it into disparate moments. Rather than depict one thing that is internally divided, picture thought represents two separate self-identical objects conceived as different only from *one another*. The notion of "moment" in Hegel is thus not a temporal idea; it is, as Jameson shows, (2010) more akin to "aspect".[3] Lacan's topology corrects the shortcomings of representational thought. The aim of this topology is, for Lacan, to provide a new "imaginary" that is better suited to the paradoxes of the real and which, as such, can paradoxically give body to that which it is impossible to incarnate, the object *a*:

> The ambiguity is due to the fact that we can't do otherwise than to imagine it in the specular register. It's precisely a matter of establishing another type of imaginarization here, if I may express myself in this way, whereby this object may be defined.
>
> (Lacan quoted in Wegener, 2016, 40)

"All space is flat" according to Lacan (ibid). Depth is an illusion created by space; it is not space itself. Lacanian topology targets the idea of psychoanalysis as "depth-psychology". Lacan held that the unconscious, as discourse of the Other, is located on the *surface*, namely at the level of everyday speech and social interaction – something entirely in keeping with Freud's discovery of *the psychopathology of everyday life*. However, if we take Lacan's notion of extimacy[4] seriously we must not forget that the unconscious, while being situated somehow "outside", is *also* deeply intimate. Thus, the notion of "depth psychology", despite some inaccuracy, should not be entirely discredited. Perhaps one should say that psychoanalysis is *a paradoxical depth psychology of the surface*. Or, we may say that depth is a diremptive remain that paradoxically enables while obstructing the speculative identity of *unconscious* and *surface*. The "purloined letter" (Lacan, 2006) is "deep", invisible to first glance, precisely insofar as it is there on the surface for everyone to see. The neurotic unconscious testifies to the paradox by which *the unconscious acquires depth precisely insofar as one fathoms that it is simply "floating" on the surface*. The phenomenology of the psychotic unconscious, where foreclosure prevails, fails to testify to this paradox; the unconscious remains out there "*à ciel ouvert*", neither "deep" nor "shallow".[5]

Insofar as the torsion on the surface gives paradoxical incarnation to the object *a*, it is synonymous with what we have christened as the diremptive remain. As such, the torsion is, at once, 1) the condition for the speculative recognition that the unconscious is on the surface and 2) the obstacle to full sublation. In other words, the kink on the surface both reminds us that there is no secret to the unconscious (it's right "there") and provides the illusion that the unconscious is somewhere "below the depths". This simultaneous *reminding* and *forgetting (reminding in the modality of forgetting)* is, of course, the very marker of *repression*, which is, for Lacan, equivalent to the *return of the repressed*. The strength of Lacan's topological surfaces is that they evoke (better than the specular image which "negativizes") the diremptive remain of the object *a*. One irresistibly feels like one got a glimpse of it and then it vanishes. More specifically, one gets the feeling that there is "depth" and then one realizes that the surface has no "inside". The topological surface is a surface with a torsion that keeps sustaining the illusion of the depth (hence depth is a diremptive remain). The constancy by which the illusion is maintained by the topological surface may be likened to Freud's "secondary repression".

Lacan casts his topological project of creating a new "imaginary" capable of giving body to the paradoxical object *a* as an endeavour that would overcome the limitations of Kant's transcendental aesthetics.: "Is topology not this no'space [*n'espace*] where mathematical discourse takes us and which necessitates a revision of Kant's aesthetics?" (Lacan, 2001a, 472, my translation). Similarly, Hegel casts his own speculative philosophy in opposition to Kant. Does this common urge to overcome Kantian ontology not further confirm the kinship between Lacan and Hegel? The Lacanian *"No 'space"* (as an alternative to Kantian transcendental aesthetics) provides the most current manifestation of the Hegelian project. The transition to Lacanian topology is thus akin to the move from the "salad" ontology of juxtaposition to Hegel's speculative philosophy via Kant's transcendental aesthetics. The pre-Kantian ontology can be likened to a flat torsion-less Euclidean surface with two sides. Kant introduces verticality with the idea of the noumenal realm beyond phenomena. Hegel, by contrast, returns to the ontology of the surface with the realization that the surface is not Euclidean. A torsion on the surface creates the illusion of depth and verticality. He did not, like Kant, fall into the trap of hypostasizing the torsion as a noumenal beyond. We may deepen this intermingling of Lacanian and Hegelian idioms by recalling the fact that for Hegel, there is, strictly speaking, no such thing as a "pure" notion. Excessive one-sidedness disparages the notion to the level of what he calls a "pure thought". Thus, Hegel argues that it is only by "giving up the *fixity* of its self-positing" that "the pure thoughts become *Notions*" (Hegel, 1977, 20). In light of this terminological clarification (notion vs. "pure thought") we could say that the Hegelian notion is a topological surface with torsion while a "pure thought" is an unwrinkled "pure" surface without a kink. Quipping Lacan, we may say: the kink, foreclosed from the flat surface of pure thought, returns as the full-blown (religious) delusion of depth. The kink on the surface, another name for the symptom, is given concrete reality as a distinct order of being while it is, in fact, nothing more than a scar of non-being (lack) within being.

Lacan took his engagement with topology and knot theory very seriously and, more importantly, also very *literally*. In response to Harry Woolf's question about whether his preoccupations with "this fundamental arithmetic and this topology are not in themselves a myth or merely at best an analogy for an explanation of the life of the mind", Lacan emphatically states that it is not an analogy. It is really in some part of the realities, this sort of torus. This torus really exists and it is exactly the structure of the neurotic. It is not an analogon; it is not even an abstraction, because an abstraction is some sort of diminution of reality, and I think it is reality itself.

(Lacan, 1970)

Lacan, by contrast to Kant, had ontological aspirations. And of course, a central contrast between Kant and Hegel consists of the latter's preoccupation with metaphysical matters which, unlike Kant, he did not entirely throw into the wastebin of noumenal unknowability. Here we should contrast Žižek's Hegel and Badiou's Hegel. Both react positively to Hegel's decision to move beyond Kant. However, a closer look at their respective sympathies for Hegel reveals a stark contrast. Badiou finds the limitation Kant places on knowledge completely anathema to his own ambitions. In his view, Hegel lifts this ban on knowledge and thereby grants us the confidence that everything is knowable (cf. Badiou, A. and Nancy, J-L. (2018)).[6] For Žižek, by contrast, the relation between Hegel and Kant is subtler in that the former does not simply lift a taboo imposed by the latter. Žižek believes that Hegel achieves a radicalization of Kant insofar as he raises the limitation on knowledge to the ontological level; if we cannot know things-in-themselves it is not because knowledge is forbidden *to us* but, more generally, because the so-called thing-in-itself is inherently unknowable. Thus, an epistemological barrier is fortified into an ontological one such that even God is denied access to full knowledge. We could say that Žižek's Hegel is "hyper-Kantian" while Badiou's Hegel is pre-Kantian. The former absolutizes the unknowability of the world while the latter does not shun the conceit to know all. An attempt can be here made to view these two different "Hegels" as *moments* of the same Hegel. The first moment lifts the limitation on knowledge to the ontological level. This means (and we are already and *immediately* at the second moment) that unknowability is an attribute of the thing-in-itself, an attribute that, moreover, we can claim to know. The speculative unity of the two contradictory moments of Hegel's philosophy renders for us the truth that the world is in-itself not knowable, that it is *not-all* as Lacan would say. Lacan's topological exploits give body to the two moments of Hegel's speculative philosophy: 1) the paradoxical-impossible surfaces incarnate a certain ontological unknowability, and yet 2) insofar as this unknowability is precisely *incarnated* (i.e. given shape in a "new imaginary") an essential ontological claim is made. The speculative unity of the two contradictory (paradoxical) moments of Hegel's philosophy gives us the complete *notion* of Hegel as opposed to accentuating one moment at the expense of the other. Of course, it must be pointed at that Žižek's Hegel as the "lower" profane element already contains both moments while Badiou's Hegel is diremptive in this regard. Žižek's Hegel, by contrast to Badiou's, attests to the Kant-Hegel identity-in-difference; a subtle *parallax shift*, rather than the grand leap Badiou imagines, takes us from Kant to Hegel.

Notes

1 I later distinguish between a diremptive and non–diremptive mirror stage (variation 7). Where the former involves a *cloning* of the "subject" (the scare quotes indicate that such a "subject" is in reality a non-subject insofar as a subject cannot be duplicated), the latter makes room for a *minimal difference* through which subjectivity can be asserted.

2 Despite reference to time (six months of age), Lacan's conception is markedly spatial if not yet topological (the French word *stade* literally means stadium – cf. Lacan (2006)).

3 The parallel with Freud is uncanny. The notion and the unconscious are outside of time.

4 The word "extimate" combines "external" and "intimate" to capture the liminal position of the object.

5 Hegel provides a proto-Lacanian expression of the immanence of the unconscious to the surface when discussing the absolute's inherence to the here and now:

> We usually suppose that the Absolute must lie far beyond; but it is precisely what is wholly present, what we as thinkers, always carry with us and employ, even though we have no express consciousness of it.
>
> (Hegel, 1991, 59)

6 Badiou's anti-kantianism is so stark that he considers himself a pre-Kantian pre-modern thinker. His influence on Meillassoux is evidenced in the latter's critique of Kant's "correlationism", his view that all knowledge is confined within the purview of the subject's historical situation (transcendental frame). For Meillassoux (2008), modern science accesses truths beyond the transcendental.

Variation 4　Vicious dialectical reversals

Žižek speaks of dialectical thinking which is not yet speculative. This, he argues, is

> the vibrant domain of the tremor of reflection and reflexive reversals, the mad dance of negativity in which 'all that is solid melts into air' – this is dialectics as eternal warfare, as a movement which ultimately destroys everything it gives birth to.
>
> (Žižek, 2015, 16)

This "vicious" aspect of the dialectic has a very clear instantiation in political struggle, where every sincere attempt towards emancipation risks not only failing but, even worse, dwindling into its opposite thereby reconfirming the rule of an even more stringent power. For Žižek, such nefarious reversals, rather than being an index of a deficiency of the actors involved, is a necessary dialectical outcome:

> From the standpoint of emancipatory struggle, it is thus crucial to take into account how, in the process of the actualization of a Notion, the Notion itself changes (into its opposite). And the purer this Notion is, the more brutal the reversal.
>
> (ibid, 36)

Far from pointing to an impurity in the intent of the revolutionary movement, the dialectical reversal is all the more brutal the purer the notion seeking actualization. According to Žižek's view, "one must first fail in reaching the goal, as the intended reconciliation turns into its opposite, and only then, in a second moment, will the true reconciliation come, when one recognizes this failure itself as the form of success" (ibid, 37). But is it not somewhat defeatist to recognize "failure itself as the form of success"? Is it always true that, "for immanent conceptual reasons, its [a revolution's] first strike has to end in fiasco, the outcome must turn out to be the opposite of what was intended" (ibid, 36–37)? Must we resign ourselves to the "impossibility of the agent's taking into account the consequences of its own act" (ibid, 36–37)?

If the *purity* of a notion leads to its dialectical demise it is because "purity" should be taken to refer to a notion's inability to recognize its identity-in-difference with its Other. It is precisely by virtue of this *méconnaissance* that the notion is led to *embody* this Other in a subsequent dialectical turn. What accounts for the vicious dialectical turn of destiny is a purity of the notion that excludes from itself acknowledgment of its speculative identity with its Other. Here "purity" designates something like diremption or one-sidedness; its result is that the Other, excluded from the notion's self-understanding, returns "in the real" of the dialectical turn. A vicious dialectical reversal is thus consequent upon diremption. Revolution would not *necessarily* lead to terror if it contained within itself its Other (i.e. the idea of a return to something prior). It is no coincidence that our word for the most radical change bringing about the most far-reaching social transformations is synonymous with the idea of something that *revolves* to a previous state. The lesson to be drawn from this etymological (non)-coincidence is that a revolution will succeed in instantiating its notion if the latter resists the pretence of standing independent of its Other. Žižek himself formulates a similar idea when he insists quite correctly that only the gesture of a *return* can bring about novelty, a point he argues *à propos* Lacan's famous *return to Freud*. We know from subsequent history that Lacan's return to Freud constituted a veritable revolution in psychoanalytic theory and practice. Moreover, we know that Lacan was driven by the pure passion of reviving Freudian theory from the straying into which it had erred in the hands of post-Freudian ego-psychology. His pure passion for Freud was akin to that of Antigone for Polyneices; he sought to provide for him a proper burial so that his legacy could live henceforth at the height of the dignity of its notion. However, this precisely pure passion of Lacan's did *not* lead to this allegedly *necessary* dialectical shift; Lacanian psychoanalysis did not "melt into air" and become reabsorbed by post-Freudian theory. It is precisely insofar as the novelty introduced by Lacan was posited in its identity with what Freud had already achieved that the Lacanian revolution did not falter into a counter-revolutionary ego-psychology. Lacan's passion may have been a pure passion but it was not a pure thought.[1]

It is likewise in the realm of human sexuality and desire. Sadism always reverts to masochism – Benvenuto (2016) puts it best quipping that "masochism is the subjectivization of sadism" – precisely because, enthralled by its own blind will to push "the suffering of existence into the Other" (Lacan, 2006), it fails to be mindful of its identity-in-difference with its victim. Sadism is anti-kenosis *par excellence*. Dirempted from the symbolic, masochism returns in the real of the dialectical shift where the splendour of sadism suddenly vanishes and "melts into air" relegating the subject to lowly self-contempt.

When a notion is actualized in the world, a gap *separates the essential principle* of that notion, namely the unity of itself and its contrary, and its *actual determination*. The greater the diremptive gap, the greater will be the dialectical shift "making good" that gap. The "corrective" work of the dialectic (uniting moments separated by diremption) will be as harsh and brutal as the purity of the actualized notion. Though this reading may smack of pre-modern mysticism granting mysterious power to a transcendental agent ("the corrective work of the dialectic"), one must not forget that Lacan provides a very similar explanation for the emergence of psychotic phenomena when he says that "What has been foreclosed from the light of the symbolic returns in the real". Both the "mystery" of the Lacanian "return in the real" and the Hegelian dialectical reversal can be understood in light of Hegel's notion of the absolute which we may take to designate the *impossible* point of the full sublation of contraries. According to de Boer, a notion suffers *"from the contradiction between what it is in itself* (the unity of its contrary moments) *and what it has actually become* (a determination opposed to its contrary)" (de Boer, 2010, 362). Psychotic hallucinations and delusions are a means of correcting the one-sidedness of the subject's notion of self – the "notion" is in this case more akin to a pure thought.[2] When Lacan says that the psychotic is spoken, we must ask: who speaks. The answer is the absolute. The excessive diremption of psychosis leads to a return of the absolute speaking through them *with a vengeance* (and *jouissance*). According to Lacan, the psychotic is the martyr of language and of the unconscious. Cast in Hegelese, he/she is the *martyr of the absolute*.[3]

The suffering of the notion (caused by the contradiction between what it is in itself and what it has actually become) points to the fact that we cannot reduce everything to what it has become, namely its actualization. The spectre of the absolute haunts all things in the form of suffering; this is true also for animal life where Hegel speaks of *pain*. The absolute casts its *spectre* on the present; it is not to be reached in the "future" but insists in all current moments. All things, through their pained contradictions, suffering and the ultimately disappointing vicissitudes of their destiny,[4] carry in varying measure the *spectre of the absolute*. If we suffer because of the gap that separates us from the absolute it must mean that we are somehow connected to it. As Žižek remarks, the absolute is nothing other than the gap that separates us from it and, we may add, thereby makes us suffer; the latter alone is the index of our connection.

Given that all things (though to varying measure) are an expression of the highest paradoxes of the absolute then the foreclosed paradox of the maximally one-sided "pure notion" will be "corrected" in time and space by a return of the foreclosed Other which is constitutive of its essential principle.[5] The universal has a certain "bias" grounded in the paradoxical nature of the absolute[6] and will "step in to the world" in order to "correct" the diremptions of one-sided notions. The key here is that this "intervention" does not happen externally-transcendentally but internally-immanently. But to actualize a "pure notion" is the will of the man of *ressentiment* whose raging fury blinds him to speculative reason. The "purity" of the notion is an un*reason*able (and thoroughly non-Hegelian) idea of the understanding. Žižek is thus right when he argues that vicious dialectical reversals are the result of a thinking that is dialectical but not yet speculative. But then one wonders why he deems wild dialectical reversals to be immanent conceptual necessities. This is to view contradiction too externally and temporally. If time, for Hegel, is an ideological category this means that the two moments of the notion (the two contradictory aspects paradoxically united together) need not be separated temporally. If, however, one insists on this separation – insofar as the actualization of any notion always bears the trace of a certain one-sidedness – then one could, at the very least, suggest the necessity of a diremptive *remain* rather than full diremption. The diremptive remain will lead, indeed, to inevitable historical vicissitudes but, by contrast to the terror, these may not entail "destroying all that one gives birth to".[7]

In his thesis concerning vicious dialectical reversals, what Žižek has therefore in mind are not notions but pure thoughts. The latter testify to the failure of achieving speculative reason. Like the zealot who, due to the actualization of his/her "notion" in pure one-sidedness, risks losing his/her humanity, the notion ceases to be a notion when it regresses to a pure thought and takes up a battle of pure prestige with its foreclosed Other. Such a pure thought degenerates into a "manic notion" or, more precisely, a "manic non-notion". Here the non-notion falls to the mercy of *jouissance* which deregulates it from all *reason*ableness. Every one-sided diremption leads to *jouissance*. Exemplary here is the dogmatism of religion where the *jouissance* generated is so strong that even the ascetic ideal (religion's most faithful ally) is impotent against it. We owe to Nietzsche the insight concerning the ascetic ideal's subordination to *jouissance*; rather than limit the latter, the ascetic ideal itself lapses into "saintly debauchery" (Nietzsche, 1998). Rather than testify to the lofty purity of the actors involved, a dialectical shift attests quintessentially to paradox experienced externally (i.e. ideologically). The integrity of the notion consists of its resilience in the face of the vicissitudes of fortune; its ability to bear contradiction internally strengthens it immanently. What Seneca says of real joy is also true of the notion: "It is a characteristic of real joy that it never ceases, and never changes into its opposite" (Seneca, 2016). *Notional joy* is speculative; its Other, which it must keep tenderly by its chest like a sister, is Freud's *common unhappiness*. The latter, far from alienating joy, immunes it to the wild dialectical vicissitudes of the one-sidedness of the pure thought of manic delight. And could the same not be humbly asked of revolution, namely that it achieves the *speculative* and thereby reach beyond the autophagic vicissitudes of the dialectic of revolution and terror?[8]

An interesting example of a vicious dialectical shift occurs when zealous devotion undermines a cause more effectively than it furthers it, something Žižek demonstrates when he critiques zealotry in favour of true fidelity which, he argues, requires constant regulation by betrayal. For Žižek, a "subject truly dedicated to his Cause regulates his eternal fidelity by means of incessant betrayals" (Žižek, 2018, xiv note 9). The dialectical shift through which a subject's zeal renders the opposite of the intended effect (undermining rather than elevating a cause) is not a dialectical necessity but, rather, the effect of the subject's position. As Žižek himself notes, "a zealot's fanatical attachment to his Cause is nothing but a desperate expression of his uncertainty and doubt, of his lack of trust in the Cause" (ibid). Relevant here is Adam Phillips' (2012) brilliant argument questioning the all too facile opposition of fidelity and betrayal in a text tellingly entitled "Judas' Gift". Phillips shows how the act of betrayal sometimes advances a cause more efficiently than it undermines it. Zeal gets caught up in vicious dialectical reversals precisely because it abandons its identity-in-difference with betrayal/doubt thereby disparaging its notion to the level of a pure thought.

In a rather enigmatic passage from *The Psychoses*, Lacan speaks of the so-called "providential function", something he likens to what we may colloquially call "karmic" retribution. Interestingly, Lacan isolates the providential function to neurosis alone. It is only when castration is operative that this function is effective. If symbolic castration is concomitant with speculative reason[9] then we may argue that this function is related to the subject's recognition of the fact that excessively diremptive attitudes will be "punished" by vicious dialectical shifts. Lacan also puts forward the idea that the superego is tied to the function of the "you" (the second person singular). We may explain this rather nebulous claim through the theoretical apparatus here put forward. The emphatic "you are ..." always rests on an implicit (if not overt) "and I am not so".[10] The function of the "you" is diremptive of the subject-other identity-in-difference;[11] it pushes in the Other what it cannot bear to see in itself.[12] Through the logic by which diremption leads to an undesired dialectical shift, the superego will eventually sting the subject with the proverbial bite of conscience. Thus, linking Lacan's reflections on the "providential function" with dialectics renders for us a certain kinship between psychoanalysis, Hegel and morality. In his *L'envers de la dialectique: Hegel à la lumière de Nietzsche*, Lebrun (2004, 203) argues that Hegelian dialectics holds a hidden connection to Christian morality which Nietzsche's genealogical method can help diagnose and overcome. Interestingly, Deleuze and Guattari (1972), also in light of Nietzsche, make a similar critique of Lacan. Is it enough to refute a theory by simply connecting it to Christian morality? Is it not, rather, testament to the genius of Christianity to have prefigured (and indeed made possible) so long ago these two pillars (German idealism and psychoanalysis) of enlightened modernity? I must add to this the proviso that there is no place in secular thought for a "providential function". However, this illusion does nonetheless *approximate* psychoanalysis and speculative philosophy by providing the subject with an inkling of castration, albeit in the disparaged mode of superstition. The commonest morality thus knows how the immoralist gets him/herself entangled in wild dialectical turns, swinging the pendulum from manic freedom and profligacy to despondent guilt and self-torment. Again, despite this proximity, Hegel's thought and Lacanian psychoanalysis are irreducible to Christian morality and, even more so, to the myth of a providential function. Where the latter splits apart the moments of the criminal act and its punishment, for Hegel the separation of moments is a quintessential ideological operation insofar as it unnecessarily introduces the dimension of time. For Hegel, the crime is its own punishment. Quipping Brecht we may ask: what is the punishment against an offense in comparison to the punishment that is the offense? The so-called law of attraction (the lynchpin of contemporary popular/ideological consciousness) does the same; it splits the thought (fear of some future event) from its realization. The problem with magical thinking is not simply that it is not based on "reality" but, more importantly, that it splits the moments of the thought and its alleged "later effect" – therein lies its ideological efficacy.[13] To fear poverty is not the *cause* of eventual poverty. The fear of poverty, much more radically, is *poverty itself.*[14] Thus, "magical thinking" errs because it is not, if I may, magical enough. It does not realize that the moments of fear and its "actualization" are identical; the "effect" is *hyper-magically* spontaneous.

Symbolic castration means that the subject must hold him/herself responsible for the dialectical setbacks consequent upon diremption. If the ego-ideal reverts to superegoic barbarism it is, by dint of the purity of the manic non-notion, consequent upon an exclusion of its Other. Could we thus not argue, in this light, that the failures of 20th century communism were consequent upon diremption? Žižek argues something of this sort when he refuses to let Marx off the hook when considering the catastrophes of 20th century communism. He holds that Marx's ridiculing of Hegel's defence of monarchy – Marx famously argued that the "Hegelian Monarch is just an appendix to his phallus" (Žižek, 2015, 368)[15] – is the weak point of Marx's thought and the possible explanation of how Soviet communism dwindled into a tyrannical bureaucratic university discourse. In the theoretical idiom here put forward, the Soviet revolution, heir to Marx's thought, dirempted the paradoxical identity–in–difference of communism and monarchism (in Kojève's (2014) estimation, Marx, unlike Hegel, lacked a theory of authority). Perhaps communism may achieve the dignity of its notion when held in identity with its Other, namely monarchy. Diremption here corrupts the concept precisely by robbing it of its Other. The dialectical shift to Stalinist tyranny would thus be tied to a specific Marxian diremption of a Hegelian insight.

Some (non)-notions are *constitutively* diremptive and are therefore immediately contradictory. For instance, according to Žižek, law, property and (loveless) marriage immediately reverse, respectively, to crime, theft and adultery (at other times, Žižek equates marriage to legalized prostitution). In the loftiness of their self-conceit law, property and marriage dirempt their identity–in–difference with their contraries and thereby pave the way to a "corrective" return in the real. Quipping Brecht, Žižek thus asks, "what is a crime against the law in comparison to the crime that is the law" or, "what is a theft against property in comparison to the theft that is property" and, finally, "what is adultery against marriage in comparison to the adultery that is a loveless marriage." Interestingly, Žižek speaks in these cases of notions that are *distorted* in order to explain the dialectical reversal but when it comes to the *massive* dialectical reversal by which the Soviet Revolution lapsed into 20th century communism, Žižek idealizes this outcome as an index of the "purity" of the notion. Does this mean that the defeat of Nazism was due to the "purity" of its notion, and that its failure provides the "form of its success"? Though my question is meant *ironice*, today's political climate may sadly force us to admit that it may harbour more truth than any alleged triumph of communism through its 20th century failure. The purity of a notion (its diremption-separation from its

Other) causes its inner distortion – through which its very notional vocation is lost – leading to whirlwinds of dialectical insanity. Each pole of an opposition remains bound within the walls of what Adorno christened as the "principle of identity" (the target of *Negative Dialectics*)[16] only insofar as its identity with its Other is denied. Paradoxically, it is when identity with the Other is admitted that the principle of identity is also overcome. With this, we witness the identity of identity and non-identity and, we must further note, it is precisely this latter paradox that enables one to claim that all cases of *identity* involve *identity-in-difference*. The principle of identity is synonymous with the principle of contradiction; insofar as manic non-notions lead inevitably to their contrary, all one-sided aims towards emancipation are thwarted leading to the impasse of contradictory identity.

We may say, at the risk of anthropomorphism, that the contradictions resulting from diremption testify to speculative reason's "vengeance" for having been pushed aside by common understanding. The superego is the psychoanalytic name for speculative reason in its vengeful guise. Hegel's notion of the "end of history" denotes the time when contradiction is sufficiently internalized as to minimize the workings of the "corrective" (dare I say, *correctional*) superego, its effort to make good the one-sidedness by which (non)-concepts have hitherto been actualized. It is likewise with the end of analysis where inner division (castration) takes the place of external opposition (superego).

Another related limitation in Žižek's thought consists of his account of current times as marked by the elimination of the "toxic" element (coffee without caffeine, love without the fall etc.). To say that love is now "without the fall" is to massively overlook the pain that love continues to inflict on frail human hearts. Dating sites and agencies do not eliminate the pain of love. The very "self-commodification" (Žižek) that takes place leads to the experience of abysmal abjection. The experience of being "ghosted", of not making enough matches, the ordeals of love at first sight based on profile pictures and other cyber-torments by no means constitute a "love without the fall" but rather open the space for a "fall without the love", a fall into abjection which Freud (1920) had christened as the deeply anguishing suicidal experience of falling form another's estimation (*Niederfallen* or *liegen lassen*). The contemporary abolition of the fall from love simply means that the fall will return with a vengeance at a later time. The two contradictory moments of fall and love are severed and forced to join each other through a temporal lag. In "traditional" love, *jouissance* and castration, namely the limit placed on *jouissance*, intermingle such that neither tendency preponderates. All the institutions that surrounded love such as marriage, religion and family enabled maintaining the semblance of harmony between the couple. In "modern love", the separation of *jouissance* and castration leads to alterations between manic bliss and melancholic despondency rather than more harmonious intermingling. Modern dating sites aim to instantiate a "love without the fall". However, insofar as such a love does not maintain its paradoxical identity-in-difference with its other (all the complications that come with love, namely the fall), such a love becomes *pure*. Finally, the "purity" of this love leads to the vicious dialectical reversal of the triumph of a *fall without the love* thereby rendering for the subject the truth that, in the last instance, purity is the greatest impurity of all.

Notes

1 The purity of Lacan's passion led to his excommunication. He was the torsion on the surface that the International Psychoanalytic Association finally foreclosed. Following the logic of the triumph of the "lower" term, I predict that eventually the International Psychoanalytic Association will become Lacanian against all its (conscious) wishes. This new Lacanianism may sadly take the form of a fanatic hyper-Lacanianism.

2 According to Pommier (2013), in psychotic hallucination, the subject's "other half" "comes back" to him/herself from the outside. This idea is, at once, Hegelian, Lacanian and Kleinian (the idea of "split off" parts of the self).

3 These are the same insofar as the unconscious is the absolute, something Lacan renders quite literally with "God is unconscious" (Lacan, 1977).

4 Heidegger (2015) provides an insightful reading of Hegel's philosophy as the epic of successive disappointments.

5 The phenomenon of a return of the dirempted Other led Hegel to wonder whether "beneath the superficial din and clamour of history, there is not perhaps a silent and mysterious inner process at work" (Hegel, 1975, 33).

6 This is most evident in Hegel's writings on religion where he says that the "deepest need of spirit is that the antithesis within the subject itself should be intensified to its universal, i.e., its most abstract extreme" (Hegel, 2008b, 310).

7 What Žižek says of love, namely that it is never "pure" insofar as "the very features which allegedly stain it … are what can effectively trigger it" (Žižek 2015, 72) is also true of the notion.

8 One could perhaps say, arguably entirely in keeping with Lacan, that the pure thought of revolution is shameless.

9 I take the absolute as synonymous with castration. Insofar as insanity hinges on the foreclosure of the latter, it implicates the subject in radical separation from the absolute.

10 Alma's emphatic "I am not like you" uttered to Elisabet in the famous monologue in *Persona* is a great instance of the "you are … I am not" dialectic. Alma denies her guilt for the rejection of maternity and finds it in Elisabet. This comes back to haunt as her denial fails to achieve its purpose. Bergman captures this failure in the fusion of the faces which immediately ensues.

11 Martin Buber's *I and Thou* is an expression of this speculative identity.

12 What post-Freudians have christened as "projection" may be recast as the diremption of the subject-other identity-in-difference.

13 All law, be it "karmic law" or "law of nature" is ideological insofar as it separates the moments of immanence.

14 As Montaigne (2009) put it best, "He who fears he shall suffer, already suffers what he fears".

15 Žižek argues that Marx's acerbic remark hit the nail on the head as the monarch is just such an appendix. Marx did not recognize the veracity of his own sarcastic claim and could not appreciate the importance of "the coincidence of the highest (pure signifier) and lowest (biology, contingency)" (Žižek, 2015, 368). A great example of truth achieved in the mode of misrecognition.

16 Adorno imputes this principle to Hegel's thought. This (false) indictment fails to appreciate that Hegel rejected such a principle to the extent of denying the existence of analytic judgments altogether.

Variation 5   Faith and reason

For Hegel, religion is a form of knowledge and, as such, is inseparable from what we understand by cognition. Even when speaking of *devotion* (*Andacht*) or *feeling* (*Gefühl*), Bernstein explains, Hegel is concerned, above all, with the cognitive aspect (Bernstein, 2002, 62). Hegel thus laments the "mutual distrust" (Hegel, 1970, 141) that plagues the relation between religion and knowledge. According to Hegel, philosophy, like religion, renounces subjective opinions in order to concern itself with God (ibid, 145). In the Middle Ages, figures such as Anselm and Abelard attested to the fact that the union of religion and philosophy was then less opaque (ibid, 146). By contrast to Kant who "found it necessary to deny *knowledge*, in order to make room for *faith*" (Kant, 1929, 29), Hegel, refusing to partake in the pseudo-religious debasement of reason, claims that "God is not the highest emotion but the highest thought" (Hegel, 1970, 184).[1] Moreover, he warns that the "opinion that thought is injurious to religion, and that the more thought is abandoned the more secure the position of religion is, is the maddest error of our time" (ibid, 185). A similar prejudice against reason is endemic of many approaches to mental health today. Among psychoanalysts, it is not rare to hear someone critique a colleague for "intellectualization". Supervisors and teachers who emphasize the importance of the "counter-transfer" insist that the clinician should stay close to his/her emotions as a measure for gauging the stirrings of the patient's unconscious. The analyst's engagement with theory is taken as a defence against the testing emotional vicissitudes resulting from the intimate bond to the analysand. The royal road to the patient's unconscious is now located in the analyst's reverie, while the latter's knowledge of psychoanalytic theory is deemed a hindrance on this arduous path. By contrast to this prejudice against the intellect we stringently hold, with Lebrun's Hegel, that "the problem of the Understanding is not 'intellectualism' but, rather, that it remains embedded in the immediate" (Lebrun, 1972, 78). According to Hegel, the opposition between faith and reason is only a stage of their mutual development. When the opposition reaches a climax the need for reconciliation arises (Hegel, 1970, 142). For Hegel, Christianity is where this takes place. It is in Christianity that the division between faith and reason grew into its most stringent opposition and therefore also here where reconciliation finally took place (ibid, 142–143). Interestingly, the increasing emphasis on counter-transference and emotionality accompanied by the progressive straying away from Freud made psychoanalysis (much like Christianity before it) another privileged locus of the heightened tension between emotion and thinking. Lacan's very *intellectual* return to Freud – mediated by encounters with structural anthropology, linguistics, game theory, philosophy and not to mention topology (to name a few) – was an opportune antidote to a tendency that increasingly sought to establish the hegemony of affect and sentiment at the cost of a general dumbing down of psychoanalysis. Lacan's return to Freud was a return to the reconciliation of reason and the unconscious – something Žižek echoes when he argues that our only hope lies at "the intersection of reason and drive" (Žižek, 2012a, 1010) – in the face of an increasing emphasis on the "irrational id" erroneously locating the origins of psychoanalysis in the Romantic celebration of intuition and emotion.

By contrast to this tendency, psychoanalysis (much like Christianity) represents the point of the highest reconciliation of the unconscious and reason. One may attest to this idea on a number of different levels. Firstly, it is false to assume that the id is unorganized; the repetition compulsion and the indestructibility of the unconscious wish have taught us that the id has *structure* (Lacan, 2006, 551). Secondly, Freud's insistence that "the possibility of the attribute of unconsciousness would be completely excluded as far as emotions, feelings and affects are concerned" (Freud, 1915b) strictly forbids the idea that the latter is a cauldron of affects. Such a misunderstanding is symptomatic of the Freudo-Marxist tradition where a rather naïve libertarian conception of psychoanalysis prevails (a kind of "wild psychoanalysis" *après la lettre*). Today this misunderstanding persists in the idea that outbursts of intense emotion (often accompanied by acting out) testify to a "failure of repression" requiring the creation of new clinical entities such as the "borderline" and the "narcissist". This ignores the fact that Freud, in his *Studies on Hysteria*, crucially posited a "proton pseudos" (false premise) at the basis of neurosis and its accompanying wild paroxysms of affect. In other words, it is precisely the repression of a certain ideational content that has aetiological importance for Freud. The will to elevate psychoanalysis to a management of emotional life has led to an outright dismissal of this central inaugurating tenet of Freudian theory. Finally, Freud's pioneering work on fantasy involved the counterintuitive discovery of infantile sexual *theories* through which the toddler addresses questions concerning sexual difference, procreation, the relation between the parents and so on (Freud, 1905). The neurotic does not suffer from "bad" emotions but from *erroneous* thoughts. The child is, for Freud, an investigator/scientist addressing the riddle of sex in a proto-theoretical manner. In brief, the *structured* nature of the unconscious, the *absence of emotions* in the unconscious and, finally, the fact that the latter is a locus of *theoretical* elaboration all testify to the fact that, quipping Hegel, *the unconscious is not the highest emotion but the highest thought*. Lacan explicitly demystifies the myth of the "emotional unconscious":

> The unconscious is neither the primordial nor the instinctual, and what it knows of the elemental is no more than the elements of the signifier ... The intolerable scandal when Freudian sexuality was not yet holy was that it was so "intellectual".
>
> (Lacan quoted in Žižek, 2015, 163)

Like Christianity, as conceived by Hegel, Lacan's return to Freud is today's privileged sanctuary for the safeguarding of the identity-in-difference of religion-faith-emotion and philosophy-knowledge-reason. Diremption has here led to the devastating de-intellectualization of psychoanalysis and the rise of contradictory notions such as *emotional intelligence, life coaching* and other like concoctions resulting from the increasingly anti-philosophical nature of our times. Lamentable here is that a certain trend of psychoanalysis has given this hostile aversion to thought a good conscience by dressing it up in the "sophisticated" attire of its own concepts.

One of Hegel's great merits is to treat concepts like human subjects: the "Notion is not merely *soul*, but free subjective Notion that is for itself and therefore possesses personality" (Hegel, 1969, 824). Conversely, Lacan deserves our praise for treating human beings as concepts[2] (e.g. the formulae of sexuation, the "mathemes" of the four discourses etc.). The Lacanian *narcissistic suicidal aggression* – the correlate to Hegel's *battle of pure prestige* – is a vicissitude reserved as much for conceptual "dead letter" (an oxymoron indeed as nothing thrives more fervently than the concept) as for living human consciousness. A little dialectic playfulness (is there any other kind?) will render the following: concepts and persons stand in speculative identity-in-difference. However, when this is dirempted they play out their dialectical unity in the disparaged mode of narcissistic suicidal aggression. This is the case today as well as with all other epochs plagued by the sombre spectre of anti-intellectualism (e.g. consider the number of derogatory words used to designate intelligent people ("nerd", "geek" or "techy")). Hegel's "anthropomorphism" of the concept and Lacan's "formalization" of the human subject are the best antidotes against this obscurantist diremption. Concepts and humans should stand in *speculative* identity rather than *specular* strife. To quip Heine, let us be warned: where they burn notions, they will too in the end burn people.[3]

Notes

1 Meillassoux (2008) argues that the limitation Kant placed on reason paved the way for hypotheses regarding supposedly less restricted modalities of knowledge. Similarly, Badiou (2003b) feels that the Romantic disparagement of mathematics led to the prevailing belief in the "ineffable" that can only be accessed through intuition.

Likewise, Hegel believes that the language of the understanding is still too representative and that, as such, it engenders the illusion of the ineffable (Lebrun, 1972, 62).

2 Bion (1959) moves in the same direction as he rightly makes the link between cognition (the linking of concepts and thoughts) and copulation.

3 In today's late capitalism, rather than view notions as people, we view corporations as persons endowing them with all the personality of souls. In this regard, Jameson speaks of "the soulful corporation" (2010, 102).

Variation 6   The paradoxes of love

For Hegel, the turbulent destinies of lover and beloved are not isolated to the human realm but form, rather, the very structure of the concept both in its relation to other concepts and, more importantly, in its self-relation. Hegel clearly states the link between the concept and love, stipulating that this love entails "the seriousness, the suffering, the patience, and the labour of the negative" (Hegel, 1977, 10).[1] More specifically, love challenges common understanding and thus pushes the subject to ascend to speculative reason. For Hegel, the paradox of love consists of the fact that in love "I do not wish to be a self-subsistent and independent person and that, if I were, then I would feel defective and incomplete" (Hegel, 2008a, 162). Love thus severs the subject from humankind's most fundamental conceit, that of autonomy or, cast psychoanalytically, narcissism (what Lacan (2006, 153) recognized as "the passion of the soul *par excellence*"). For Hegel, "Love is at once the producing and the resolving of this contradiction" (Hegel; 2008a, 162) and as such it pushes us to go beyond the doxa of the understanding (and thus narcissistic self-conceit) and take on the challenge of speculative thought. Following Hegel's idea that love provides the structure of the logical concept, I will put forward various paradoxes of love and consider the resulting contradictions ensuing from diremption.[2]

Love is the site of intense dialectical tensions insofar as it involves the paradoxical identity-in-difference of a number of opposed terms. In *Anxiety*, Lacan makes the surprising claim that in love man does not have the phallus and woman is not the phallus. It is as though love requires that each partner flounder on the path of ordinary sexuation. Love is thus, firstly, the place of the identity-in-difference of winning and losing. Woman must lose her femininity (being the phallus) while man must lose his masculinity (having the phallus) so that love may arise. Love's triumph rests on the lovers' defeat. The touching beauty of Haneke's *Amour* consists precisely of staging a love where old age has robbed the woman of being the phallus and the man of having it. Here age shows that love has endured the loss of phallic triumph. It is easy to love when blinded by the splendor of youth. The true test comes when that has faded and idealization no longer provides a support for passion. Also, it is important to further note that the dichotomy by which man *has* and woman *is* the phallus hinders the path to sublimation. One must here distinguish idealization from sublimation. Where the former rests on a woman's admiration of a man's phallic potency and, correlatively, on a man's fixation to his partner's beauty, the latter, by contrast, rests precisely on the opposite, namely the realization regarding the partner's failure to meet that phallic standard. This realization is what sublimation proper consists of. As Žižek puts it rather poetically, "if it's true love, then I don't love the woman for her smile, eyes, legs, etc. – I love her smile, eyes, etc. because they are hers" (Žižek, 2015, 21). True sublimated love requires phallic demise where blind idealization gives way to insight that *chooses* to remain silent about the beloved's flaws, not out of ignorance, but out of the modest humility of love. Idealization rests on a diremption of the very paradoxical identity-in-difference of the beautiful and the ugly. The ugly is beauty's Other; without it the latter dwindles to mere decorative finery. Nietzsche's aesthetic genius explicitly posited the paradox by which beauty finds its origin in the experience of ugliness: "What would be 'beautiful', if the contrary to it had not first come to awareness of itself, if ugliness had not first said to itself: 'I am ugly'?" (Nietzsche, 1998). Žižek gives voice to a similar idea with the following subchapter title: *The Birth of Beauty Out of the Abject*. The psychoanalytic commonplace, by which idealization is said to rest on splitting, can now be sharpened with the idea that it is, more precisely, the splitting of beauty and ugliness that is at stake. Can the beauty of woman, of the "fairer" sex, be separated from the abjection of woman, that she stands as the bearer of the literal mark of castration? Is her greater attunement to the arts of aesthetic refinement not dialectically bound to the horror she hides?

Secondly, in love only a lack has the power to fulfil. In love, Lacan explains, one is not asked to give one's overabundance, one's excess or one's resources. Under the demand of love, one is not even invited to give one's joy but, simply, what one does not have. Lacan (2001b) reminds us that, according to Plato, it is only sorrow (*Penia*) that can give birth to love (*Eros*). Echoing an old evangelical saying, Lacan (2001b) repeatedly states that the "rich man" cannot access love. The whole comedy of love lies precisely in the fact that a lack comes to play the role of excess. One can also find in this paradox the key to understanding the tragedy of love. In love, Lacan explains, the lover seeks a non-existent object in the beloved. The disappointment of love, its tragic dimension, emerges when the discrepancy between what is sought and what the beloved has is revealed. Thirdly, there is no love that does not stand in dialectical union with hate. Love without hate flounders into the contradiction of passionless adoration:

> the more a man can believe a woman confuses him with God, in other words, what she enjoys, the less he *hates*, the less he *is* – both spellings are intended[3] – and since, after all, there is no love without hate, the less he loves.
>
> (Lacan, 1998, 89, emphasis mine)

A love worthy of its name must not shy away from the aggressivity and hate that constitutes the kernel of my *jouissance*. When Freud (1930) explicitly refuses to *love the neighbour*, Lacan sees there a fleeing from aggressivity and hate, one's own as well as the Other's:

> We can found our case on the following, namely, that every time that Freud stops short in horror at the consequences of the commandment to love one's neighbor, we see evoked the presence of that fundamental evil which dwells within this neighbor. But if that is the case, then it also dwells within me. And what is more of a neighbor to me than this heart within which is that of my *jouissance* and which I don't dare go near? For as soon as I go near it, as *Civilization and Its Discontents* makes clear, there rises up the unfathomable aggressivity from which I flee, that I turn against me, and which in the very place of the vanished Law adds its weight to that which prevents me from crossing a certain frontier at the limit of the Thing.
>
> (Lacan, 1986)

To love the neighbour, for Lacan, means to embrace the kernel of hate-evil-*jouissance* that inhabits my neighbour and myself. In loving the Woman-neighbour-Thing, man must be willing to hate and explore the realms of evil. Interestingly, Lacan (1998) recalls that Freud makes use of Empedocles' idea that "God must be the most ignorant of all beings ... insofar as he does not know hate". Freud was, perhaps more than any of his predecessors, aware of the intricate tie linking love and hate, and yet, he fails to love the neighbour out of a fear of aggressivity and hate. If, as Benvenuto argues, "Eros is making the other the finality of my subjectivity" (Benvenuto, 2016, 154) we must also recall that the courage for aggressivity is crucial on this path. With Lacan we may say that "as long as it's a question of the good, there's no problem" (Lacan, 1986). The true test consists of accommodating the neighbour's evil as well as our own.

Fourthly, for Badiou (here following Lacan), love and *jouissance* are distinct and opposed precisely insofar as the former inaugurates the Two as the minimal form of collective – Badiou poetically claims that "love is communism" (2003a) – while the latter further fortifies the hegemony of the One. We may here add, however, that Badiou's definition of love misses another of its fundamental paradoxes, namely that love at once marks the decline of egotism[4] and represents the height of narcissism (Lacan, 1988).[5] As Radiguet (2004) put it, "love is the egotism of two". Is *Genesis* not a story of self-diremptive love, namely the colossal egotism of love that leads frail humanity to the conceited defiance of God? Badiou's diremption of this paradoxical identity-in-difference pertaining to love may account for the somewhat idealistic views he holds in this regard (cf. *Éloge de l'amour*). He cannot appreciate what psychotic lucidity alone could unveil, namely the fact that love, despite its healing powers, is undeniably also a fatal disease (for Lacan (1998), the greatest student of the psychotic, love is also a form of suicide).[6] We cannot allow idealistic and/or cynical simplifications to obfuscate the dialectical tension between Badiou's love as communism and its obverse love as egotism.

Consideration of the fifth paradox of love requires a brief foray into Badiou's reflections on love in general and, more specifically, his thesis according to which true love, understood as "the immanence of the Two", is atheism (Badiou, 2003a). In *What is Love?*, Badiou (2000) attempts to distinguish *veritable* love from four "simulacra" of love: fusional, oblative, purely sexual and Platonic/asexual love. These are experiences that may be mistaken for love but which fall short of the Event of love because they do not attest to the sexual disjunction:

1. In fusional love, the disjunction is foreclosed in the name of the One. The two lovers constitute a unity and difference is entirely *obliterated*. Here the real of the disjunction is obliterated through a striving for unity which may even culminate in death.
2. When love becomes a mere affect of tenderness towards the other, the dimension of ambivalence and hence disjunction is *veiled* over.
3. A pure sexual encounter cannot attest to the disjunction as each partner remains entirely at the level of masturbatory jouissance. For Badiou, sex taken alone keeps two partners solipsistically isolated from each other. Badiou, in *Éloge de l'amour*, explicitly states that desire separates the two partners. Žižek often expresses the view that the sexual act is "masturbation with a real partner" (Žižek quoted in Zupančič, 2000, 293). Here the dimension of the disjunction is indeed experienced but then arrogantly and selfishly *disregarded*.
4. Platonic love outright *refuses* to experience the disjunction through sexual abstinence.

The sexual disjunction is the psychoanalytic name of the biblical fall. The derivative modes of love represent yearning for prelapsarian bliss, namely the desire to *obliterate*, *veil*, *disregard* or simply *refuse* the truth of the sexual disjunction. This temptation must be resisted. True love is atheistic resignation where the fantasy of paradise beyond disjunction is abandoned. To Badiou's reflections, I would simply add that love is, indeed, atheism but it is also deepest piety and *faith*. The fusional, oblative, erotic and Platonic conceptions mark as much of a straying from true atheism as they do from veritable faith. True faith, as true atheism, can only be achieved after the fall. One must have faith in the name-of-the-father in order to reach the atheism of sexual disjunction.

In *Encore*, Lacan argues that recognition of the impossibility of the sexual rapport opens the path of wisdom. Could we then say that to love is to give up the fantasy of finding the person that is "right for us"? The following anecdote illustrates this idea. It is said that a married couple asked Socrates whether their son should wed a particular woman.[7] Socrates immediately replied "He should marry at once". Puzzled, they asked how he came to such a rash decision without reflection. "There are two possible outcomes", he replied. "Either she will be right for him or she will not. If she is, there is nothing else to be said. If she is not, one also need not worry as he will then become a philosopher". To this anecdote, I add the following sequel which will deepen the idea of love as a paradoxical expression of identity-in-difference. Let us imagine the concerned parents respond thus:

> We entirely understand what you are saying but the problem here is a bit more complicated, as our son is certain of one thing alone, namely that he wants to become a philosopher. As a result, the most dreaded outcome would be, in fact, that she is right for him as that would put all his ambitions to peril.

Should we not all likewise seek in our beloved someone who will help fulfil our philosophical vocation, someone not "right for us"?

Finally, another paradox of love revealed by psychoanalysis is the incongruity between love and the feeling of love. Lacan (1977) defines the psychoanalytic process as a movement from $i(a)$ to a, namely from the specular image to the object that slips from that image and therefore plays the part of *cause of desire*. Psychoanalytic treatment moves from the narcissistic field to that which disturbs it; it transitions from $i(a)$ or the field of love to a, that of desire. In *Encore*, however, Lacan defines the analyst discourse as love. On the one hand, we have a narcissistic love based on the libidinal investment of the specular image and, on the other hand, we have the psychoanalytic process, namely what was formerly defined as the patient libidinal *dis-investment* of the image. Insofar as psychoanalysis is equated with the latter form of love, it is safe to surmise that it is deemed the wiser love, commensurate with the slow ascension of the concept. It is certainly the more *speculative* love, insofar as it must endure the paradox of giving up the feeling of love pertaining to the narcissistic domain. Psychoanalysis begins with love (transference to the supposed subject of knowledge) and ends with the deeper more paradoxical love, namely dis-investment from the first love. To borrow again from Hegel, the first is mere "disporting Love" while the latter testifies to the "labour of the negative" (Hegel, 1977, 10). The love that pertains to the narcissistic field is the love of the other who matches my ideal; it is the index of a happy correspondence between my fantasy and the other's appearance. This love, simple and there from the start, must be relinquished through the slow and arduous work of abandoning the narcissistic field (the feeling of love) and taking the challenge of a paradoxical love. Philosophical love is the transition from the *specular* to the *speculative*.

The wisdom required by love is that of speculative reason insofar as love is the intense expression of the identity-in-difference of 1) triumph and defeat, 2) plenitude and lack, 3) love and hate, 4) communism and egotism, 5) piety and atheism, 6) the person not "right" for us and the one who will raise us to the heights of philosophy (the concept) and, finally, 7) true love is at odds with the feeling of love.[8] Love is lost when it is deprived of its dialectical unity with its contraries. The "lower" profane terms take ghastly vengeance when dirempted by the snobbery of the "higher" term's conceit. This leads to *sick love* manifesting in the one-sided triumph of despondent defeat, abysmal lack, appaling hate, dreadful egotism, sinful impiety and discordant incompatibility. Insofar as the concept emerges from the experience of the dialectical tensions of love, the loss of love entails a concomitant loss of the concept – something widely attested to in the endemic anti-philosophical tenor of our times. One may argue that the rise of generally anti-Hegelian postmodern philosophies attests, if you will allow me the malice, to new modes of *thought without the concept*, an undertaking as tepid as it is decaffeinated.

A shortcoming of Badiou's thought lies in repeatedly missing the importance of this profane element. His excessive *fidelity to fidelity* castrates his thought from appreciating the paradoxical intertwinement of betrayal and fidelity. This is an ever more acute problem when dealing with the specific question of love which, as we know from the many paradoxes it entails, is far from a simple matter of fidelity. Badiou (2009) is, in this regard, too quick to dismiss Proust's insistence on the link between love and jealousy. With Proust (and Freud insofar as he placed Oedipal triangulation at the heart of human passion), we must insist on the centrality of jealousy and betrayal in love. Badiou misses the crucial point that the emphasis on fidelity in love (a specifically feminine demand) is there precisely to counter the *inherent* threat of betrayal, infidelity and jealousy. If perfidious deceit and suspicious distrust did not *constitutively* plague love from within, why would vows of fidelity play a central role between lovers? One cannot but notice the very feminine traits of Badiou's thought. This is not, of course, a reproach in itself but only in that its one-sidedness hinders Badiou's philosophy of love from accounting for emergences of masculine profanation as sexual infidelity. Insofar as the masculine is prone to attacks of profanity, man is subject to attacks of betrayal (temptation). Femininity, standing for the *constitutively* profane, is inherently betraying and is therefore immune to attacks in the form of *exception*. Lacan (2006) even argues that the feminine demand for fidelity is tied to a projection of her own constitutive infidelity to the male partner. Just as fidelity that dirempts betrayal becomes zealotry, love that is not also betrayal is tantamount to idolatry, namely pure sacralization that has dirempted profanation. To love requires, at the very least, the betrayal of the first incestuous other. The subject incapable of this profanation-betrayal is doomed to impotent love. The impasses of male and female homosexuality lie precisely in that in one case we have an excess of profanation in the form of attacks of betrayal while, in the other, we have a quasi-paranoid demand for fidelity faced with the excessiveness of constitutive infidelity.[9]

Notes

1 Freud (1915a) also put forward a theoretical apparatus based on a consideration of love and its contraries. He distinguished three polarities of the mind (economic, biological and real) built upon the principal contraries of love, namely *to be loved, indifference* and *to hate*.

2 This, I hope, will provide further insight regarding the structure of the concept, something that will be indispensable at the end of the treatise when I consider the notion of the human.

3 The original French plays on the homonymy of "*il hait*" (he hates) and "*il est*" (he is).

4 Freud (1911) quotes the Persian mystic poet Rumi: "when the flames of love arise, the self that ruthless tyrant dies".

5 Hegel also disregards this aspect in his account of the paradox of love.

6 As Lafontaine said it: "Love, Love when thou holdest us/ One can well say: 'Farewell prudence'". www.aesopfables.com/cgi/aesop1.cgi?jdlf&iv1jd&iv2l.jpg. Though there is much to be praised in love there is much to be warned against too (*Romeo and Juliet, Tristan and Isolde* etc.).

7 This is evidently an untrue story for which I cannot even find a source. That said, the anecdote is informative for our purposes.

8 Lacan and Badiou opted for a logic of love: "It is thus necessary to keep the pathos of passion, error, jealousy, sex, and death at a distance. No theme requires more pure logic than love" (Badiou, 2000, 266).

9 On the impasses of homosexuality see Morel (2000) and Soler (2000).

Variation 7　The paradox of identity

In the spirit of Freud's discovery of the psychopathology of everyday life, the Lacanian subject emerges only in shadowy glimpses and ephemeral moments such as slips of the tongue, dreams, jokes and so on. As soon as one has taken the slightest glimpse of the subject it vanishes. When Lacan claims that "a signifier is that which represents the subject for another signifier" he means that there is no signifier that discloses the subject entirely; no slip of the tongue will completely unveil the unconscious. All signifiers point to other signifiers – the subject emerging transiently between two signifiers. It is likewise with the object which, insofar as it is "negativised" from the imaginary (i.e. "reality"), may be glimpsed only in fleeting moments. The psychoses provide, once again, a challenging exception to this rule concerning the ephemeral nature of subjectivity and, concomitantly, the transience of the object. Clinically, the former is most vividly attested to in the hardened identifications of the psychotic where the subject is reduced to the level of mere meaning: "when the subject appears somewhere as meaning, he is manifested elsewhere as 'fading', as disappearance" (Lacan, 1977, 218). With respect to the object, it has failed to be constituted for lack of separation. Scotomized pregnancies and the phenomenology of hoarding testify to this phenomenon. We thus find ourselves facing two homologous paradoxes at the level of the subject and the object. Firstly, we see that *there is a subject only insofar as it disappears*; a diehard clinging to identification only leads to *aphanisis*, the disappearance of the subject. The caricature of an army private zealously attached to his duties most comically attests to this fading. Guyomard (1992, 19) gives very eloquent expression to this paradox when he argues that the less we have identifications the more we have an identity (in a truer sense of the word). One must, however, avoid the misleading dichotomy of "true" and "false" selves as that too would be diremptive. To further complicate matters (in our dialectical paradigm complications are always welcome), Lacan (2006) argues that "the *I* and the *ego* separate and overlap in every particular subject". In other words, what *blocks* the subject is also what *is* the subject. The true and false selves are not merely opposed and, as a result, the army private's false pretences will inevitably give way to instances of subjectivity even in the very effort to hide these. Secondly, we see *that the object emerges only on the background of its loss* without which it is reduced to the inert stasis of a heap of junk.

In *Archive Fever*, Derrida argues that mourning is already desire. To lose the object is already to find it again and, conversely, to find it already implicates the subject in loss. This identity-in-difference remains massively hidden from the perspective of melancholic diremptivity. In "Melancholia and the Unabandoned Object" Russell Grigg puts forward a compelling critique of Freud's idea linking melancholia to loss. Against Freud, Grigg (2015) argues that "the melancholic response arises because of the proximity of the object through its failure to have become lost". By contrast, I hold that little is gained by simply swinging away from Freud. Melancholia is neither simply the outcome of an unconscious loss (Freud) nor is it tantamount to the object "not being lost". It is crucial to posit the concomitance of the object and its loss and maintain that melancholia emerges precisely where this is dirempted. More precisely, diremption may take two forms depending on which moment of the identity-in-difference is occluded. Where loss is emphasized to the detriment of the object, we have melancholia. Where the object's presence is noted at the expense of loss, the subject falls prey to mania. Ultimately, the direction of diremption hardly matters as melancholia and mania form an anxious dialectical unity in the manic-depressive psychoses, where we testify to the contradiction of depressions that are themselves manic. We no longer have a mere alternation between polarized states but a ghastly fusion of a subject at once manic and depressed. As one suffering subject put it, "My depressions were tornadolike – fast-paced episodes that brought me into dark rages of terror" (Leader, 2012).

The dialectical shifts between mania and melancholia represent two moments of a concept disparaged through *the ideological work of illness*. The subject, incapable of seizing the contrary moments in speculative unity, experiences discord between massively contrasting affective states. The separation of moments can also occur through the ideological distortion of space where two insufficiently differentiated subjects each stand for one of the moments in its "purity" (e.g. a perennially elated man married to a woman suffering from unipolar depression – a model instance of *woman as symptom of man*). Here the kinship between Hegel and Klein becomes apparent. Where the depressive position hinges on the ability to sustain the speculative unity of contraries, the paranoid schizoid position results from diremption dividing and intensifying the two logical moments. Mania's frantic denial of depression leads to the triumph of the latter "lower" term. Depression is the truth (subjectivization) of mania, as much as the aforementioned woman is symptom of her frenzied man.

Here the proud *jubilation* of identification (cf. *The Mirror* Stage) is hardly distinguishable from the defeated despondency of destitution. The mirror stage – the process by which identity is formed – protects the infant from these mad alternations or, what is equally distressing, the rigid fixation to either extreme. The infant acquires a self-image through the experience of recognizing him/herself in the mirror and thereby gains respite from inner bodily incoordination. For Lacan, the infant's initial inner self-experience is marked by motor insufficiency. Identification with his/her body image allows for the illusion of bodily unity, which has real effects insofar as it allows the child to gain increased motor agility. In a nutshell, the mirror stage brings about a divorce from the body proper for the sake of an engagement with the body's image. The result is an extraction of *jouissance* insofar as the body, in its palpitations and tremors, is partially forsaken for the sake of a fascination with the self-image. This is how the structure of neurosis is established, a structure where the image of the self reigns supreme. The neurotic becomes henceforth engrossed in how he/she is *seen* by others and him/herself. The psychotic, by contrast, is without body image and will therefore not benefit from the ego's capacity to limit *jouissance*. It is no wonder then that it took Nietzsche whom, quipping Žižek (1999), we may christen the "psychotic philosopher if there ever was one") to wake Western philosophy from the slumber of its ascetic denial of sensuality – a denial which is, paradoxically, itself imbued in sensualist *jouissance*. Psychotic grandiosity has nothing to do with excess narcissism but is, rather, consequent upon the lack of a consistent ego. Freud often referred to the psychoses as the "narcissistic neuroses" with the idea that such subjects are so deeply engrossed in "primary narcissism" that transference to an analyst would take place only very problematically. This idea fails to appreciate the extent to which the psychotic lacks any properly sustained image of self, something we see most explicitly in the phenomenology of the schizophrenias. According to Lacanian theory, the psychotic, far from exhibiting an overly infatuated self-rapport, is so engrossed in the Other that his/her "self" has hardly formed. In the face of an absence of cathexis of the body image, psychotic *jouissance* risks exploding beyond measure. This is the source of the grandiosity; excessive *jouissance* rather than self-infatuation. The lack of an ego in the psychoses results at times in an acute preoccupation with the *jouissance* of body. This is most explicitly attested to in schizophrenic "organ speech" (Freud, 1915b) as well as the various forms of psychotic hypochondria, not to mention the experiences of bodily fragmentation consequent upon depersonalization. The transition from object of *jouissance* to object of desire may be understood in light of the mirror stage. The formation of a self-image requires the gradual "phallicization" of the child's body, namely the process by which different parts of the body enter into the metonymy of the mother's desire ("he has his father's eyes" and so on). This process drains the body of *jouissance* leaving behind only localized remainders in the form of partial objects and erogenous zones.

This movement from the inner sensation of the *jouissance* of the body to a fixation to the externally imposed image of the body has an earlier philosophical correlate in the thought of Schopenhauer (1966), who distinguished between the experience of the world as "Will" and as "representation". The former involves the experience of the world through the feeling of one's visceral *inner* sense, while the latter involves an experience of the world mediated by what one *sees* rather than feels. We could say that the mirror stage marks the transition from an experience of self as "Will" or *jouissance* to an experience of self as "representation" or ego. The Nietzschean (1999) re-appropriation of Schopenhauer's distinction, under the rubrics of the Dionysiac and the Apolline, also evokes a duality between the body as *jouissance* and the body as image.

The mirror stage involves the following identity-in-difference: *one can have a "healthy" relation with the body (i.e. some minimal mastery) only if one is alienated from that body.* The Apolline will rise in beauty only at the cost of relinquishing Dionysiac ecstasy. Arguably, the psychotic and pervert's deeper awareness of *jouissance* is the effect of the diremption of the mirror stage's paradox. Psychosis and perversion thus attest to the contradiction of an over-investment in the body (rather than its image) accompanied by radical anomalies in the subject's relation to the body.

We may here distinguish between a diremptive and a non-diremptive mirror stage, where the former would be incomplete, insofar as identification with the specular other is not followed by an equally important process of dis-identification.[1] Such a mirror stage is reducible to master discourse (*"le discours du maître"*) centred on a delusional sense of self-mastery founded upon the ego's fallacious sense of having substantive being (*"le discours du m'être"*) (*Encore*). We are here at the level of *jubilation* where the subject is veritably enthralled by the image. Feelings of extreme despondency may follow every time the fixity of the identification is challenged by the vicissitudes of life. Such diremptive forms of mirroring mark the contemporary cult of the "selfie". Here the subject's jubilant cry is sometimes tragically followed by death, thereby staging the ironic contra-diction by which solipsistic self-mastery overlaps with the most literal staging of subjective destitution. The paranoid subject too testifies to this diremptive mirror stage; the pathos of *narcissistic suicidal aggression* manifests as the contradic-tion of *suicidal homicide* or, where the will to preserve the Other persists, as *homi-cidal suicide*. All the depersonalizations of the schizophrenic also belong here, as identification without dis-identification is as fragile as the proverbial unbending tree. Shame is not operative in the diremptive mirror stage. This leads to the painful contradiction of *shameless humiliation* so beautifully captured by Julien Green: "God, unable to make us humble, made us humiliated" (quoted in Goddard, 2014). The obsessional neurotic's total disdain for his/her body is also a result of this diremption at the level of identification. He/she is so wedded and infatuated with his/her image that the body proper is entirely forgotten (e.g. Narcissus, so deeply enamored with his image, did not notice he was drowning). A non-diremptive mirror stage, by contrast, includes identification and dis-identification alike. What is at stake is an image of the self that includes lack. We have here the non-specularizable object that is, paradoxically, crucial for specularity. Without the object *a* which slips out of the image we do not have a self-image at all. Moreover, the identity-in-difference of shame and dignity is here operative. The humble subject of the non-diremptive mirror stage enjoys solemn self-respect. Shame is speculative. We may here delight, as Hegel surely would, at the speculative coincidence of the meaning of the words *shameful* and *shameless*; despite contrary suffixes they mean the same thing.

The distinction here put forward between a diremptive and non-diremptive mirror stage can aid us in giving added theoretical precision to André Green's (2007) differentiation between "life narcissism" and "death narcissism". Where the latter would involve diremptive identity formations, the former would be more attuned to the paradoxes of identity. However, to maintain the rigour of our Hegelian reading we must immediately add that the diremptive mirror stage is but a "moment" of its non-diremptive counterpart. For Hegel "being evil means singularizing myself in a way that cuts me off from the universal (which is the rational, the laws, the determinations of spirit)" (Bernstein, 2002, 62). However, Bernstein also adds that this is a necessary stage in the development of the I (ibid, 63). The jubilatory moment of the mirror stage is the diremptive "evil" moment where I cut myself off from the Other in triumphant exaltation. If we bear in mind that, for Hegel, evil is the source of all problems but also the place where reconciliation finds its source (ibid: 63), then we may suggest that the non-diremptive mirror stage is a sublation of the diremptive mirror stage. Self-diremption, Bernstein notes, brings about evil but it is also the condition for the sublation of evil (ibid: 63). Likewise, jubilation brings with it strife and conflict, but without it the conditions for reconciliation and love would also be lost.

For Hegel, the subject is "what maintains itself in being-other-than-itself" (Hegel quoted in Althusser, 2006). To be "I" one must be "not-I".[2] This paradox is, indeed, what radically separates Lacan's mirror stage (heir to Hegel) from Winnicott's (1971)[3] "mirroring" or Fonagy and Target's "mentalization". The latter miss the fact that what guarantees the minimal consistency of identification is precisely the very thing that contests it. This is the object *a*, that which gives the image its consistency precisely by resisting inclusion in the image and thereby contesting that consistency. The ego holds together only on the basis of an *extraction*.[4] Traditional ontology posits a substantial subject that has full being, while postmodernism denies the notion of the subject altogether (e.g. Foucault's "the death of man"). By contrast to these two insufficient alternatives, Lacanian psychoanalysis posits (with Hegel) the paradox of a subject who acquires a substantive "essence" precisely from his/her lack of substantiality. Many non-Lacanian schools of psychoanalysis attest to a regression to traditional ontology. This is evidenced by the prevalence of notions (pure thoughts, I should say) such as "character" (Reich) and a continued adherence to biologistic conceptions of the human libido. The aforementioned theory of mentalization as a means of acquiring a robust identity also adheres to this mirage of traditional ontology. Thus, beyond the mirror stage's dramatization of a certain paradox at the level of the imaginary ("I" = "not-I"), we now attest to the expression of a paradox at the level of the real or the object *a*. The object's obstinacy – forever slipping out of our grasp – denies the completion of our self-image and through this denial, paradoxically, gives the image its consistency. The subject maintains itself precisely by perpetually losing a part of itself; to be "I" one must be "I minus *a*". The drive thus becomes a *death* drive, insofar as it emerges primordially as the fool's despairing attempt to remedy this paradox through vain aggressive attempts to desperately secure a hold on the ever-fleeting object. The logic according to which I must lose something of me in order to be me is the source of aggression in the mirror stage where this structural necessity is blamed on the specular other, accused of robbing me of my identity in the very gesture by which it grants me this identity. The mirror stage dramatizes this paradox, thereby confusing a structural necessity with the contingency of an imaginary other's presumed will. When André Green asserts that the death drive is narcissism (2007), he may be drawing inspiration from Lacan's theory of the imaginary, according to which the subject wants to destroy the source from where he/she acquires a self-image. The specular relation thus accounts for aggressivity and the death drive is indeed tied to narcissism.

Notes

1 Moncayo (2014) also asserts that identity functions according to the law of contradiction.
2 As Lebrun puts it, "Spirit harbours within itself its own opposite" (1972, 57, my translation).
3 Winnicott erroneously found in Lacan's *mirror stage* a predecessor to his mirroring. As Bowie (1991) aptly argued, Winnicott's Lacan is "Lacan without Lacan" insofar as the reference to alienation is missing.
4 This conception takes us very far from self-psychological models, seeking to make good "deficits" of self-image prevalent in "disorders of the self".

Variation 8　Subject and collective

When Lacan claims that "the collective is nothing other than the subject of the individual", we must sharply differentiate collective, subject and individual. For Lacan, psychoanalysis is not a science of man/individual insofar as "there cannot be a science of man since science's man does not exist, only its subject does" (Lacan 2006, 730).[1] The "subject of the individual" is the gap (subject) in the ego's (individual) imaginary edifice signalling a point of impossibility in the subject's self-representation. As Žižek puts it most eloquently: "the subject is nothing other than the impossibility of its own signifying representation" (1989). The subject emerges precisely where the Other's signifiers fail the ego in its self-representation. Only against the background of the lack in the Other is subjectivity possible. When Lacan thus claims that the subject is "the collective" or, in similar vein, that the "unconscious is the social", we are left all the more puzzled insofar as the subject is here *equated* with the social Other. This is, seemingly, a blatant contradiction of the idea that the subject of the unconscious is a *gap* in the Other. This paradox re-inscribes itself in the following paradox as well. On the one hand, Žižek shows, we have the universality of language and social otherness that inhibits the subject from realizing itself:

> does not Hegel's *Phenomenology of Spirit* tell us again and again the same story of the repeated failure of the subject's endeavor to realize his project in social Substance, to impose his vision on the social universe – the story of how the "big Other", the social substance, again and again thwarts his project and turns it upside-down?.
>
> (Žižek, 1999, 76)

On the other hand, however, the subject will only arise out of the ponderous edifice of language and social substance if, and only if, he/she agrees to partake in the collective social bond. The solution here is to recognize the paradox by which *one may reduce the suffocating weight of the Other (thwarting the subject's project) by getting close to it (making it extimate) and joining the social substance (accepting thrownness, to put it in Heideggerian terms* – see variation 17*).* In other words, the Other ceases to be "substance" as the "individual" approaches it less frightfully. At that "magical" point of encounter between subject and Other (a point of extimacy one may christen as "cure") "substance" becomes "collective" and "individual" becomes "subject". Subject and collective are thus two synonymous words for the point of intersection at which individual and Other meet; this point of intersection is a point at which both are lacking. In Hegelian terms, where individual and substance are pure thoughts, subject and collective are, by contrast, notions. Once the transition to the notion takes place, the big Other ceases to be a massive obstacle to the subject's self-realization (turning his/her plans "upside down"). The vicious dialectical reversals thwarting the subject give way to milder and more reasonable fluctuations. As with revolution's turn into the terror, these failures of the subject are not (contra Žižek) *necessary* dialectical outcomes; they are, rather, the result of diremption. Though failure does indeed provide "the form of success", failure may be held in speculative identity with success as its Other such that the two need not split as massively separate temporal/historical moments of a dialectical shift. Indeed, the subject who maintains his/her success in speculative identity with failure (common morality christens him/her as *modest*) is less likely to succumb to devastating miscarriages.

Psychoanalysis' starting point is the collective, namely the space where subjectivity emerges. Herein lies the importance of projects aiming the treatment of the psychoses within institutional spaces. Guy Dana (2010) argues that the aim of the clinical work within institutional spaces is to create a plurality of locations in such a way that the question of the subject awakens through the tension created by the whole. Groups are created where patients can speak to each other and where partial identifications are made. This creates the possibility for socialization and allows the subject to loosen the hold of previous identifications now rendered unnecessary. In neurosis, the subject emerges between signifiers. In psychosis, the plurality of institutional places replaces the plurality of signifiers. It is thus hoped that the subject may appear in the interstitial zone between these spaces. With only one institution (the hospital), Dana argues, the collective is lost and so is subjectivity; paraphrasing Lacan, we may quip that the subject of psychosis fades behind the ponderous presence of the hospital-signifier. Within a pluralistic arrangement, substance is more likely to transform into collective insofar as the interval between spaces may institute a lack in the Other. Paradoxically, it is by relinquishing itself as universal (i.e. abolishing the universality of the hospital) that the institution truly universalizes itself as a collective. The hope is that a similar logic would occur at the level of the subject such that the psychotic would slowly rework and partially abandon a terrifyingly specular imaginary built around the (false) universality of the primal mother/father in order to then achieve the (true) universality of a subject recognized by the collective (rather than recognized only by a primal mother/father as the latter's object of *jouissance*). The introduction of space and lack (or "interval", as Dana tellingly names it) allows for "the dialectic" by which the individual may "universalize [his/her] particularity" (Lacan, 2006, 148) and thereby gain recognition by a collective that has also universalized itself by relinquishing its hegemony. The foreboding space of the hospital is a place where precisely this dialectic of universality and particularity is dirempted, leading to the ominous contradiction of subjects (patients) entirely cut-off from social otherness and yet entirely drowned in the discourse of the Other (psychiatry) with its weighty signifiers in the guise of the unequivocal "pseudo-scientific" language of the DSM from which little respite can be envisioned. The distinction between a hospital and a pluralistic clinical institution may now be given more precise theoretical acuity with the formulation according to which the former is a pure thought while the latter is a notion. The subversive and curative potential of the clinical institution lies precisely in the fact that it functions as notion and hence *symptom* for the subjects. The pluralistic nature of the institution prevents any one sector from assuming the aura of a pure thought or master signifier. The fact of constituting *one link in a chain* prevents any link from asserting itself as pure thought. Laudable projects such as Dana's embody the great communist ideal as it is sung in the International: "We are nothing, let us be all". The psychoanalytic institution is indeed a collective of "nothings" (subject's reduced to *bare life* through the vicissitudes of fate) seeking to create together a veritable "all", namely a universal that is free of the hegemony of the One. The great medieval Persian poet Attar's *The Conference of Birds* tells the tale of thirty birds *(si morgh)* flying together in pursuit of a God/leader *(simorgh)*.[2] At the end of their journey they realize that God is nothing other than the collective they have created. A perfect tale, indeed, of *nothings* becoming *all!*

The diremption of the subject-collective dialectical unity goes hand in hand with the failure of intimacy. According to Dana (2010), the psychotic is not capable of constructing the Other as *intimate*. His/her Other is either intrusive, totally untouchable or both. Schreber's God provides a paradigmatic example insofar as He is, at once, massively invasive and curiously ignorant of human affairs. Both extremes testify to a failure of intimacy that we may tie, more generally, to the failure of accomplishing neighbourly love.[3] Love, for the psychotic, entails a cosmic catastrophe – hence all the efforts to deflect it through the grammar of paranoia (Freud, 1911). To slightly sharpen Dana's claim, it is perhaps more accurate to say that it is the domain of extimacy that has not been duly constituted. The psychotic cannot constitute the object since the latter is, by definition, extimate; it is both external and intimate – it touches the subject at his/her most intimate core while, nonetheless, retaining a radical exteriority. The clinical picture testifies to great difficulty in separating from the object; as Lacan (1969) famously quipped, "the psychotic carries the object in his pocket". The object is, so to speak, grafted onto the body. The most striking example is that of a scotomized pregnancy where the object (baby) is reduced to an extension of the self, such that the mother does not even recognize it. Alternatively, we have the mother who knows she is pregnant but speaks, without irony or metaphor, of the baby as "the monster". In one case, the baby is in no way made *external* while in the other case it is so utterly and literally foreign that no *intimacy* is achieved at all. To be theoretically accurate we should say that in both cases the object-baby has become neither external nor intimate. Extimacy has not occurred insofar as its achievement involves recognizing *the paradox of an object made intimate precisely through becoming external.* For the psychotic, the baby is either a foreign intruder or a mere extension of the mother, seamlessly sewn onto her body without a trace of separation. To experience the object as extimate is a veritable achievement akin to acknowledging the unconscious, the intimate-external Thing *par excellence.* As the by-product of the discourse of the Other, the unconscious is, indeed, a foreign entity and yet also what is most internal.

Grave problems ensue precisely when the subject chooses the path of voluntarism rather than that of the sacrificial emptying into the Other. We may argue that the diremption of the identity-in-difference of kenosis and self-realization leads to the severe impasse of the "beautiful soul"[4] with its ungodly contradiction, so elegantly expressed by Jameson, of a "desperate dialectical unity" of "philanthropy and paranoia" (Jameson, 2010). One may here add that philanthropy and paranoia are in-themselves sites of contradiction as both represent the height of narcissistic conceit manifesting as excessive preoccupation (negative or positive) with the external world. This is arguably the reason for Lacan's suspicion of philanthropy expressed with vigour as early as in *The Mirror Stage*: "we place no trust in altruistic feeling, we who lay bare the aggressivity that underlies the activity of the philanthropist, the idealist, the pedagogue, and even the reformer". Here we also stumble on a central shortcoming of Foucault's thought. The ethics of the so-called care of the self does not appreciate the fact that the path to self-realization must go through the channel of kenosis-evacuation. This misrecognition inherent to Foucault's ethics may be the reason why Žižek (1999) baptizes him as "the pervert philosopher if there ever was one". Foucault's diremption of the paradoxical self-realization through kenosis leads to the contradiction of *narcissistic perdition* where a subject's narcissistic practise (dieting, asceticism and so on) furthers alienation.

Hegel believes that fear emerges insofar as the subject flees kenosis (Hegel, 1970, 189). We could say that Lacan's "Other" or Hegel's "World Spirit" is a symptom of the subject.[5] When Jameson (2010) claims that "Spirit is the collective", we may add that spirit is the collective insofar as the latter is the symptom that the subject must identify with lest he/she fall in the tumultuous vicissitudes of diremption and the consequent triumph of the "lower" term. Lebrun thus notes that for Hegel, "all suffering is the price that the particular pays for obstinately maintaining its difference" (Lebrun, 1972, 48, my translation). The refusal of kenosis is tantamount to rejecting this symptom and may lead, in the worst instance, to paranoia (a return of world spirit – the "lower" term from the standpoint of the pretence to autonomy – in the guise of a persecutor). In Freudian terms, we could say that the refusal of kenosis disparages the homosexual social bond to the disparaged modality of "the grammar of paranoia" (Freud, 1911). The refusal of kenosis is tantamount to a subjectivist self-assertion that paradoxically leads to de-subjectification. Adorno (2009) comes to a similar idea when he argues that the "more reification there is, all the more subjectivism will there be". The refusal of kenosis represents a heightened stubborn assertion of self which leads to a reified (non)-subjectivity. Rather than sacrifice in the form of kenosis we have real sacrifice such as terrorism and the self-sacrifice for capital.

For Hegel, the refusal of kenosis brings about the anxiety of total loss and is, moreover, the condition for the subject's relinquishing of responsibility (the plight of the beautiful soul). Žižek explains that we experience our destiny as an external fate despite the fact that we are creating it every day (Žižek, 2012a, 984). We see as the working of the Other what is in fact our own doing. As Dupuy puts it,

> destiny is here this exteriority which is not exterior, since the agents themselves project it out of their system: this is why it is appropriate to talk about auto-externalization or auto-transcendence.
>
> (quoted in ibid, 984)

For Hegel (1970, 189), kenosis is equivalent to the abolition of dualism. By emptying itself into the Other, the subject-Other dichotomy is dissolved, paradoxically making possible a modicum of self-assertion. Through kenosis and the positing of the identity-in-difference of the subject and Other, the subject re-appropriates what was projected outwards and "destiny" is, at least partially, transformed into agency. A kind of madness ensues as the subject dirempts the dialectical unity of subject and Other. Paranoia involves the impossibility of re-appropriating what has been auto-externalized such that the Other becomes a mere mirror reflecting the subject's own partial drives. Thus, Žižek's claim that those who cannot relate to the presupposition of "a spectral or virtual substance" (i.e. the "big Other", an "objective order" emerging "out of the interaction of individuals" and "experienced by the individuals involved as a substantial agency which determines their lives" (Žižek, 2012a, 972)) are psychotics (ibid, 972) is not entirely accurate insofar as psychotics do relate to such an entity. Indeed, the risk of a total and literal hypostatization of the Other is much more likely in psychosis. The most accurate rendition of this problem, I claim, is to argue that the psychotic's absolute diremption of the identity-in-difference of the subject and the Other leads to the contradiction of a subject at once entirely related to the Other (Schreber is intimately, indeed *anally*, connected to God) and also totally detached from the Other (this same Schreber reduced much of humanity to the evanescence of "fleeting improvised men" and, as aforesaid, his God was utterly ignorant of human affairs, and hence remarkably absent in His asphyxiating presence). The aim of analysis is to reduce the weight of this diremption.

The paradox of the Lacanian "big Other" is that it is an effect of the actions of the individuals that make up a society and yet it is irreducible to those individuals whose actions it, in turn, regulates. As Žižek notes, the Other "is experienced by the individuals involved as a substantial agency which determines their lives" (Žižek, 2012a, 972). The individual is faced with the speculative challenge – and this is the very basis of subjective responsibility – of recognizing this "spectral or virtual substance" (ibid, 972) as his/her self-reflection. The psychotic, and more generally the Hegelian *beautiful soul*, cannot grasp the paradox that the Other is the result of his/her own self-reflection. As a result, he/she is relegated to the destiny of rectifying in the Other a moral flaw pertaining to him/herself. Interestingly, we may redefine foreclosure (and perhaps also, though to a different extent, the negations involved in repression and disavowal) as the subject's failure to fathom the self-reflexive relation he/she maintains with the Other. The result of this failure is a re-emergence of this Other ("in the real" according to Lacan's famous quip) as an externally perceived Other whose dialectical relation to the subject remains entirely opaque. Laplanche's reduction of Lacan's Other simply to that of "others" (as in "other people") fails to grasp the self-reflective relation that subsists between the subject and the Other.[6] Laplanche's revision thus regresses to a salad ontology obfuscating the Hegelian dialectical opposition crucial for understanding the elementary phenomena of psychosis resulting from foreclosure.

The following example helps elucidate how the spectral Other comes to be and gives an idea of the myriad ways a subject may relate to it. Imagine a young man from a conservative family where homosexuality is still an absolute taboo. It is conceivable that after some time all the members of the family would know about it. A secret would thus emerge that would be paradoxically known by all. The only "person" that would remain ignorant of it would be the big Other. In other words, the continued effort to maintain the "secret" would serve only the function of protecting this spectral non-existent entity which, though resulting only from the behaviour of the actors involved, is irreducible to any one of them or even the sum of them all; the proof, of course, lies in the fact that this very Other is now *determining* the agents' behaviours. Thus, Hegel advocates for "the substantiality of the ethical order" for which "individuals are accidents" (Hegel, 2008a, 161). However, insofar as "Ethical life is not abstract like the good, but is intensely actual" (ibid, 161) this order is not an abstract universal placed from above on human subjects; it is rather the product of the real interactions of the agents themselves. No one can escape from this spectral entity, and if any modicum of autonomy is to be achieved the subject must take cognizance of the fact that the Other is a product of his/her self-reflection, i.e. that subject and Other stand in identity-in-difference. To return to our example, the secret is kept for the sake of the Other (which is instituted by nothing other than this effort to retain secrecy), and, more importantly, each subject will relate in his/her own way to this Other, or, more accurately, each subject will *constitute* this Other in accordance to his/her own subject position. For instance, for the anxious man who stays in the closet, the Other is the stand-in for his own inhibition, while for the parents, fearing the loss of social dignity, the Other is the reflection of their own shame. Both will have *complaints* (the marker *par excellence* of the refusal to take responsibility) to the extent to which they cannot appreciate their involvement in the creation of the Other. Where the parents will say "our friends will laugh at us", the son will say "I have no freedom". A modicum of freedom will be achieved only when all recognize and perhaps alter their involvement in the situation that they bemoan. The degree of madness and paranoia a person will experience is a measure of the denial of his/her role in the constitution of the Other. A subject who *absolutely* forecloses any involvement in the emergence of the Other will feel persecuted by this Other as by a totally foreign entity that cannot be re-appropriated.

The spectral Other is thus ineradicable. Hegel makes this point lucidly evident in the following notable passage:

> The educational experiments, advocated by Rousseau in *Émile*, of withdrawing people from the common life of every day and bringing them up in the country, have turned out to be futile, since no success can attend an attempt to estrange people from the laws of the world. Even if the young have to be educated in solitude, one should still not imagine that the fragrance of the spiritual world will not ultimately permeate this solitude or that the power of the world spirit is too feeble to gain mastery of those outlying regions. It is by becoming a citizen of a good state that the individual first comes into his right.
>
> (Hegel, 2008a, 160–161)

The remarkable notion of "the fragrance of the spiritual world" points presciently to Lacan's notion of the big Other, namely an entity that lacks concrete existence and which is yet impossible to escape. Hegel's definition of language as "the most spiritual existence" (2008a) is further evidence of his incredible prescience. Like psychoanalysis, Hegel is interested in providing a modern/secular outlook concerning intangible things. This is the true meaning of materialism: to view "spectral" or "spiritual" things (the Other, language, God, miracles, ghosts) in a non-spiritual way. Symbolic castration faces the challenge of the following speculative proposition: the essence of the spectral is the material and, conversely, the essence of the material is the spectral. Ignoring the spectral altogether is tantamount to scientism, while resorting to spiritual explanations involves the pre-modern hypostasis of otherworldly realms. The tightrope upon which Hegel and Lacan (and we with them) walk is situated precisely between arrogant scientism and ignorant obscurantism. Fortunately, we are accompanied by topology on this tightrope; it tells us that the spectre is nothing other than the torsion on the surface creating the illusion of height and the fear that we may fall. This should give us the courage to skate along the surface insouciant of the imagined perils that plague our foes.[7]

Symbolic castration requires the difficult task of reckoning with the spectral dimension without recourse to superstitious obscurantism. This requires fathoming the theoretical concept of structure. Structure denotes a domain irreducible to constitutional inheritance (Freud's phylogenetic schemata) as well as experience (Freud's theory of seduction). More specifically, the idea of structure marks the identity-in-difference between that which is *necessary* and that which is *external* or *foreign*. Essentialism weds the category of necessity with that which is internal: the human being is said to be *necessarily* and *innately* predisposed to an inclination. By contrast, social constructionism brings together the *contingent* and the *external*: a subject is said to be this way because of a *particular externally* imposed norm/experience. Structure rejects these commonplaces and proposes, instead, the paradoxical category of something *necessary* yet *external*. With this, we reach the idea that the human being's "essence" – much like the torus' centre of gravity – lies outside of him/herself. The diremption of this paradoxical category has led to the contradiction by which the intellectual good conscience of our day vacillates between the two aforementioned conflicting and equally insufficient alternatives (though more palatable to the common understanding) of biologistic essentialism and social constructionism/relativism.[8] One could reframe the debates between Žižek and Butler (Butler, Laclau and Žižek, 2000) in terms of this paradoxical notion of external necessity. According to the Lacanian/Lévi-Straussian view espoused by Žižek, the symbolic order is a universality that is irreducible to biology or anything "internal" to subjects (it is an external universality/necessity). For Butler (and Derrida (2014) whose work she closely follows in this regard), by contrast, the symbolic is reducible to the social, i.e. the set of contingent customs, laws, ideals and so on that shape a group of people. By contrast to Derrida and Butler, the view espoused by Chomsky does not reject the category of universality. Chomsky holds that there is a universal capacity for language. However, by contrast to Lacan, he locates this universality within an innate biological disposition. The radicality of Lacan's view lies precisely in achieving the paradox of an external universality.[9]

But how are we to grasp the *externality* of this necessity? Is this to be simply conceived as something distinct from the subject? If so, this would take us back to the ontology of juxtaposition. In light of what was discussed above regarding the subject's task of recognizing the Other as his/her symptom (i.e. as the result of his/her self-reflection), we may argue that what here "acts" *externally* (language, the Other) on the subject is *its own Other* which, paradoxically, reveals itself as the locus where it always had all its signification. However, in order not to fall into Kant's ontology of opposition by which this otherness is conceived merely conventionally, we must also add that the subject-Other relation is not reciprocal; the Other is symptom of the subject and *not* vice-versa. For Lacan, what is ultimately decisive, as far as psychoanalysis and the analysis of the unconscious are concerned, is the subject's relation to the Other of speech and language; the relation to others, the counterparts that populate our lives, is but a special case of that determining relation. This move already takes us away from the ontology of juxtaposition (a world made up of counterparts) and beyond Kant's ontology of opposition (where the subject and the Other are opposed though a mere quantitative consideration) to the Hegelian schema here put forward. The shift of emphasis away from *others* to the symbolic Other of speech and language represents a generalization much like that of the shift from Newtonian physics to Einstein's Relativity. Gravity for Newton is a force between two bodies while, for Einstein, it is the result of a curvature of space-time. Thus, for Einstein it is not the relation between bodies that matters but the relation of each with the medium in which they are all embedded, namely space-time. For Lacan what is likewise decisive is each subject's relation to the medium in which he/she is embedded, namely speech and language (the symbolic Other). The intersubjective relations between subjects are of secondary importance. Where Einstein's field equations state that "mass tells space-time how to curve and curved space-time tells mass how to move", [10] Lacanian psychoanalysis holds that "the subject receives his own message in an inverted form from the big Other". In our analogy between Einstein and Lacan, the subject corresponds to "mass" while the Other corresponds to "space-time". The subject free associates to the Other ("mass tells space-time how to curve") who, in turn, returns this message to the subject in an inverted form ("curved space-time tells mass how to move"). In the analytic setting, *transference* stands for "the curvature of space-time". If the transference moves the subject hither and thither, it is due to "the ripples in space-time" caused by his/her own "mass", i.e. speech. Kenosis involves the subject's recognition that the institutions that govern his/her world are the products of his/her own doing. Failure in this regard relegates the subject to the paranoid position of taking all objective institutions as *imposed* on him/her in order to limit his/her freedom from without.[11] Jameson explains that for Hegel, the law is "a desperate attempt of *Verstand* to think immanence by separating its moments: inside from outside, before from after, cause from effect, possibility from actuality" (Jameson, 2010, 70–71). In the ethical domain, we may say that the law is the result of the understanding's diremption; incapable of recognizing that the Other is his/her symptom, the subject conceives of the Other as a law imposed on him/her as an external limit to his/her freedom and subjectivity. The more vehemently the subject persists in this diremption, the more he/she "founders on the impossible contradiction of the very notion of 'law'" (ibid, 70).

The subject-Other identity-in-difference overlaps thematically with the dialectical unity of the private and the public.[12] The dissipation of the boundaries separating public and private involves diremption of the identity-in-difference between externality and interiority, namely the idea that intimacy/interiority require sociality. Joan Copjec captures this well in her splendid analysis of Kiarostami's *The Wind Will Carry Us,* where she argues that rather "than protecting women from exposure, the limitation of their access to public forums can only turn them inside out, externalize them completely" (Copjec, 2006). Simply put, deprived of public life the subject also loses access to interiority. The failure to fathom this identity-in-difference has arguably led to the contradictions involving the encroachment of private obscenity into public space and vice versa (e.g. social media) as well as the contradictions related to sexual life attested to in the growth of sex without love/intimacy (the increase of pornography and dating sites) and in the rise of love without sexuality (sexless marriages).[13] Numerous ways in which Lacan theorizes this identity-in-difference could be isolated: 1) the notion of extimacy, 2) the topology of the Moebius strip which arguably elucidates the working of all paradoxical identities-in-difference and 3) the claim according to which the "unconscious is politics" (Lacan, 2002).

Notes

1 Lacan follows Heidegger's critique of all sciences that reify *Dasein* into a "human being" with positive qualities (Heidegger, 1967, 45–52). However, by contrast to the "anti-humanism" of Althusser, Lacan holds that a subject exists.

2 Attar plays on the Persian homophony between thirty birds *(si morgh)* and phoenix *(simorgh*, the bird that would be their eventual leader).

3 Reinhardt (2006) argues that the psychotic has failed neighbourly love insofar as he/she "loves his delusion as himself".

4 For Hegel, this is one who cannot appreciate his/her complicity in the situation that he/she bemoans.

5 Benvenuto (2016, 98) aptly reveals the kinship between Lacan's Other and Hegel's "World" or "Objective Spirit":

> Ultimately, Lacan's theory tries to provide clinical substance for what to Hegel was the objective spirit: a subjectivity that does not identify with the individual mind but that determines it, while at the same time being anonymous, collective, logical, and formal.

6 "The theory of seduction affirms the priority of the other in the constitution of the human being and of its sexuality. Not the Lacanian Other, but the concrete other: the adult facing the child" (Laplanche, 1999a, 212).

7 Could the alleged necessity of terror after revolution not be such an imagined danger?

8 For Badiou, the event is contingent. It graces only the few. The notion of structure tells us, by contrast, that we are all graced *and* cursed by this necessity.

9 The postmodern aversion to dialectical thought (is there any other thought?) is captured in Baudrillard's sweeping claim that "there is no dialectic in primitive societies, no unconscious in primitive societies" (Baudrillard quoted in Pagès, 2015, 36). Could there be a more blatant case of what Lévi-Strauss (1991) called the "archaic illusion", namely the ideological mystification involved in fathoming an otherness so exotic as to not even share with "us" the very structure of thought?

10 Retrieved, February 22, 2018 at: www.youtube.com/watch?v=9_vYz4nQUcs

11 Jameson (2010, 112) feels that the modern subject is burdened by precisely this kind of paranoia.

12 Jameson gives expression to this link in the following:

> This simultaneity of the coming into being of my individuality and its being-for-others ... is however itself the moment of a second unexpectedly complex and paradoxical dialectic: one in which ... my private "I" will vanish behind the public "I" ... kenosis, as Hegel will call it, in which the private is emptied out in order to make way for the public.
>
> (Jameson, 2010, 38–39)

13 A rather pernicious instance of the violation of the private by the public is attested to in the current state of psychiatry. Benvenuto notes that "the object of psychiatry, a discipline of the private world *par excellence*, remains paradoxically *public*: like no other discipline, it depends on public opinion, on the idols of town squares and (pharmaceutical) markets" (Benvenuto, 2016, xxv).

Variation 9 *Ausstossung* and *Verwerfung*

In a passage from *Less Than Nothing* concerned with no less than "the negativity which founds the symbolic order itself" (Žižek, 2012a, 860), Žižek argues that Freudian "primordial repression" is not the repression of something into the unconscious but, rather, a repression constitutive of the unconscious. Insofar as it involves the expulsion of the real into the symbolic, this "*Ausstossung*" appears diametrically opposed to the Freudian "*Verwerfung*" entailing the foreclosure of a signifier into the real. In the first case, we have a movement away from the real towards symbolization, while in the latter case we are dealing with the violent expulsion of a signifier outside the symbolic network. Žižek paradoxically argues, however, that *Ausstossung* and *Verwerfung* occur simultaneously in the founding gesture of the symbolic order. The expulsion of the real into the symbolic cannot occur without the exclusion of a signifier from the symbolic order thus constituted: "The price the symbolic has to pay in order to delimit itself from the Real is its own being-truncated" (ibid, 863). The simultaneous interplay of *Ausstossung* and *Verwerfung* implies that "there is no Other of the Other"; the symbolic order is deprived of a signifier completing it. Symbolic castration involves the recognition that *Ausstossung* and *Verwerfung* are part and parcel of the same process; integration into the symbolic and expulsion into the real belong together. For the symbolic order to have consistency it must, paradoxically, be deprived of something. As Maleval puts it, the primordial *Ausstossung* "assures the consistency of the signifying chain only by de-completing it" (Maleval, 2000, 63, my translation). The failure to recognize this identity-in-difference (the symbolic order's lack is also its support) involves diremption, the most radical form of which is the specific foreclosure involved in psychosis. The notion of a general foreclosure, or *Verwerfung*, constitutive of the symbolic order is thus to be distinguished from the specific foreclosure involved in psychosis where it is a question of a very particular signifier, namely that of the Name-of-the-Father (Maleval, 2000). Interestingly, however, there may be a way of relating these together. The specific foreclosure of psychosis is tantamount to the diremption of the general foreclosure constitutive of the symbolic order and subjectivity. The failure to fathom the constitutive paradox of the symbolic order (a lack completes it) relegates the subject to the central contradiction of psychosis, namely a "full" symbolic order devoid of lack which, paradoxically, is all the more depleted. The emergence of the subject, concomitant with the founding of the symbolic order, also requires the simultaneous operation of *Ausstossung/Verwerfung*. If *Ausstossung* corresponds to the expulsion of the real through the intervention of speech and the articulation of desire, *Verwerfung* points to the ineradicable alienation such an articulation of speech and desire entails: "desire is *inarticulable* precisely insofar as it is articulated in a signifying chain" (Žižek, 1996, 6). The subject is decentred in the Other ("desire is the desire of the Other") and, Žižek reminds us, this Other is also decentred. The act of speech through which the subject asserts him/herself is equivalent to the moment of ineradicable alienation. The movement away from alienation is not only alienating but is alienation itself. As Žižek notes, Agamben shows that "'desubjectivization' ('alienation') and subjectivization are thus the two sides of the same coin: it is the very 'desubjectivization' of a living being, its subordination to a *dispositif*, which subjectivizes it" (Žižek, 2012a, 984). The psychotic subject, neither "desubjectified" nor alienated, is all the less "subjectified". According to Agamben, this individual reduced to total obedience and hyperbolic "normality" is taken to be the terrorist. The more "normal" one appears today the more one risks being taken for an assassin (ibid, 986).

Ausstossung/Verwerfung occurs through the paternal proclamation of the law. Prior to it, we are at the level of the primal "symbolic" mother who has not yet become "impossible" and who makes law in a capricious way. The way out of this monstrosity is through the father's word which sets in motion the operation of *Ausstossung/Verwerfung*. The cost of this *Ausstossung* is that the symbolic order thus constituted is de-completed, insofar as the empty place of the law can no longer be filled in with a primal father. The correlate to this, at the level of the subject, is an ineradicable alienation in the Other. The operation of *Ausstossung/Verwerfung* requires elevating the father's particular enunciation to the status of a universal law. The difficulty of the paternal function lies in that it involves the gesture by which a particular poses as the voice of universality. Here we encounter the discrepancy between the real and symbolic father. The latter places himself beneath the law that he proclaims. In terms of Lacan's formulations on sexual difference, the symbolic father says: "all are subject to castration" (for all x, Φ x). By contrast, the *real* father, as agent of castration, cannot enforce this law "democratically". He imposes castration while excluding himself from this prohibition insofar as he sexually enjoys his wife. Drawing again on the formulae of sexuation, the father now seems to say: "there is one that is not subject to castration" ($\exists$x, notΦ x). The point from which the incest taboo is pronounced is a point of its radical transgression.[1] To institute the All of castration, we must accept the One of the paternal exception embodied by the real father in the family kinship structure. Here too, however, we must be attentive to the logic of identity-in-difference, lest we overlook the fact that the father's potency hinges precisely on his castration. If the father can successfully transgress the law, he proclaims it is because he has submitted to his own father's law. It may be arguably the case that the diremption of this identity-in-difference (castrated father = potent father) has led to the contemporary crisis of paternity marked by the virulent contradiction of the simultaneous rise of "humiliated" fathers, on the one hand, and perverse seductive ones on the other – not to mention that these two opposed figures are often imagined to co-exist in the same person.[2]

For Lacan, the father is a "*père-version*" insofar as there is no pure symbolic father without a perverse underside, sustaining his law in the autocratic mode of the exception. Without it his word is deprived of the *force* of law. The father may reign as a name only insofar as he is supported by what Žižek (1992) refers to as the superego figure of the father as enjoyment, a father deriving *jouissance* from his status. For Žižek, the father represents "the most radical perversion of all" (Žižek; 1992, 25). The father's position does not allow for rivals. Insofar as he assumes the place of exception, despite being the voice of the universal, his position cannot be duplicated; there cannot be two exceptions. As Allouch (2004) says, the father is non-specularizable insofar as he is the One and only exception to the All of castration. The paradoxical identity-in-difference of the symbolic father of universal castration and the perverse superegoic father provides yet another index of the difficulty to fathom castration.

Interestingly, Žižek defines radical evil as a particular's pretence to pose as the universal. Evil is thus not "particularity as such but its false, 'perverted' unity with the universal". It is a presumption "that inverts the proper relationship between the particular and the universal". In evil, the universal is debased "to a mere means of my self-assertion" (Žižek, 1996, 15). If the paternal function requires a living, breathing, particular father to represent the universal incest taboo then we must conclude that the subject's acceptance of this universal interdiction requires a paradoxical acceptance of a paternal radical evil. In proclaiming the Law – and yet exempting himself from its jurisdiction – the real father becomes a figure of radical evil; the father's *voice*, in all its *jouissance* and particularity, poses as the agent of universal castration. If we take seriously Lacan's claim that the father is "a sacred reality, more spiritual than any other" (Lacan, 1981, 244, my translation) and Žižek's (1996, 18) Schellingian quip according to which evil is "incomparably more spiritual, remote from sensual *Genuß*, than is the Good", are we not forced to conclude that the father is the embodiment of a radical "spiritual evil" insofar as he represents, as Žižek's Schelling would say, the "false unity of Ground and Existence"?

Before yielding to the conclusion cynically equating paternity and evil, we must remember that the father's intervention will be *seen* as evil, only insofar as the subject does not accept the paternal word as an equitable law above all. The child needs to harbour the belief that the father submits to his own law – that he represents something beyond the parents[3] – even though things are not entirely such (recall that the father is an *exception*). Symbolic castration thus involves an act of faith on the part of the child akin to the Latin *Credo quia absurdum,* "I believe it because it is absurd".[4] This is why Lacan speaks of the necessity to be *duped*[5] for the symbolic law to have efficiency. The real father may facilitate this duping if he assumes his position with a sense of irony. If, like the proverbial king, the father really thinks he is a father, difficulties will arise; we would then be really dealing with radical evil, namely a particular man debasing the universal to his own self-assertion. The unduped subject sees evil in the field of the Other and he/she will respond with evil, his/her only means of protest. Instead of a subject assuming alienation in a symbolic order that is itself decentred, we have two figures of radical evil in a struggle of pure prestige. Firstly, we have the evil of the symbolic order imposing its *particular* symbols in a false pretence to universality. Secondly, we have the evil of a subject who refuses to acknowledge his/her reliance on these symbols in a posturing of autonomy. A subject who does not relinquish his/her defiance against the paternal law will transform the latter, in fantasy or delusion, into a monstrous Thing. As Hegel says, "Evil resides in the gaze itself which perceives the object as Evil" (Žižek, 1998b).

Notes

1 Lacan (2001a) speaks of the fact that "the parent of the same sex appears to the child as both the agent of sexual interdiction and the example of its transgression" (Lacan, 2001a, 46 my translation).

2 Another important paradox here is that the father's power (power in general) must remain hidden to hold sway:

> The real in the background that serves as the ultimate guarantee and support of the public power is thus a spectral entity – not only does it not need to exist in reality, if it did appear and directly intervene in reality, then it would risk losing its power, since, as Lacan made clear, omnipotence (*toute-puissance*) necessarily reverts into "all-in-potency" (*tout en puissance*): a father who is perceived as "omnipotent" can only sustain this position if his power remains forever a "potential", a threat which is never actualized.
>
> (Žižek, 2015, 54)

We may add *power* to the list of spectral entities of concern to any true materialism.

3 The mother's role in enabling the father to assume this function must not be underestimated. Lacan emphasizes the importance the mother "attributes to [the father's] speech – in a word, to his authority – in other words, with the place she reserves for the Name-of-the-Father in the promotion of the law" (Lacan, 2006, 482).

4 This phrase is attributed to Tertullian's *De Carne Christi* (cf. Wikipedia https://en.wikipedia.org/wiki/Credo_quia_absurdum).

5 Lacan plays on the French homonymy between "*les noms-du-père*" (the names of the father) and "*les non-dupes errent*" (those who are not duped err), in order to stress the importance of taking the leap of faith with respect to the paternal law, allowing oneself to be its dupe.

Variation 10 Symbolic murder and suicide

Relating to the Other requires that the subject become its dupe; this is the act of faith through which symbolic castration occurs. Paradoxically, this opens the way for a possible subversion of the Other, its ideals, injunctions and imperatives. In psychosis, both of these are lacking. The subject is not duped by the Other and remains passive with respect to the Other. Being duped by the Other and subverting the Other are two sides of the Moebius strip. They are the two symbolic deaths necessary for sociality; the subject must die (i.e. give up some of the *jouissance* tied to being the Other's object) and the Other must die too, opening the path for the child's subjectivity. The paradox of being the Other's dupe and subverting the Other is beautifully captured by the tension between two contradictory stories of enormous import for psychoanalytic thought. The first is the myth of the murder of the primal father and the second is the Biblical story of Abraham and Isaac.[1] The former narrates the tale of the necessity of sacrificing the primal father who stands in the place of the Other of *jouissance*; the primal figure of obscene enjoyment must be abolished for desire and social co-existence to emerge. The latter, by contrast, relates the need to sacrifice the son. Rather than choose between these alternatives, we must posit their identity-difference such that the murder of the father (i.e. the subverting of the Other) may *only* take place as the subject assumes his/her own castration or symbolic death. Insofar as the vocation of man is, first and foremost, that of a *son* we must all first die by a suicidal act of faith through which symbolic castration occurs – this is Isaac submitting himself to Abraham's knife. Only then, paradoxically, will we have successfully killed our fathers and opened for ourselves a margin of freedom. Interestingly, the story of Isaac and Abraham contains within itself the dialectical tension between the death of the subject and that of the Other. Is the focal point of the story Isaac's *submission* to the knife (i.e. the child's castration and symbolic death) or is the principal motif that of God tearing Abraham's hand away from his son (i.e. the castration of the father)? Or does it concern God's own indecision and internal division?

The unexpected identity-in-difference of the primal murder and the subject's own symbolic death should make us attentive to the centrality that we, following Freud, have granted to the theme of patricide. Lacan will abandon this theme as it involves the obfuscation of the father's castration. He controversially argues that the Oedipus is a "dream of Freud's" that veils the father's mortality by falsely positing the alleged wish as the cause of his death (Lacan, 2007). In this light, Freud's theoretical insistence on patricidal fantasies appears as a diremption of the identity-in-difference of the father's "death" with his ability to function as the representative of castration. Aphoristically, we may put forward the following speculative proposition: only a *dead* father *lives* up to his symbolic role. Lacan's progressive de-Oedipalization of psychoanalysis, for better or for worse, could be understood as intended to counter this alleged Freudian diremption.[2] Aligning psychoanalytic theory with Kantian philosophy, Copjec reads the Freudian primal murder as a "noumenal" event that cannot be an object of experience. She further introduces the notion of "subreption" to denote the operation through which "a supersensible idea" is "falsely represented as if it were a possible object of experience" (Copjec, 1996, xx). The subreption of the primal murder, she explains, corresponds to representing this event as something one may experience, a deed not yet realized. This has "the effect of both exonerating us of the murder and making us guilty of its nonaccomplishment" (ibid, xxii). The subject thus falls prey to the cruel logic of the superego that punishes "severely every failure of will to realize itself" (ibid, xxii). Any external obstacle hindering the realization of this heinous crime is vilified as the impediment to a delusional sense of freedom. By locating the primal murder in the noumenal realm, Copjec achieves a decisive step towards reducing the spell of the patricidal theme haunting psychoanalytic theory. However, following Hegel's dissolution of the noumena-phenomena divide, must we not relocate the primal murder within phenomenal experience? But would this not implicate us in the dangerous error of "subreption"? Can we rethink the primal murder within the order of phenomena without regressing to a subreption?

Copjec is right in warning against falsely envisioning the primal murder as an act that remains to be accomplished. Her theorizing is a laudable achievement in the way of traversing the fantasy and freeing the subject from the duty of realizing this act. However, a more thorough crossing of the fantasy could be achieved if the primal murder is thought anew in light of its identity-in-difference with its Other, namely the subject's own symbolic death. Such a perspective, informed by speculative reason, would free the subject from the superegoic injunction to "kill the father" without unnecessarily positing a fictitious noumenal realm where this would have allegedly already taken place. In brief, the notion of subreption involves the diremption of the identity-in-difference of phenomena and noumena. As such it entangles Copjec's thinking in *the ideology of time* insofar as she expects salvation or grace to occur in some imaginary future day of judgment. A Hegelian perspective, by contrast, would not unduly separate the moments of 1) symbolic murder (having *already* taken place) and 2) grace that will occur at a *later* time. The speculative positing of the identity-in-difference of murder/suicide immediately entails the moment of grace in the here and now.

One must here beware, however, of falling prey to the idealization of a totally harmonious phenomenal realm; neither Copjec's efforts to cast the primal murder into noumenon, nor the Hegelian move of equating the primal murder with an act of faith will rid the world of aggressivity. The good will here not entirely sublate evil as one can not take their identity-in-difference as a statement of their *absolute positive unity*. As a result, despite the insight of Lacan's critique of the Freudian patricidal theme, one should remain Freudian in this regard insofar as the movement towards the universality of law occurs through this radical "crime". Though Freud's patricidal theme involves a diremption of the identity-in-difference of the father's *death* and his ability to *live* up to his role, one needs to bear in mind that, insofar as identity-in-difference is never complete, one cannot fully abandon the Oedipal-patricidal theme which will always persist as an ineradicable diremptive remain. Here, evil functions as the protest through which the subject and the symbolic order arise. We must avoid idyllic readings that emphasize the primordial "yes" or "*Bejahung*" to the father without underscoring the crime at the base of peaceful co-existence. Where the constitution of the subject and the symbolic order are concerned, evil has primacy over the good. Radical evil, or the death drive, makes possible the advent of the subject; it is, Žižek argues, "the primordial act by means of which I choose my eternal character" (Žižek, 2007, 69) or, in Lacan's words, "the unsoundable decision of being" (Lacan, 2006, 145).[3]

It is a delicious bit of irony that Lacan's de-Oedipalization of psychoanalysis and concurrent critique of the patricidal theme achieves precisely what Lacan was preaching against, namely the symbolic murder of Freud his (Oedipal) father. Lacan's "return to Freud" may arguably be part and parcel of a greater ambition to kill the master-father through the duplicitous means of flattery and idealization. For everyone, this symbolic murder is an essential step in the transition to subjectivity. Every subject must move beyond Oedipus through a symbolic murder. This may occur either through the psychoanalytic process (in light of the paradoxes of psychoanalysis Leclaire could have also titled his piece *A Parent is Being Killed* or, to echo the Biblical story with an added sado-masochistic twist, *A Parent's Hand is Grabbed*) or through the ascension to sexual love through which the subject surmounts the castration of latency. For those subjects living out their loves in the intellectual realm, this symbolic murder may take the form of a theoretical *lèse majesté*. I venture the controversial claim that "beyond Oedipus" is a mere "dream of Lacan's", murder in effigy. One is not "beyond Oedipus" from the outset; a transformation is required to get there. This may occur through *amorous* sexual love, the arduous path of *analysis* or the toils of *theory*. Lacan's "beyond Oedipus" fails to recognize the Oedipus as a *necessary* diremptive remain and, ironically, this "foreclosed" diremptive remain returns in the "real" of Lacan's (patricidal) relation to Freud. Lacan's *statement* regarding the Oedipus as a "dream of Freud" is immediately contradicted by the evidently Oedipal nature of his *enunciation*. It is thus Lacan, rather than Freud, who *falls prey* to diremption, insofar as he underestimates the fact that what allegedly keeps us bound to the Oedipal (this "dream" of the neurotic) is also what may liberate us. As diremptive remain, the Oedipal dream/wish is, at once, the obstacle to and the condition for sublation. In short, what escapes him is the following speculative proposition: *only the Oedipus can take us beyond the Oedipus.*

Notes

1 Leclaire's masterpiece tellingly entitled *A Child is Being Killed* begins with a reference to the story of Abraham and Isaac as a metaphor for the psychoanalytic process. The child that is "killed" is the "imaginary phallus", namely the object of maternal desire that forms the kernel of the ego formed in the mirror stage. It is a site of alienation from which treatment seeks to liberate the subject.
2 On Lacan's de-Oedipalization of Freud see Demoulin (2002) and Van Haute and Geyskens (2012).
3 Note the euphemism involved in recasting the act as a "decision". Is it speculative reason or pusillanimity at work here?

Variation 11 Generational difference: parent and child

In *Le Sacrifice*, Rosolato (2002) isolates three principal differences that organize mental and social life, namely sexual, generational and power difference. Firstly, we have the opposition of man and woman. Second, we have parents distinguished from children and finally, we have, to put it in Kojève's words, "the principle of the essential difference between those who exert it [authority] and those who are subject to it" (2014). I attempt to show that each of these is founded upon an essential identity-in-difference, the diremption of which leads to the obliteration of these differences thereby relegating the subject to an undifferentiated (non-)space where the peace and respite afforded by clear boundaries is lacking.

With respect to generational difference, it is evident that the parent-child relation cannot be conceived in terms of the classical ontology of juxtaposition; a parent and a child are not different in the same way that any two randomly chosen subjects differ. Moreover, Kant's ontology of opposition is also insufficient insofar as the two terms considered are not interchangeably different; it is not a matter of indifference who is called the parent and who the child. Moreover, two generations are not separated by a mere quantitative differentiation; a certain difference in age, for instance, does not suffice to establish the abyss separating father from son. Following Hegel's notion of self-reflection, if we look at the parent in him/herself we see that becoming a parent requires a subjective transformation: one must relinquish one's infantile position. A child has to die for a parent to be born.[1] This process is complicated, however, by the fact that the very desire to become a parent arises, paradoxically, "from the position of the child" (Pommier, 2013, 149). Pommier explains that, for a potential parent, "a child can appear as the payment of a debt since she has been conceived fantasmatically *of* the father or *for* the mother of the man who is her progenitor" (ibid, 150–151). A paradox thus plagues the assumption of a parental role; the desire to be a father or mother requires a transition away from childhood and yet this desire is itself rooted in an infantile wish. What further complicates matters is that two subjects engaged in a sexual relationship (i.e. in a sexual non-rapport marked by impossibility) will tend to regress somewhat to their respective Oedipal complexes where their infantile sexualities played themselves out. The family constellation will thus involve as many Oedipus complexes as it has members. The difference, however, between the adult couple and the child in their respective experiences of sexuality is that the interdiction is suspended for the adults. It is as though the inherent madness of the couple ("there is no sexual rapport") is tied to the fact that the couple involves a transgression of the incest taboo (Apollon, 1997, 148). Being in a sexual relation complicates the possibility of assuming a parental role. The sexual rapport suspends the Name-of-the-Father in such a way that the parents become the real children in the family: "there are no other children in the family but the parents" (Lacan, 2006, 482). The fact of being involved in a sexual relation – a precondition of parenting – ironically complicates assuming a parental role. In Hegelian parlance, the self-reflection of the parent leads it to pass over into its Other. Conversely, insofar as children are the ones who, unlike their parents, respect the incest taboo, we may say, inverting Lacan's quip, that "the are no other adults in the family but the children". One must not forget that couples often decide to have children in the (unconscious) hope that this change in the family constellation will somehow make the sexual rapport a little more "possible". As such, children are – even prior to their birth – placed in the role of the Name-of-the-Father, namely the signifier that grants some inkling of possibility to the sexual rapport. Papageorgiou-Legendre (1990) discusses the tradition where a father names his son after his own father. She interprets this custom as pointing to the unconscious knowledge that one's relation to one's children often repeats undesirable aspects of one's relations to the previous generation. Insofar as this repetition occurs, one forces one's children into the position of one's parents, to the extent that one has failed in undergoing the necessary internal transformation required to become a parent. Here again, we see that the parent–child opposition is partly mitigated by a hidden identity-in-difference which comes to light only after speculative reason's theoretical effort to bring each into self-reflection.

Despite insisting on the radical *difference* of parent and child one must also acknowledge the concealed *identity* that this difference obscures. Denying the *difference* represents an outright assault on the most basic tenets of decency. Transgressions of the incest taboo (the sexual exploitation of children) hinge precisely on the denial of this difference, something that Ferenczi (1949) took care to address in his seminal "Confusion of the Tongues Between the Adults and the Child". However, to ignore the *identity* also leads to nefarious outcomes such as parents who have entirely relinquished their infantile positions. Such parents think of themselves as the founders of a lineage, as if they were born *ex nihilo*. This fantasy of omnipotence creates a parent without lack (a parent as one-sided pure thought), something that could lead to an eventual psychotic structure in the child. The diremption of the child's passing over into his/her Other is also not without its own hazards. A child who in no way echoes or evokes the parent's infantile attachment to his/her own parents is, simply put, an undesired child. Such a child will remain, instead, an object of *jouissance*. The development of a child requires that the mother ceases (or, at the very least, limits) *enjoying* the child and begins, instead, to *desire* him/her. This distinction is not one of mere words. For a mother to *desire* rather than *enjoy* her child requires a deep recognition, on her part, that the child belongs to a larger kinship structure. In this way, the child is both dethroned from his/ her regal status as "his majesty the baby" (Freud, 1914) and, more importantly, rescued from a suffocating position and granted sanctuary in a more modest but also more liberating place as a member of the family and, eventually, society at large. When the mother can say of her baby something like "he has his uncle's nose" or "she has her aunt's smile" and "her father's gaze" the transference to desire takes place. Tragically, in the case of a child born with a birth defect such analogies are sustained with difficulty, precisely because the child's appearance makes such comparisons difficult. As such the child cannot enter into the meto-nymic chain of the objects of his/her mother's desire and retains a position as object of her *jouissance*. The transition from object of *jouissance* to that of desire requires that the child be partially *identified* with the figures populating the mother's desires and fantasies. Insofar as these will have formed in her infancy, her own parents will be the central figures here. As a result, the crucial process of "phallicization" by which the child acquires a sense of self-worth as this person's daughter or son involves the paradox by which he/she be also identi-fied with this person's mother or father. A great store of libido gets transferred to the child form the parent's own infantile attachment to his/her own parents.

Thus, the diremption of the paradoxical identity-in-difference by which the self-reflection of the *child* and that of *parent* pass to their respective Other has the potential consequence of leading to foreclosure and psychosis. In order to rightly secure the abyssal gap separating parent from child one must paradoxic-ally also posit their identity. The key to the process of self-reflection by which an element reaches its Other is that it is only this way that each term retroactively also becomes "at home" with itself. This latter point is crucial for grasping the gap separating Hegel from Kant; without it one falls into the ontology of opposition, according to which parent and child differ only in name and where, therefore, the distribution of tasks and responsibilities fitting to each generation dissolves into abomination. Lacan's idea according to which "children are the symptoms of their parents"[2] succinctly captures the identity-in-difference here put forward. As what is most intimate, a subject is in a relation of identity to his/her symptom. Yet, insofar as this relation is not reciprocal/symmetrical – parents are not a symptom of their children – difference is not abolished through the positing of identity. Indeed, the whole tenor of the Hegelian argument here put forward is that difference perdures paradoxically only under the auspice of an identity revealed through self-reflection.

Hegel argues that "parents are, for their children, an obscure and unknown presentiment of themselves" (quoted in Kojève, 1980). Perhaps we could say that the symbolic permutation of roles (Papageorgiou-Legendre, 1990, 56) alters a subject by elevating him/her to the dignity of his/her notion (something of which they acquired a "presentiment" in childhood through their parents).[3] The psychotic collapse that occurs when faced with paternity is the inverse of this elevation to the notion. The vertigo caused by the elevation to the height of notional dignity leads the subject to seek refuge in the collapse to a pure thought, namely madness. The idea that a child is a symptom of his/her parents means that the opposition can neither be conceived of *horizontally*, where parent and child would be reduced to mere counterparts akin to siblings, nor simply *vertically*, where one term (the parent) would stand "higher" than the other "lower" term (the child). Rather, the relation characterized as *symptom of* implies a horizontality with a torsion. If parent is the surface, the child is the invisible kink that permeates it all over (the infantile is indeed ubiquitous). Or, to put it somewhat differently, parent and child are paradoxically on the "different" sides of a surface with only one side. The parent who, seduced by the ideal of false freedom, resists recognizing in his/her child the symptom of his/her own being is a perverse parent, an infantile parent, who through his/her diremption pushes the child into increased infantilism and stubborn defiance. Here the parent–child relation degenerates into a petulant battle of pure prestige, where the specular imaginary triumphs over any semblance of communication. The child-symptom may then get motivated by angry *ressentiment* and become a *hyper-symptom* of the parents precisely in his/her forceful refusal to be symptom of the parents. This is the plight of the psychotic child (heir to the perverse parent) who incarnates the contradiction of *a hyper-symptom orphan child* of his/her parents.

Notes

1 Interestingly, the symbolic transmutation of roles required to become a parent entails a surprising dialectical reversal of sexual position. In becoming a mother, the woman assumes the phallic position of *having* the baby–phallus and, conversely, in becoming a father, a man takes on the feminine position of paternal *exception* (the place of exception is quintessentially feminine).
2 Nietzsche (1996) seizes this beautifully: "What was silent in the father speaks in the son, and often I found in the son the unveiled secret of the father".
3 A person need not literally become a parent. What is required is a paradoxical maturing through reconnecting with childhood. This may occur by becoming a (good enough) parent or simply though the painstaking *conceptual* labour of reaching for that imaginary point at infinity christened *adulthood*.

Variation 12 Power difference:
analysand and analyst

A prototypical instantiation of the difference of power, one highly pertinent for this enquiry, is that between analyst and analysand, namely the pair forming the phenomenon of transference. Reverting back to the analogy with Einstein, we could say that the end of analysis marks the moment when the subject realizes that it was he/she who all along told "spacetime how to curve". Such an assumption of responsibility is nothing other than symbolic castration. For this to occur the subject must achieve two difficult realizations. Firstly, he/she must see that the complications plaguing his/her relations with others is but a reflection of the more general context (linguistic, cultural, familial and so on – all that is subsumed under the rubric of the Other) in which these intersubjective exchanges take place ("it is not this or that body that causes me to move this way but, rather, the general curvature of spacetime"). This is the transition from the ontology of juxtaposition to Kantian opposition. Secondly, he/she must also recognize that this Other (the curvature of spacetime), when considered in-itself, reveals itself to be the place where he/she had firstly placed ("projected" some would say) all of his/her own significations ("the curvatures of space time are due to my mass"). This last step takes us to the Hegelian ontology of an alterity that is not reducible to mere convention. In other words, it is not a matter of indifference who is named the analyst and who the analysand. The power-differential between analyst and analysand is what prevents the regression to the ontology of opposition conceived as convention.[1] Through the artifice of the *subject supposed to know* the subject empties (kenosis) his/her unconscious knowledge on the figure of the analyst. The final re-appropriation of this knowledge confirms that the initial evacuating into the Other-analyst was not a loss but the condition through which the subject can realize him/herself as the Other of its Other. If there is any validity to Lacan's "there is no Other of the Other" it is simply because *you yourself* are this very Other. The end of the treatment ideally brings about the subject's self-reflection by which he/she can recognize him/herself as the Other projected all along on the person of the analyst. At this point, the analyst is revealed both in his/her radical alterity and in his identity with the analysand ("it was my own knowledge that I had displaced in him/her all along"). This may explain Lacan's reluctance to fully appropriate the notion of counter-transference into his psychoanalytic lexicon. He insisted that the transference is a unitary phenomenon between analyst and analysand and that, as such, it should not be divided into two parts. In the idiom here developed, breaking this unity into transference and counter-transference is a diremption of the identity-in-difference of analyst and analysand; this diremption (as all others) leads to the dissolution of each in their specificity and, consequently, also to the gap that separates one from the other. Following Lacan, we may quip that *the analyst is the symptom of the analysand*[2] – perhaps something akin to what Freud had in mind in devising the notion of *transference neurosis* – in the hope of asserting the identity of the two in a way by which their radical difference is also posited. In this light, what we call transference is the diremptive remain of the impossible total sublation of analyst-analysand, leader-follower and teacher-student, to name the various relationships that constitute Freud's (1900) notion of "the impossible professions", namely psychoanalysis, governance and pedagogy.[3] The impossible professions (insofar as they involve transference) are notional rather than one-sided. The diremptive remain of transference, at once, enables and hinders the self-reflection of each term to its Other. All the impossible professions concern *love* above all else, namely the very model for the notion – recall that for Lacan (1998) the psychoanalytic discourse is equivalent to love. Working with psychotics, by contrast, puts the profession at the risk of becoming *impotent* rather than impossible; here the work may undergo the vicissitudes of vicious dialectical shifts consequent upon the reign of the pure thought. Transference that is denigrated to the one-sided instability of pure thought disparages into full-fledged *suggestion,* where the identity-in-difference of analyst-analysand is completely dirempted. This is, of course, most prevalent in hypnosis (the quintessential *impotent* profession) where the relation between the two subjects is totally vertical. It is also an imminent outcome of badly handled psychotherapy. We could thus translate Lacan's idea according to which "transference without interpretation is acting-out" (Lacan, 2004) to the following adage: notional transference without interpretation disparages to the one-sidedness of acting out and suggestion. Transference is notional while suggestion and acting out are one-sided pure thoughts. For this reason, the former is erotic while the latter are either entirely desexualized or overtly erotomanic.[4]

We may expand on this Hegelian recasting by considering the structural differences of transference in various clinical structures. Schizophrenia, Soler (2012) explains, is marked by an avoidance of transference. However, Soler (ibid) notes, the absence of transference does not mean that there is no relation. A simple object relation (different from transference) is nonetheless possible and beneficial results may be obtained from it. Here there is no opposition in the transference, the analyst does not occupy the position of the Other; he/she is just another person.[5] The clinical work is confined to the ontology of juxtaposition. In paranoia and its variations (erotomania, delusional jealousy), the analyst functions as a mirror of the subject's partial drives. For Schreber, God is in the place of the small other rather than the big Other:

For the psychotic the only other is the small other. It is true that Schreber talked about god, who was the main personage of his delirium, but for him god wasn't a third term; god was just another image of himself.

(Safouan, 2004, 37)

God (and also Dr. Flechsig) embodies Schreber's own drives returning in the real. Here the imaginary is reduced to a specular mirroring where symbolic positions (doctor, patient, God, creature) merge into one another in a merely nominal opposition. This is the level of the Kantian opposition by mere convention. Indeed, the "grammar" that Freud (1911) discovered in the paranoias amply attests to how fluidly interchangeable the positions of self and Other are in this structure. Here the analyst is not just any other person insofar as the relation of opposition is in place. For Freud and Lacan, one major difficulty in the treatment of paranoia consists of the fact that the transference constitutes a triggering element (Soler, 2012, 19). Soler explains that the mobilization of the subject supposed to know is equivalent to an appeal to the Name-of-the-Father (ibid, 19). How are we to avoid this nefarious consequence without entirely cowering in the face of the clinical challenges posed by paranoia? A few words regarding the theory of transference will prove invaluable.

In classical psychoanalysis, transference is viewed as a repetition of an object relation. Lacan (1977), by contrast, distinguished transference from repetition as two *distinct* "fundamental principles" of psychoanalysis. The emphasis on repetition diminishes the specificity of transference as a phenomenon particular (though not exclusive) to the analytic setting. Such a conception remains at the level of an ontology of juxtaposition, insofar as the specificity of the subject–Other opposition enacted in the transference is obfuscated. We may say that only the imaginary dimension of the transference is brought to light. Lacan (2004) provides a precise definition of transference as the introduction of the symptom into the field of the Other. The symptom, he explains, is nothing but a bit of botched *jouissance*. As such, it is perfectly masturbatory. If love is what brings subjects together, *jouissance*, by contrast, is what separates them. When the symptom becomes too painful, when *jouissance* becomes unbearable suffering, the subject may seek help. This is the beginning of transference as the symptom is minimally removed from its autoerotic shell and brought into contact with the Other. Henceforth, the knowledge hidden in the symptom is transferred on to the analyst. This is why the analysis can cause a mild "paranoia" – one assumes the Other knows something. The neurotic transference constitutes a "healthy" paranoia insofar as it is the source of a curiosity that ignites the taste for truth. The analysand wonders about signs from the analyst. This is a great source for the elaboration of fantasies. By contrast, transparency destroys the power of the transference. A certain enigma needs to be maintained. Some "paranoia" can even be triggered in the spouse of the analysand. There may be fear that he/she will be "found out" through the partner's analysis (as an internet meme has it, "someone's therapist knows all about you"). One's own unconscious is also at stake in the analysis of one's loved ones.

The use of the word "paranoia" may be surprising to those who limit paranoia to the psychoses. Strictly speaking, some may argue that in neurosis we have transference love, while psychosis is where paranoia proper may arise. However, if we retain the link between love and paranoia established by Freud's grammar of paranoia then the idea that neurotic transference love involves a mild "paranoia" would not be so strange.[6] The difference with psychotic paranoia is that in neurosis the love (and hence "paranoia") is mitigated by the fact that knowledge is only *supposed* in the analyst – we may say that the love is erotic-fantasmatic rather than erotomanic-delusional. As a result, the initial deflection of knowledge will, over the course of the analysis, be undone such a that the end of treatment will mitigate transference love and terminate the mild "paranoia" consequent upon the deflection of knowledge. This is the achievement of symbolic castration where the *knowledge* deflected on to the analyst is re-appropriated as the analysand's own subjective *truth*. Such an outcome is less likely in psychosis where the deflection of knowledge and the consequent paranoia is more radical and literal.

In short, we may distinguish the mild notional "paranoia" of neurosis from the veritable paranoia as pure thought in psychosis. In the latter case, transference testifies to paranoia imbued with certainty rather than doubt. Alternatively, in the case of schizophrenic indifference, there is no paranoia at all and the transference thereby becomes flat and affectless. We either have an attachment that has no common measure, namely delusional transference love, or very little to no attachment. Either way, the transference does not lead to curiosity about the unconscious. The function of the subject supposed to know involves serious risks here as it may be replaced by the conviction in a subject that *knows* (the element of *supposition* being eliminated) accompanied by the belief in the *jouissance* of an Other taking the subject as target. In paranoia, the clinician–patient relation assumes the topology of total verticality. The paranoid subject is incapable of making a *symptom* of his/her analyst and, instead, looms over the clinician as a towering despot. Lacan explains that the psychotic enters discourse as master. This is because he/she experiences subjective division (castration) as *fragmentation* and *depersonalization*. To avoid this, he/she assumes the role of the undivided master (S1). Of course, this decision is not without its impasses as the master's position is fraught with diremptions. Reticence, the general refusal to speak, is another protection against this always-imminent threat of depersonalization. However, given the logic of the triumph of the "lower" term, a sudden dialectical turn will immediately transform the clinician into a towering figure hovering above an indigent and persecuted patient. In schizophrenia, the clinician–patient relation assumes the topology of a flat surface. The two terms co-exist on a simple horizontal plane without symptomatic torsion. Only in neurotic transference do we testify to the kinked surface where the clinician and patient occupy "different" sides of the Mobius plane. So, once again, how to avoid the dangers of triggering the madness that transference poses for the psychotic without entirely giving up on the efficiency of the clinical work?

The analyst's position is precarious as it risks wavering between the safe place of a secretary and that of a persecutory knowing Other. To prevent being put in the place of the persecutory Other, we have no other choice than to be the witness or "secretary" (Lacan) of what the psychotic has received from the Other. Otherwise we may be conflated with that Other. It is best to let the psychotic retain the position of subject supposed to know while we are his/her secretary. The madman and the analyst are both witness to the Other's cruelty/*jouissance,* although the madman is a closer witness than we are. Allouch (2015) elegantly shows that the kinship between the analyst's and the madman's relation to the Other explains why Freud felt that Schreber's memoir was so much like his own theory of libido. The psychotic forces us into transference while he/she occupies the position of subject supposed to know.[7] Accordingly, Allouch argues, the psychotic transference is a reversal of the neurotic transference. In the same spirit, Maleval holds that in "the case of neurosis, the analysand addresses the analyst insofar as he is supposed to know. In the case of psychosis, the analysand presents a certitude with which he tries to interest the analyst" (2015). More specifically, the inversion of the transference is typical of paranoia. The reason for this inversion does not lie in narcissism but in the difficulty of subverting the Other. If he/she begins to love the analyst transferentially this may entail either total indigence or the various vicissitudes of love in paranoia ("she loves me", "she hates me" etc.). Changing the direction of transference love is an important manoeuvre used to avoid this. Again, this is not due to narcissism or self-love but, rather, to a lack of self (a failure of narcissism) resulting from a total failure to subvert the Other. As the secretaries of their testimony we help them outwit the Other and reduce something of the mortifying *jouissance* they are subjected to. Love, including transference love, is a cataclysm for the psychotic. In Hegelese, psychotic love is not yet notional-sublimatory but a one-sided idealizing pure thought under which the subject is crushed to lowly destitution. The danger of such one-sided transference consists of the risk of vicious dialectical shifts and the triumph of the "lower" terms by which love is disparaged, as aforesaid, to one-sided lack, hate, egotism, impiety and incompatibility.

To summarize, transference can take various forms each corresponding respectively to the ontologies here outlined. In schizophrenia we have the ontology of juxtaposition, while in paranoia and its variants we have the Kantian ontology of opposition. In the latter case, it is more important than ever to refuse the position of subject supposed to know as the subject's evacuating (kenosis) of unconscious knowledge onto the analyst will lead to a paranoia that may proliferate endlessly without the respite afforded by a subjective re-appropriation in the form of truth. Here kenosis becomes a literal self-evacuation leading to radical transference hate or total infatuation and idolization of the analyst. Insofar as the Kantian ontology of opposition posits an otherness that is merely nominal, the analyst must here invest in a surplus of vigilance by making sure the transference does not indifferently alternate directions. In other words, it is crucial that the paranoid subject's position as knowing subject be fixed securely since madness will likely ensue if the analyst takes the role of subject of knowledge. It is only in the neurotic transference proper that kenosis-transference is irreducible to pure perdition. At the termination of treatment the "cured" neurotic finds him/herself paradoxically "at home" through the process of passing over into his/her Other, namely the analyst-symptom.

Finally, a clinician who resists his/her dialectical unity with a patient is not a psychoanalyst though he/she may be a psychiatrist or a psychologist. Such diremption places the clinician in the position of the "higher" term and the patient in that of the "lower" without recognition of the complexities of dialectical unity. This is the hallmark of the university discourse. Only a clinical approach that takes seriously the vicissitudes of transference and counter-transference can heed to the complications of the dialectical relation. If the clinician accepts the speculative identity-in-difference then the roles are reversed from their common acceptation and the analyst comes to occupy the lower abject position (the symptom) while the analysand takes up the higher more dignified position. In the psychoanalytic setting, it is the analysand who snubs the analyst-symptom. Freud's clinical acumen is not separable from the *dignity* he grants to the speech of patients. The onus falls on the analysand to not *resist* his dialectical unity with the analyst thereby paving the way towards subjective destitution and the universality of castration.

Notes

1 In some parts of the world (e.g. Toronto) mental health clinicians are asked to be transparent with patients by disclosing aspects of their own lives ("safe and effective use of self") and, if asked, by revealing case notes. Within such a space, the required power-differential for triggering transference is flattened. Here the analyst-analysand relation is reduced to the ontology of juxtaposition or, at best, to the Kantian ontology of opposition by mere convention.

2 Like the symptom, the analyst is the person we all want to get rid of but panic as soon as the prospect of separation becomes imminent.

3 The following from Freud is telling: "And it must dawn on us that in our technique we have abandoned hypnosis only to rediscover suggestion in the shape of transference" (Freud, 1916–1917).

4 In variation 13, we will consider how desexualization involves the disparagement of notional eroticism to desexualized pure thought.

5 This absence of transference is never absolute as there is always some confrontation with the Other (Zenoni, 2013, 115).

6 Lacan explicitly likened the analytic work to a guided paranoia: "Far from attacking it head on, the analytic maieutic takes a detour that amounts, in the end, to inducing in the subject a guided paranoia" (Lacan, 2006, 89).

7 The idea that the psychotic occupies the place of the subject supposed to know seems to contradict the aforementioned idea that he/she deflects all knowledge (unmitigated by the dimension of supposition) in the analyst. The clinical reality is that in

psychosis we either see a deflection of knowledge on the analyst without possibilities of reversing the process or, by contrast, certainty about knowledge residing in the subject. The latter (namely the reversal of the transference) is a preferred outcome and the suggested clinical technique aiming to ward off the deflection of knowledge on the analyst insofar as that may aggravate paranoia and trigger insanity.

Variation 13 Sexual difference: man and woman

Sexual difference too rests on a crucial identity-in-difference generally obfuscated by common understanding while underscored by Freudian theory. From a psychoanalytic perspective, the son inherits his father's masculinity only at the cost of a prior submission to the father's phallic power. Without this primary feminization the eventual advent of masculinity will founder. Aphoristically, it is only the *daughter* in the *son* that will ever grow to become a *man*. The erect male penis comprises the co-existence of two contradictory moments. It is testament to masculine power and attests to sad need, akin to a homeless wanderer seeking warm shelter. These two moments correspond to the masculine and feminine perspectives on the male phallus. To a heterosexual man, another male phallus is a threat, an insignia of his potential domination – and, *mutatis mutandis*, his own phallus is the marker of his triumph. To a heterosexual woman, by contrast, the male phallus is "filled to the rim with tears" (Duras, 1983 – my translation). Agamben's view (1998) that "there is no man ... who does not want to be a despot when he has an erection" is markedly one-sided insofar as it fails to appreciate precisely the sad tears that this pretense to tyranny veils. When the "higher" perspective, granting pure power to the male organ, dirempts its speculative identity with the "lower" (truer) perspective, it paradoxically leads to the triumph of the latter.

The diremption of the identity of masculinity-femininity (positive and negative Oedipus complexes) has led, at the social level, to various contradictions regarding gender, which are, I believe, emblematic of our contemporary situation. On the "conservative" end, we have excessive masculinity co-existing with impotence (various men's movements growing as a result of the current frustration of masculinity), while on the "liberal" end we have the discourse of transsexualism which thinks itself forward-thinking and subversive while anachronistically appealing to the essentialist idea of an "error of nature".[1] At a theoretical level, the diremption of sexual identity-in-difference leads either to 1) the impasses of essentialism where sexual difference is solidly grounded in nature or 2) postmodern approaches where difference is relegated to the ruses of ideology. Regarding the latter, a central error of Butler's (1997) work on gender is that she takes a certain contradiction regarding sexual orientation – heterosexuality as "melancholic" identification caused by the un-mourned loss of the homosexual other – as constitutive of sexuality rather than as a specific outcome of the contemporary diremption of sexual identity-in-difference. Where the essentialist posits difference as incontrovertible, the postmodernist stubbornly insists on identity. Both miss the specific dimension of sexual identity-in-difference upon which alone castration is sustained.

More specifically, Butler treats the masculinity-femininity divide as a Kantian opposition. In what appears as Hegelian self-reflection she shows that masculinity and femininity pass over, respectively, into male and female homosexuality. The first problem with her argument is that she places sexuation (masculinity and femininity) on the same plane as object choice (heterosexuality and homosexuality). Secondly, she misses the asymmetry of the two processes in question. Masculinity does not pass over into femininity in the same way that the latter passes over into the former. As we will soon see the relation is not symmetrical. Finally, she also misses the point that the failure of sexuation constitutes its very success. To reduce sexuation to a "melancholy gender" is to miss the crucial Hegelian idea according to which kenosis is not tantamount to total perdition but is, rather, the means of self-realization. The diremption of the paradoxical identity of the failure of sexuality (we may call it sexual-kenosis) and its (always partial) success relegates Butler's work to the contradiction by which it wavers from a blatant denial of sexual difference and hence castration ("undoing gender") to the aggrandizement of the latter to the grand scale of melancholic despair. Hegel may indeed have fallen prey to a naïve optimism claiming that the "wounds of the Spirit heal, and leave no scars behind" (Hegel, 1977, 407), but Butler's inflation of the wound of castration to the proportions of a universal "melancholia of gender" is no less hyperbolic.

Here an important question emerges: why should the loss of homosexual attachments have such dire consequences (i.e. melancholia)? Why is it not the same for all the heterosexual attachments that one may never make or mourn? Why do these losses not contribute to identification with the other sex? It seems that Butler implicitly takes sexual difference as a given insofar as she grants such an importance to homosexual attachments over heterosexual ones. If one were to mourn every lost possible object of love, every missed encounter and every forbidden pleasure, the world would be reduced to a psychic memorial, a cemetery of buried possibilities in the realm of love. Adam Phillips, in his response to Butler, argues that one cannot do away with exclusion and difference. The wish to live in a world with no lost attachments and no exclusion or difference is, he argues, part of our primary process tendencies (i.e. our wishes unconstrained by the reality principle): "Every child rightly wants to know whether there is a position beyond exclusion or difference or separateness – a world in which leaving and being left out disappears" (Phillips, 1997, 158).

Each gender must pass over into its Other in order to be "at home" with itself. The man who refuses all feminization and flaunts a pure, untarnished manhood will founder in the face of the contradiction that makes "virile display in human beings seem feminine" (Lacan, 2006, 584). If the man has the phallus while the woman is deprived of it, one must remember that her lack remains irreducible to total privation. In the symbolic order, Lacan explains, absence is itself a form of presence: "However, to not have the phallus symbolically is to participate in it by way of absence, it is thus to have it in some way" (Lacan, 1994, 153). Likewise, for the boy to have it, the possibility that he does not have it must also subsist. Being castrated is essential in the ascension to having it (ibid, 186). Thus, rather than simply claim that the boy *has* the phallus, Lacan prefers the equivocal litote, according to which the boy is "not without having it". The self-reflection of *having* (in the case of the boy) takes it to its Other, namely not having. It is indeed a commonplace of Lacanian theory that the burden of castration actually falls mainly on the man. This is well attested to by the clinical phenomenon of stuttering, something that one sees almost exclusively in men. Likewise, the self-reflection of *not having* it (concerning the girl) passes it over to its Other (i.e. having it). Interestingly, this idea is corroborated by Lacan's controversial claim according to which a woman cannot be castrated. This dialectical procedure by which *having* and *not having* pass into each other explains how Verhaeghe (1999, 49) came to conclude that penis envy is actually more of a man's issue while the fear of loss of the object is primarily a woman's concern. Lacan famously put forward the idea that woman *is* the phallus while *man* has the phallus. However, here too ambiguities prevail. If *being* the phallus means being the object of desire, then one must not forget that the achievement by which a woman succeeds in winning over a man's desire entails acquisition of the phallus. Thus, to be the phallus reveals itself as somewhat akin to having it. Likewise, when a man seeks a woman, Chiesa explains, "he unconsciously repeats in the fantasy his Oedipal offering of himself as an imaginary phallus that would fully satisfy the mother" (Chiesa, 2016, 189 n.71). Just like *having* and *not having*, the opposition between *having* and *being* is subject to dialectical reversal.

In today's liberalism, the identity-in-difference of masculinity and femininity is dirempted, with the resulting triumph of the ontology of juxtaposition and its concomitant notion of *diversity* taking the place of that of *difference*. We have a proliferation of sexual identities, with numbers increasing every day. According to the ontology of juxtaposition, there are as many genders as people out there.[2] Derrida's (1990) plea for a "plurivocal" conception of sexual difference belongs to this regressive ontology where the dialectical tension between man and woman is absolved in a diremptive move that shuns the horror of castration. Elsewhere it is the interpretation of sexual difference as Kantian opposition that results from the diremption of Hegelian identity-in-difference. Here masculine and feminine are akin to Yin and Yang (see Salecl (2000) who speaks of the "New Age Jungian resexualization of the universe"), two equal forces in opposition which can interchangeably be called positive and or negative.[3] This Manichean nominalism of sexual difference fails to heed the fact that the dialectical shifts between masculinity and femininity are not reciprocal and/or symmetrical. Sexual difference is not a matter of Kantian opposition. Insofar as there is a *real* of sexual difference, it is not a matter of indifference who is called *man* and who *woman*.

The self-reflection of *man* and *woman* paradoxically asserts each term in its own specificity precisely by passing it over to its Other. Through this process alone can *man become a man* and *woman a woman*. I am here quipping Legendre (2000) who, in the face of the postmodern near-abolition of sexual difference, claims that "a man is a man and a woman is a woman". Of course, this proposition, if it is not to flounder to patriarchal diremption, should be taken as a speculative, rather than tautological, proposition.[4] The repetition of the words "man" and "woman" both as subject and predicate should be taken to designate the contrasting moments of the respective terms. The shortcoming of patriarchy, McGowan explains, is that it fails to appreciate the contradictions of femininity by which a woman may be, at once, a caring mother as well as a sexual object, innocent and yet coquettish and so on (McGowan, 2019, 81). Ordinary feminism is, interestingly, also diremptive in this regard. As Benvenuto (2016) explains, it is a masculine ideal that most feminists seek to erect, thereby dirempting, no less than chauvinists, the feminine moments of the woman-notion.

Insofar as Hegelian self-reflection precludes symmetry between the sexes, we reach Lacan's controversial "woman is a symptom of man". It is precisely as *symptom* that the feminine has suffered throughout the ages and, still today, all the heinous vicissitudes of diremption. As symptom, woman is a torsion of man, the kink on the Mobius strip. Lacan's claim that "woman does not exist" is entirely commensurate with her status as symptom; the torsion on the surface of Moebius strip does not exist and yet it is also, for that very reason, ubiquitously dispersed on the surface. The torsion is, at once, nowhere and everywhere. We may thus supplement Lacan's claim with the equally valid assertion concerning woman's omnipresence, namely the ubiquity of the feminine *not-all*. Sexual difference understood according to the ontology of juxtaposition envisions a flat surface without torsion. Here difference is abolished. Patriarchy, by contrast, posits a stark hierarchy where the "higher" masculine term diremps the "lower" feminine term with the paradoxical result of the triumph of the "lower" symptomatic term. The demise of patriarchy is undoubtedly tied to this diremption and triumph of the "lower" term, something that is attested to widely by the contemporary crisis of masculinity. One could say, not without accuracy, that the *kink of femininity*, foreclosed from the surface, returns in the real of the demise of patriarchy. This "elementary phenomenon" at a large-scale social level is subsequently "symbolized" with the paranoid delusion, rampant among "men's groups", through which women have staged an arduous plan to bring about the demise of men.[5] What is missed here is the subject's assumption of the responsibility of his/her diremptions. The absence of woman in the male homosexual couple means that the kink on the surface has been likewise obliterated. In this case the kink returns in the form of the extreme hedonism of sado-masochism rampant in the gay community.[6]

In woman, man encounters his own castration and must therefore *choose* whether he will accept or oppose this incorporation into the feminine.[7]

The explicit oppression of women is a modality of diremptive refusal. Here, the "higher" term dominates the "lower" without recognizing in her a reflection of itself. Ironically, however, this oppressive attitude, fuelled by the violent repudiation of the feminine, reduces men to effeminacy and impotence. Nothing smacks more of meekness than a man's wrathful repudiation of the feminine; an insight that popular-colloquial consciousness arrives at when mischievously equating this wrath with feminine menstrual pain. One should also not underestimate the diremption involved in the "lower" term's refusal to be symptom of the "higher" term, namely woman's repudiation of femininity, her hysteric refusal to be symptom of man. When this refusal is motivated by *the spirit of revenge*, we get a vicious dialectical reversal by which woman becomes instead the *hyper-symptom of man*.[8] The obstinacy of both male and female "camps" increasingly aggravates the conflict between one-sided notions unwilling to meet within the sane space of acknowledged identity-in-difference. A paranoid climate ensues where anything can be expected but love and reparation. It is here noteworthy that the conservative and liberal understandings of sexual difference reproduce the vicissitudes of sexual difference in their encounter with one another. Liberals emphasizing sameness (difference as a social construction) do so from the feminine standpoint while conservatives emphasizing difference (usually understood by them as rooted in biology) do so from the masculine-patriarchal perspective. The contradictions inherent to these positions are that the masculine-conservative-patriarchal, by positing *difference*, unwittingly upholds the feminine, while the feminine-liberal, by insisting on *sameness*, endorses a masculine view – from a psychoanalytic point of view, the feminine stands for difference while the masculine/phallic denotes sameness.[9] To Benvenuto's claim that some feminists advocate for a phallic ideal of femininity, I would add that the flag-bearers of the masculine-patriarchal ideal speak from a position of feminine "impotence". It is as though the *statements* they pronounce are, in both cases, *a priori* contradicted from the position of *enunciation* from where they are uttered.

Finally, let us take a brief foray into the dialectics and erotics[10] of power. Psychoanalysis has taught us that power and eroticism belong together such that sexual tension can only be maintained through an *ambiguity* within power relations between subjects: "Our point here is not merely that the relationship of domination in a sexual contact is always tainted with ambiguity, but that it is the very ambiguity, 'undecidability', of a Master/Servant relationship that 'sexualizes' it" (Žižek).[11] Power, much like the mercurial phallus, is a *symbolic* "object" that flutters equivocally between participants, thereby creating, precisely through this indistinctness, the tension required for erotic passion. Freud (1905) isolates three central obstacles to sexuality, namely shame, disgust and morality. In an effort to sharpen Freud's metapsychology, I venture to claim that all three of these constitute specific effects of the more general phenomenon of *power disambiguation*. De-sexualization occurs when the *dynamics* of power falter into the *inertia* of sheer domination. When it becomes all too clear where the locus of power resides, we have the flattening of the erotic tension. Here shame, disgust or morality set in. Wielding too much power over another who refuses to even feign the slightest resistance leads to guilt and resentment (morality), shame in both parties or simply disgust at the lowly position assumed by the victim. The resilience of a subject's sexual desire in the face of heightened power disambiguation constitutes the measure of his/her perversion. By contrast, the more readily de-sexualization sets in when confronted with the slightest power disambiguation gives us a measure of a subject's neurosis.[12]

Notes

1 Regarding the use of the phrase "error of nature" in transsexualist discourse see Gherovici (2010, 165).
2 In a 2014 article ABC News isolated 58 different gender identities found on Facebook. (retrieved on June 27, 2019 at https://abcnews.go.com/blogs/headlines/2014/02/heres-a-list-of-58-gender-options-for-facebook-users/). Salad anyone?
3 Shannon Bell's (2010) "fast feminism" not only reduces sexual difference to this Kantian opposition but also uncannily resorts to a literalized version of Kant's "negative size". Bell speaks of the "female penis" differing from the male only in size. Her public displays of orgasm show that women can cum *just as much* as men. In this grotesque display we attest to a literalized parody of Kant where the latter's laudable theoretical notion is degraded to a puerile "mine is as big as yours". The agonal has veritably given way to the gonadal.
4 Or perhaps both, namely a paradoxical speculative-tautological proposition. We will consider another such proposition in variation 25.
5 Some of Jordan Peterson's conjectures on "cultural Marxists" are not far from such assumptions.
6 Benvenuto (2016) explains that the lack of difference in the male *homo*sexual couple leads the partners to search for that lost difference in the excesses of varied sexual practices. We may wonder whether the over-used term "hetero-normativity" (with all its negative connotations) is not a contradiction insofar as the "hetero" may be the best chance to break out of the closure of "normativity" (see Soler, 2000 and Morel, 2000).
7 The proverbial masculine fear of "commitment" is exemplary of this refusal.
8 Nietzsche's "misogyny" targets the vengefulness of woman as hyper-symptom rather than women altogether.
9 A man will be relieved to find other men dressed like him at a party while a woman may drown in dread faced with such a discovery. Where sameness fortifies masculinity, it abolishes the feminine.
10 Is there anything more erotic than dialectics? Was Nietzsche (1999) not one thousand times right when he sacrilegiously christened Socrates (the eternal dialectician) as the "true eroticist"?
11 www.lacan.com/frameXI2.htm
12 Insults and profanations offer a delicious spice to the exquisite delights of the forbidden fruit. However, when these break a certain threshold sexual tension is flattened, thereby paving the way to the triumph of the comic or the tragic. A joke testifies to this. A young woman tells her partner that she finds it kinky to be insulted during sex. In the midst of their next sexual encounter, he thus

exclaims: "I shit on your father's grave". Of course, he missed the subtle mark of the sexual. If at that moment she did not burst out laughing (comedy) she would have fallen instead into tears or deep rage (tragedy). What was surely missed was the orgasm as she pulls her body away from the stunned boy, leaving his sword unsheathed, hanging ridiculously in the stupefaction of man's ignorance of the feminine.

Variation 14 The paradox of a
boundary without a limit

The three central differences structuring psychoanalytic theory all hinge on the identity-in-difference of opposed terms such that, upon self-reflection, each passes over to its Other. Paradoxically, it is this very loss of self through the transfer to the Other that secures the specificity of the term in question. We may here recast Santner's (1996) notion of a *crisis of investiture* in terms of our Hegelian idiom. A symbolic title will hold if its self-reflection brings it to pass to its Other. Only in this way, paradoxically, will it not flounder into a plethora of other determinations. Our late modern crisis of investiture is thus a special case of a current crisis of diremption. Symbolic positions (child, parent, man, woman, analyst, analysand) can only perdure when their identity-in-difference with their Other is posited. Only this way will a title's status as *notion* be secured; the crisis of investiture means that titles have disparaged to pure thoughts. The diremption at the level of sexual identity-in-difference has led to the contradictory pansexual-asexuality defining our contemporary culture of *jouissance*. Each of the three paradoxical identities-in-difference should be conceived as asymmetrical relations where one term stands as the symptom of the other.

The establishment of these principal differences structuring mental life is concomitant with the creation of the unconscious. More precisely, these differences, despite constituting the unconscious, do not themselves hold in the unconscious. Since the unconscious does not know time (Freud, 1915b) generational difference is absent there. The notion of an adult is a fiction; at the level of the unconscious we are all infants. If there were at all any such thing as an adult, it would involve someone who has, paradoxically, achieved much in his/her reconnection to the "child within". Winnicott's (1971) reflections on the importance of playing testify to the paradoxical identity-in-difference by which a human being *matures* only through a return to *infantile* frolicking. Moreover, given that for Freud there is only one masculine libido (in Lacan's words, there is only one (phallic) signifier to denote sexual difference), the unconscious ignores sexual difference too.[1] It is likewise with respect to the difference of power. The clear boundary separating those who exert power from those subjected to it is inoperative in the unconscious. In short, at the level of the unconscious there are only men and children co-existing in a wild primal state anterior to the imposition of the master signifier through which the difference of power is established. However, this very unconscious can only be constituted as an *unconscious* (rather than subsisting in the open *à ciel ouvert*) once these differences have been established. In an effort to locate these principal differences topologically we may say that they are found at the periphery of the unconscious in a place of extimacy. They are the stitching that separates the unconscious from the preconscious and the conscious. As such, the institution of these three central differences is tantamount to the work of primary repression. They are the very torsion on the surface of the unconscious; they are, at once, absent from it and yet ubiquitously present.

To state the identity-in-difference of two terms does *not* simply entail stating their unequivocal sameness. The self-reflection of an element does indeed lead it to its kenosis in the Other. However, this is the condition for the term's accession to its own notion. Through its kenosis to woman, man gains his virility; emasculation (*Entmannung*) and feminization (*Verweiblichung*) occur when that specific kenosis fails. What is at stake is the question of the notion of a limit or boundary. How can we establish the separate identities of each term without establishing a diremptive boundary between them such that one term arrogantly snubs its other? Here it may be useful to consider Hegel's distinction between a limit/boundary (*Schranke*) and lack. Where the former is imposed externally on the two entities in question, the latter arises immanently within each term as an expression of its internal division.[2] To cast it in the vocabulary we have developed throughout this treatise, a boundary needs to be imposed when diremption is operative.[3] Man's diremption of his identity-in-difference with woman leads, paradoxically, to his feminization. To counter this, he may resort to various artificial limits and semblances to re-establish his masculinity. What is reviled, not without a smidgen of hysteric embellishment, as "toxic masculinity" is linked to this desperate re-claiming of the masculine in the form of a quasi-paranoid barricading intended to prevent intrusions of the feminine. However, as the deadlocks of patriarchy have shown, this kind of bulwark against the threat of waning masculinity has its impasses. What is required is a "boundary" created immanently through self-reflection rather than imposed externally from above, i.e. as the doing of the "higher" term threatened by the force of the symptomatic "lower" term. If the "higher" term receives the "lower" as its *symptom,* then each term accedes to its notion and the required separation is established in the paradoxical modality of identity-in-difference. Stability can only be achieved through the immanence of the speculative.

The process by which man, parent and analysand take their respective Others (woman, child and analyst) as their symptom has an affective correlate, namely shame. Kant had already come to an explicit formulation of its importance in regulating the relations between the sexes. Moreover, he specifically argued that shame (modesty) prevents the sexual exploitation of one sex by the other:

> It is true that woman would not be content if the male sex did not appear to pay homage to her charms. But modesty (*pudicitia*), a self-constraint that conceals passion, is nevertheless very beneficial as an illusion that brings

about distance between one sex and the other, which is necessary in order that one is not degraded into a mere tool for the other's enjoyment.

(quoted in Žižek, 2015, 60)

Similarly, Lacan argues that in the absence of a sexual rapport, modesty (*pudeur*) is the only virtue (Lacan, lesson of March 12, 1974). The lack of a rapport implies an absence of any kind of natural "harmony" that would guide the behaviour of one sex towards the other. This absence makes more likely occurrences of sexual exploitation. As a result, shame is required as a *signal affect* warning the subject of a possible traumatic intrusion. Earlier, we saw the importance of shame in establishing for the subject a non-diremptive identity. The same can now be said regarding the subject's appurtenance to his/her gender. A sense of modesty in a man is an index of his femininity (to blush in modesty is characteristically feminine) and, paradoxically, it is, precisely for this reason, the ground for his masculine power, namely his ability to approach woman. Through a similar speculative process, a woman's modesty, though providing the quintessential insignia of her femininity, protects her from the undesired man; the blush to her face will either signal her flight away from him or, even more expediently, tell him to back off.[4] In this light, her blush functions as a phallic shield. Shame (modesty) is thus the affect that regulates the relations between men and women precisely insofar as it is the correlate to self-reflection. For Hegel, love and shame allow for the restraint that enables sexual relations to remain ethical. He thus defines "the ethical aspect of love" as "the higher aspect which restrains purely natural impulses and puts it in the background. Such restraint is already present at the natural level in *shame*, and it rises to chastity and modesty as consciousness becomes more specifically spiritual" (Hegel, 2008a, 167). We thus see a kind of progression from shame to love and finally to chastity and modesty, with the latter deemed to be the most spiritual. We must not, of course take this progression in a teleological sense or, even worse, in an instinctual-biological sense *à la* Karl Abraham. What is at stake, rather, is the movement from external opposition to inner division; it is a question of recognizing that the Other as *symptom* is the product of one's own self-reflection. When Lacan states that for man and woman, woman is the Other sex, this means that woman is symptom of both men and women. Woman thus stands for the symptomatic "lower" term that every subject (male or female) must decide to embrace or dirempt. The more spiritual affect of modesty entails the greatest recognition of the symptom as a kernel of one's own being rather than a foreign abject entity to be discarded.[5]

Modesty also regulates the relations between different generations. Talking about sexual matters between parents and children brings about a feeling of unease akin to shame. Its function is to protect the individual from the threat of incestuous desire. For the child, the acquisition of shame guards him/her from the *confusion of tongues* that could lead to sexual seduction. Shame was listed by Freud (1905) as one of the chief obstacles to sexuality along with morality and disgust – the latter two are less spiritual in the Hegelian sense and thus more akin to a diremptive limit/boundary. Finally, the relation between analyst and analysand also requires the operation of shame in order to properly handle the eroticization of the transference. Here the requirement of the psychoanalyst's neurosis, as opposed to perversion/psychosis, is central. The analyst should be capable of desexualization when faced with the conscious or unconscious advances of a seductive patient. By modelling modesty for his/her patients, the psychoanalyst can aid them to achieve that required movement by which external opposition gives way to internal division. The analysand's seductions obfuscate the analytic work and hinder the progress of the treatment. They are the quintessential expressions of resistance. As such, these seductions function as a rejection of the analyst-symptom. Through this manipulative manoeuvre the patient dirempts his/her identity-in-difference with the symptomatic "lower" term embodied by the clinician. This leads, paradoxically, to the triumph of the rejected "lower" term attested to in the high propensity of acting out in the erotically heated moments of an analysis. Refusing to work with an analyst-symptom, the subject inadvertently reduces him/herself to a literal "walking-symptom" (acting out and *passage à l'acte*). Such a subject, in the grips of a momentous diremption of the analyst-symptom, imagines (through projection) that it is the analyst that rejects him/her in his/her disparaged and self-imposed position as abject symptom. Needless to say that hate may follow in the transference and that aggressivity towards the analyst will accrue. By valiantly bearing this aggressivity (cf. Winnicott's "The Use of an Object"), the analyst may be able to instil an effect of shame and thereby enable the analysand to realize that he/she (like the aforementioned (pseudo)-feminist is waging a war with his/her own diremptions. Again, shame functions here as the rampart against diremption and the correlate affect to self-reflective kenosis.

What is common to the three relations that constitute the three principal differences is that they all involve sexuality in a central way. In the case of the parent-child relation sexuality is what must be at all costs resisted, while in the man-woman relation it is a requirement to transgress the taboo. For the analyst-analysand couple, sexuality is also barred but the taboo is not as severe as with parent and child. In the relation between man and woman, the erotic must remain notional so that it does not wane into tepidity. Many patients who come to the analyst for problems related to their conjugal life complain of lack of passion; for them, the notion of love has given way to the desexualized pure thought. We try to help them revive *the notion of eroticism* precisely through *the eroticism of the notion*, namely a *talking cure*. In the analyst-analysand relation, the eroticism of the notion should not be obliterated but should be mitigated through the functioning of shame and modesty. The taboo needs to be in place at the level of the act, but it need not be so stringent at the level of fantasy. The free associative work, the notional activity of language *par excellence*, requires maintaining an *as if* eroticism without which the efficacy of the work dwindles into the placidity of the one-sided pure thought and, more worryingly, the possible dialectical shifts it may lead to (these latter two extremes refer to a mortified non-transference and to a wild erotomanic non-transference). Finally, in the case of the parent-child relation, notional eroticism must completely give way to the pure thought of desexualization, mostly in the form of disgust. Without this near total disparagement of the erotic notion, the child is at the risk of severe mental illness. Needless to say, these ideal vicissitudes seldom transpire as the imposition of the taboos in their appropriate form requires the arduous and patient labour of self-reflection by which a term accedes to its notion through the paradoxical kenosis to its Other-symptom. This achievement requires, of course, nothing less than that most difficult love which Christian wisdom has christened *love of the neighbour* and which psychoanalytic sagacity may rename as the *love of the symptom*. The parent must love his/her child-symptom as man must adore his woman-symptom and, finally, the analyst must love the patient sufficiently to agree to be his/her abject-symptom regardless of all the wild dialectical vicissitudes this may entail. Only through this difficult love can a paradoxical *boundary without a limit* be achieved that will safeguard these principal differences such that each term may endure at the height of the dignity of its notion.

Notes

1 Soler (2000) speaks of the "homosexual unconscious".
2 It is remarkably prescient and proto-Lacanian of Hegel to speak of "lack" with respect to the manner of maintaining boundaries through internal *division* rather than external imposition.
3 More precisely, a boundary is a diremption and as such it leads to impasses and contradictions. For Hegel's discussion of the contradictions inherent to the concept of "limit" see de Boer, 2010 (372), and Hegel, 1969 (127 onwards).
4 The dialectical nature of shame is most evident in that the slightest nuances in a woman's blush will make it clear whether she signals desire or disgust/unease. The same affect with nearly identical external insignia indicates two opposed meanings.
5 Much of the (pseudo)-feminist reviling of men is likely based on the following mechanism. A woman rejects her femininity casting it out as a rejected "lower" term that blemishes her masculine ideal of womanhood. However, unaware of her own diremptive tendency she projects it on to men ("they hate and vilify the feminine") against whom she then stages a battle of pure prestige. She thus wages war against her disavowed diremptions displaced on to men.

Variation 15 Good and evil

Žižek argues that evil contains itself only by becoming infinite/absolute evil. Evil cannot be contained by a transcendent power. Only evil has, paradoxically, the power to properly contain evil. The good is thus not an overarching higher principle controlling/containing evil from above.[1] The stringent opposition of evil and the good is the result of the diremptions the understanding that cannot see that violence is contained by violence. Controversially we may say that Nazism is arguably the result of the diremption of this identity-in-difference. National Socialism sought a good that it conceived as starkly opposed to evil, thereby failing to recognize an essential unity of opposites. Fascism does not consist of an insufficient separation of good and evil but rather from an over-stringent division. Žižek argues similarly when he claims that "barbarism is not the opposite of culture, but rather, it is pure culture – culture without civilization" (Žižek in Badiou, 2010, 163). For Žižek, "it is no accident that Hitler was Austrian, fanatically devoted to Wagner and in thrall to German *Kultur* much more than to Prussian militarism" (ibid, 163). Fascism is the result of a good that rejects its formal unity with evil. The "higher" term's diremption of the symptomatic "lower" term led to a generalized and ubiquitous evil. What is more evil than the pretence to pure good? Interestingly, the identity-in-difference between violence and the restraint of violence is also operative in what Dupuy notes as the paradoxical relation between interdiction and ritual: "Often, the ritual consists in staging the violation of … prohibitions and violations" (Dupuy quoted in ibid, 975). With this added insight we may shed light on the relation between the rise of violence and the decline of symbolic rituals. If these two are linked it is not because ritual enacts a prohibition but, to the contrary, because it stages a violation. The decline of symbolic ritual leads to violence because we have lost the means by which to contain violence through the paradoxical process of making it "exorbitant". As Bernstein puts it, evil is necessary for the sublation of evil (Bernstein, 2002, 68). Political correctness is diremptive in this regard. It is based on the puerile fantasy that thinks we can eliminate violence and aggression by making a taboo of everything. This effort has created a civilian-ruled police state dressed in the false attire of benevolence.

Following Girard, Žižek explains that under Christianity the logic of sacrifice becomes inoperative. By telling the story of sacrifice from the perspective of the victim, scapegoating is undermined insofar as the innocence of the victim is asserted (Žižek, 2012a, 975). Sacrifice becomes fake and the containment of violence through sacrifice is also lost, thereby opening the space for uncontained violence. The loss of sacrifice and, concomitantly, the loss of the containment of violence through violence have brought about a central contradiction of our time by which the cessation of sacrificial violence has unleashed a state of global civil war. Here violence emerges as the "implicit admission of impotence" (ibid, 998). These times of ubiquitous combat testify to the contradictory dialectical unity of riots and terrorism where, according to Žižek, the former represents a zero-level protest sustained by no desire while the latter acts "on behalf of that *absolute* Meaning provided by religion" (ibid, 998). The aforementioned suspicion cast on the intellect among certain psychoanalysts is related to the fact that evil and knowledge, according to Hegel, belong together. The biting of the apple of knowledge led to the fall into evil (Bernstein, 2002, 62). However, knowledge, though forbidden, is also what makes us human (ibid, 64). One must pass through evil-knowledge in order to eventually sublate it. If we admit that knowledge in psychoanalysis must be sublated (otherwise psychoanalysis becomes a university discourse) we must also add that this sublation can, paradoxically, only take place under the auspices of an "exorbitant" knowledge. Lacan's intellectual forays into a plethora of academic disciplines are a necessary step on the way towards this sublation.

The ethical act, Žižek (1996) argues, has the same formal structure as radical evil insofar as both are unmotivated by simple egoistic concerns. Žižek thus posits the identity of good and evil with the claim that "Evil is 'Good in becoming'" (Žižek, 2003, 88). Is the murder of the father then an ethical *act* or an instance of evil? It depends on the perspective. If the father's enunciation of law is seen as evil (a particular debasing the universal for its own self-assertion), then the correlative murder of the father will be felt as evil too. The subject may literally kill the father insofar as the symbolic murder has failed. If the father's proclamation of law is seen as an instance of a particular sacrificing itself for the universal, then the subject's own symbolic murder will be less tarnished with guilt. It will then become evident that the father's law and the primal murder are, in fact, part and parcel of the same process of the expulsion of the real into the symbolic. By proclaiming the law, the father "dies" insofar as he subordinates himself to the law. He lessens the burden of the symbolic murder and allows the subject to take responsibility for his/her act. The father's law, though it involves a particular posing in the place of the universal, is not a case of evil but represents, rather, a prime instance of the good. Good and evil are thus formally the same. For Badiou, evil is not the outcome of ignorance (i.e. a state of unknowing or "innocence") but is, rather, the consequence of a "truth procedure" that has not been properly limited. Evil is thus the outcome of an "over-fidelity" to a truth:

As can be seen with scientism, or with totalitarianism, there is always a
desire for the omnipotence of the True. There lies the root of Evil. Evil is
the will to name at any price. Usually it is said that Evil is lies, ignorance, or
deadly stupidity. The condition of evil is much rather the process of a truth.
(Badiou, 2003a, 66–67)

Good and evil are separated by a mere quantitative consideration; evil is the
good that has lost its sense of measure. The challenge of symbolic castration is
here felt with all its ethical weight as the subject is beckoned to recognize a
kinship between the most heinous evils and the loftiest goods. The failure to
recognize this formal identity relegates us to the mediocrity of compromise
formations in the realm of ethics. Today's emphasis on compromises attests
to the veritably reformist times in which we live. Nietzsche had presciently
diagnosed this long ago: "This modernity made us ill – this indolent peace,
this cowardly compromise, the whole virtuous filth of the modern yes and no"
(Nietzsche, 2005, 4).

Likewise, the symbolic murder of the father, as an act of pure defiance, is
radical evil from one perspective and the height of good from another. This act
is essential for the advent of the symbolic order and the subject. It is the radical
Ausstossung through which the subject gains respite from the monstrosity of
the primal Thing. The symbolic murder is an exorbitant evil that creates the
good. This primordial *Ausstossung* manifests as a decision to speak and articulate
desire. The subject abandons the silence of infancy and joins the community of
speakers. However, insofar as *Verwerfung* must accompany every *Ausstossung*, the
subject's speech will always be tainted with an ineradicable stain of falsehood.
He/she is forced into a minimal lying gesture as the truth may be spoken only
through the medium of untruth. If symbolic castration occurs, this minimal lie
at the basis of all enunciation will not be seen as evil. For the psychotic subject
for whom castration is inoperative, the lie which accompanies all truth as its
shadowy other side plagues him/her with melancholic guilt when observed in
him/herself and paranoid rage when witnessed in the signs emanating from the
Other. What the psychotic cannot fathom is the identity-in-difference of truth
and lies. Strictly speaking, it is not accurate to say (as has become commonplace) that the psychotic cannot lie. The clinical experience amply testifies to
the opposite. The psychotic cannot fathom that a lie is a means to truth.

Evil has primacy over the good, which must, therefore, allow itself to be
incorporated by it. The man poised to do the "good" must recognize his act
as a mere moment of evil, the principal element (symptom) of the conceptual
pair, in order to avoid the delusional self-conceit of the over-virtuous. Lacan
asks us nothing less than to recognize our good as a moment of evil when he
reminds us that psychoanalysis places "no promise in altruistic feeling" (Lacan,
2006, 80) in that it lays "bare the aggressiveness that underlies the activites of
the philanthropist, the idealist, the pedagogue, and even the reformer" (ibid,
80–81). Much of post-war twentieth century philosophy falls prey to the error
of embracing the good prior to its incorporation by evil. Exemplary here is, of

course, Levinas' critique of Heideggerian fundamental ontology. Like Levinas, Badiou too misses the dimension of evil antecedent to the good. In both cases, an *ethical* decision for the diremptive remain of the good is taken as the *ontological* priority of the good over evil. Badiou and Levinas explicitly and avowedly follow Plato for whom, as Pagès explains, dialectic designates the knowledge of Ideas and, as such, the science of the good, namely the Idea that gives to all other Ideas their unity and force. Plato takes the diremptive remain of the good as ontologically grounded and therefore prior to the speculative process rather than as a question of ethical choice made *a posteriori*.

Žižek puts forward a similar critique of Badiou:

> In Badiou's affirmative approach, Evil is a defective mode of Good, and the hypothetical subject is a defective mode of the subject as agent of truth, while from the Hegelian (and Lacanian, I would claim) perspective, the negative move comes first: loss is prior to what it is the loss of, betrayal is prior to what it is the betrayal of, the Fall is prior to what it is the Fall from.
>
> (Žižek, 2015, 79–80)

The Greeks too fall prey to the same error:

> The Greeks lost their moral compass precisely because they believed in the spontaneous and basic uprightness of the human being, and thus neglected the 'bias' towards Evil at the very core of humanity: true Good does not arise when we follow our nature, but when we fight it.
>
> (Žižek, 2015, 132)

By contrast, for Hegel "the gesture that opens up the space for the Light of Logos is absolute negativity, the 'Night of the World', the point of utter madness in which fantasmatic apparitions of 'partial objects' float around" (ibid, 184). Kierkegaard also chooses the good/sacred over the evil/profane. However, unlike Badiou and Levinas, for Kierkegaard faith is a *leap* and, as such, it cannot be grounded in any ontological priority of the good. Tertullian's faith is interesting insofar as it is not only not grounded in any sense of the good's primacy but is, rather, chosen despite awareness of profanity's precedence; as is famously known, Tertullian claims to believe *because* it is absurd. Philosophies that choose the diremptive remain of the good speak from a masculine position. The possible pitfalls of these philosophies would thus mirror the impasses of masculine sexuation; by choosing the good, evil may return in the form of "attacks of evil". More accurately – and to be fair to such thinkers – it is a question of whether the good is chosen as a diremptive remain, with the recognition of the speculative identity of good and evil, or whether the good is chosen in strict opposition to evil, in a diremptive act that posits a pure good untainted by evil. Only in the latter case would "attacks of evil" be an imminent possibility. By contrast to Badiou and Levinas, Nietzsche's celebration of cruelty and his disparagement of morality are tied to his fidelity to the diremptive remain of evil, namely what he argues an older and more noble morality considered the good (Nietzsche, 1998). Evil is less diremptive of the identity-in-difference of evil and good. The good insists more fervently on the abyssal difference with evil. Evil better recognizes that evil and good are brethren; the good makes claims to much higher pretences than evil. Everyday language has a term to designate the "holier than thou" but the opposite, namely to designate someone as "more profane than thou" smacks of absurdity.[2] Where evil is on the side of the real, the good provides the shelter of semblance. It is, as Lacan would have it, the penultimate barrier to the real (Lacan, 1986). Nietzsche, de Sade, Schmitt, Machiavelli and Hobbes choose the diremptive remain of evil and thus speak from a feminine position. Rousseau is ambiguous in this regard. In his general assessment of his contemporaries he sees evil everywhere and yet, as though to buttress this acute consciousness, he posits, almost as an afterthought, the primordial existence of a noble savage, a mythical repository of the good.

Notes

1　Also, clinically, one cannot impose on the analysand a higher principle by which he/she could limit aggression. This would be re-education rather than psychoanalysis.
2　In *Seven* (Fincher, 1995), the murderer shows that he and the cop are both sinners. He knew it all along. The cop, however, lived in the convenient illusion of their radical difference.

Variation 16 Truth and lies

If the early Lacan (of the symbolic order) emphasized the importance of sense while the later Lacan (of *jouissance* and the real) shifted attention to non-sense, we may bridge these together thereby positing the continuity of the Lacanian oeuvre with the idea of a paradoxical sense from non-sense. We may here speak of a paradox at the level of meaning insofar as sense hinges on the presence of an ultimately nonsensical phallic signifier. For Paul de Man (1979), every text is an allegory of its own unreadability. This elegant definition may also be applicable to the "text" of the unconscious and thus provide an interesting model for the direction of the psychoanalytic treatment. A subject is "cured" when he/she can come to better terms with the unreadability of the unconscious rather than rage against it with fixed narratives, master signifiers and static constructions. The aim of interpretation would consist of simply puncturing such rigid significations, forcing the subject to narrate their ego anew. Where psychoanalytic constructions would move towards the further consolidation of meaning, interpretations would move in the direction of revealing the fault lines that ultimately make every text "unreadable". Such a technique, consisting of revealing the points of impossibility-illegibility of the subject's free association, would work only in the neuroses. In the psychoses, it may lead to disastrous effects such as depersonalization and fragmentation, as the undoing of the ego may not easily be rectified by new discursive productions. This will either lead to increasingly paranoid elaborations with greater weight cast on the specular imaginary or to a depressive void of subjectivity. If, as aforementioned, meaning (the imaginary) is stable only if it is not univocal, then the equivocating interpretation may result, in the psychoses, in forms of speech testifying to a radical and dangerous instability such as attested to by manic proliferations, depressive silences and paranoid constructions. In the neuroses, where the aforesaid paradox of meaning is operative, one can more confidently hope that the puncturing of meaning through interpretation will lead to broader and more flexible constructions from the analysand.[1] Only in this case can the allegory of the text's unreadability retain its metaphoricity; otherwise it may slide into the dangerous realm of the literal where the text's unreadability will be experienced as a real and concrete threat not only to identity but also to the body proper. This reference to non-sense at the basis of sense is also crucial for understanding how subjective responsibility can be assumed through the analytic process. The interpretation, insofar as it aims primarily to deconstruct, is most efficient when ambiguous. The link between interpretation and enigma is therefore not arbitrary. It is only in this way that the space of non-sense can be preserved so that a novel sense may emerge. Cast in Lacanian parlance, the analysand can take responsibility only for a message received in inverted form, i.e. upside-down and somewhat nonsensical. Interpretations that focus too stringently on meaning further alienate the subject who will respond with either total obedience or maintain a position of defiance. With the formulation according to which "the subject receives his own message in inverted form", Lacan takes us further away from the Romantic (post-Freudian) misunderstanding of the unconscious as a cauldron of wild unorganized affects. By stark contrast to this Groddeckian and (pseudo)-Nietzschean "unconscious", Lacan's dictum reveals once again that the unconscious has structure (one could not, otherwise, speak of *inverted* messages) even if such structure precludes the presence of unequivocal meanings. The idea of signifiers unhinged by signifieds gives the unconscious the form of music (a symbolic system of signifiers without signifieds, as in mathematics). Moreover, the importance of the motif of *inversion* as the very form of interpretation engages the analytic couple in a *contrapuntal* exchange where the analyst offers *variations on themes* introduced by the analysand.

This particular topology by which interpretations *invert* the analysand's speech only to paradoxically better render it on its feet is intimately tied to the dialectic by which truth and untruth mutually implicate each other. Where symbolic castration is operative, the truth is negated such that it re-emerges *half*-said (*mi-dit*) within the interstices of quotidian discursivity. Truth and untruth are not radically opposed insofar as the former manifests itself partially only through the latter. Undoubtedly, Lacan draws inspiration from Heidegger's (1967) notion of truth as *a-letheia*, according to which truth and untruth form a unity rather than stand opposed. Heidegger's penchant for etymologies served him well here insofar as the Greek word for truth (*a-letheia*) involves a negation; the "a" prefixing "*letheia*" denotes that truth is the negation of oblivion ("*lethe*"). For Lacan, as we have seen, this translates into the idea that truth manifests itself as fiction. This means that the unconscious manifests itself clinically in the guise of lies: "there is no truth that, in passing through awareness, does not lie" (Lacan, 1977). The Lacanian-Heideggerian thesis concerning the identity-in-difference of truth and untruth (*a-letheia*) implies that truth emerges only as negated.[2] What makes truth inoperative in psychosis is, quite paradoxically, the fact that it has not been repressed.

A brief analogy with photography may help. To obtain a photograph we need, firstly, a negative that we may then develop. If the final picture is to be labelled "truth", its production requires the negative that we take to the lab. The contradiction of psychotic foreclosure is that, on the one hand, it represents a much deeper rejection of truth and/or castration[3] than repression while, on the other hand, it involves a *failure* of the negation of truth. This apparent inconsistency is resolved if we remember that truth is its own negation.[4] There is no "raw" truth prior to its suppression; the truth emerges as the result of an arduous play of concealment and dis-concealment emerging in the dialectical process of psychoanalytic treatment. Reverting back to our analogy, the "truth" in psychosis is reduced to the bit of "brute reality" sitting "out there" waiting to be photographed. From a psychoanalytic point of view this does not constitute truth *proper* insofar as no *symbolic* inscription of that "reality" has taken place given the failure to *register* it in a *negative* that may be then developed into a photograph – the latter alone would correspond to the psychoanalytic notion of the return of the repressed truth. Something is surely lost in every photograph, and it is precisely this loss that allows the photograph to represent for us the "truth" of the recorded event more efficiently than our actual lived experience of the moment. It is usually when looking at old photographs that one realizes what one really had and is now lost. The experience of the present moment is always tainted with a kind of hypomanic disavowal (something akin to *ingratitude*). Looking at old photographs requires a decidedly *depressive position* that facilitates the access to truth. Insofar as the identity-in-difference of truth and lies is radically dirempted through foreclosure we may argue that the latter puts truth altogether out of efficiency. In this light, it may be arguably the case that the so-called disenchantment of the world has made more difficult our access to truth. Interestingly, the immense popularity of video games and virtual reality testifies to a return to fiction, thereby marking our contemporary situation with the contradiction of a heightened reality principle accompanied by a need to bury oneself entirely in the unreal. Psychoanalysis resists this contradiction by holding on to the paradox of truth-fiction. As apogee of materialism, it represents the paradoxical unity of the pre-modern mythological and the modern scientific.[5]

The result of this diremption is that truth is reduced to the dimension of knowledge.[6] Thus, the pursuit of knowledge (as opposed to truth-fiction) would be solidary with a will to ignorance: "there is no knowledge which doesn't emerge against a background of ignorance" (Lacan, 1992, 171). The apex of this will to ignorance is found in psychotic foreclosure, thereby rendering *paranoid*, according to Lacan, the very structure of knowledge. The diremption of the truth-fiction identity-in-difference leads to the contradiction of paranoid knowledge; the rejection of the dimension of fiction, rather than leading to a more lucid vision of the world, gives rise to paranoid systems of thought. Scientism is a degradation of truth-fiction to knowledge-paranoia arising from the vain attempt to access a "pure" truth untainted by fiction-untruth. Modern American psychiatry, behaviourism, cognitive science as well as 19th century physiognomy and phrenology hinge precisely on such a degradation of the dimension of truth-fiction. The upshot of this scientistic diremption is an immediate reification of subjectivity into something akin to physical matter. As Findlay notes in his foreword to Hegel's *Phenomenology of Spirit*, if Hegel were alive today he would rail against the contemporary reifications of consciousness:

This treatment of conscious inwardness as if it had the contingency and the singularity of external, natural being, leads, however, inevitably to attempts to physicalize consciousness, to identify it with a thing, or a set of things, that we find out there in the natural world. Had Hegel lived in the present age we should now have had a long treatment of the behaviourisms of Watson and Tolman and Skinner.

(Hegel, 1977)

Interestingly, Findlay continues, Hegel would not have fallen in despair faced with this kind of scientistic reductionism insofar as he would retain hope that, through a dialectical reversal, matter (rather than mind) would be reduced and, consequently, mind would be able to reassert its primacy:

All that is important in Hegel's long attempt to make dialectical sense of these primitive exercises is the final outcome: that if self-consciousness can be reduced to something like a bone or a bone-structure, then a bone or a bone-structure must be credited with all the intentional negativity, and the negation of this negativity, involved in self-consciousness. The manoeuvres of reductionism are accordingly vain: if mind can be modelled by matter, matter must be possessed of every intricate modality of mind. Nothing has been achieved by the "reduction", and, since the phenomena of self-consciousness are richer and more intrinsically intelligible than the limited repertoire that we ordinarily ascribe to matter, it is matter rather than mind that is thereby reduced. This conclusion is what Bertrand Russell would call "malicious". Hegel, however, is not ashamed of the vengeful ingratitude of consciousness and spirit: it overreaches its pitiable "other", and reduces it to itself.

(ibid, xix)

We have, firstly, the paradoxical dialectical unity of truth and fiction. Secondly, we have the scientistic diremption of this identity-in-difference leading to the contradiction of paranoid knowledge. This is finally followed by the "vengeful ingratitude of consciousness and spirit" by which matter is reduced and spirit finds again a path to self-assertion freed from reification. If Russell deems this a "malicious" operation, it is arguably because truth's final triumph by reversal is *seen* as malicious from the standpoint of the paranoia of knowledge; it is the envious eye of diremption that perceives *its own malice* in the Other. Today's scientistic reductionism casts matter as the "higher" term unaware that its diremptive snobbery of mind only further fortifies the latter's ultimate triumph.

Maleval (2000, 16) aptly argues that the pharmaceutical industry uses neuroscience as its veil of modesty. This, we may add, is a ploy by which it hides its impudence (Soler, 2011, 94) as well as its "malice", namely its own will to perceive the subject's resistance to scientistic reductionism as malice, something the subject often tragically pays the price for with the straitjacket. Another possible outcome of the diremption of truth-fiction is the rise of what we colloquially christen as "bullshit". Bullshit is undeniably less spiritual than lies which, unlike the former, retain a dialectical kinship to truth. In *On Bullshit*, Harry Frankfurt puts forward such an argument when he claims that where "the liar cares about the truth and attempts to hide it; the bullshitter doesn't care if what they say is true or false, but rather only cares whether or not their listener is persuaded" (Frankfurt, 2005, 61). Perhaps we should here ask ourselves the following daring question, leaving it for posterity to find an answer: is Modern American psychiatry an instance of the paranoia of knowledge, or, more innocently, is it the quintessential manifestation of bullshit?

Political correctness, that most pusillanimous of delusions, is also diremptive of the truth-lies identity-in-difference insofar as, according to Žižek, it abolishes the domain of "sincere lies." Following Kant, Žižek locates this paradoxical realm somewhere "between the two extremes of pure inner morality and external legality"; it is the domain of *politeness* which is "both more than just obeying external legality and less than pure moral activity" (Žižek, 2015, 60). Politeness involves the paradox of *sincerely* saying things which, upon deeper self-reflection, we know we do not really mean (e.g. asking people how they are doing, wishing them well and so on). With political correctness, "in place of spontaneous customs followed in a non-reflexive way, we have explicit rules ('blacks' become 'African Americans', 'fat' becomes 'weight-challenged', etc.)" (ibid, 151). This threat to the order of sincere lies leads to the contradiction of *politically correct impoliteness*. Here the "higher" term (the pretence of political correctness) dominates the lower term (the "incorrect"). Yet it does so in a thoroughly impolite manner; what is more truly incorrect than to tell people how to speak while falsely waving the flag of tolerance and diversity? We thus come to the contradiction by which the politically *correct* reveals itself as the quintessentially incorrect and impolite. Political correctness veers into sheer rudeness precisely insofar as it refuses to see in the "incorrect" (sincere lies) its symptom and truth. Political correctness is held captive to the illusion of pure and unadulterated politeness-correctness. This provides yet another instance of the disparagement of the "higher" into the "lower" term consequent upon diremption. The impasses of political correctness are akin to those of the obsessional demand for truth entirely untainted by lies. Here the moral trumpeter stands for the "higher" term radically censoring all lies. The upshot is that he/she can do so only from a position of *constitutive* insincerity.

What we see, at many levels of social life, is the rise of rudeness and impudence with explicit right-wing effrontery at one end and the (pseudo)-left-wing conceit of dictating to others how they should speak at the other end. What joins the *ubuesque*[7] leaders of the far right and the eternally wounded social justice warriors of the (pseudo)-left is precisely their shared foreclosure of the domain of sincere lies which, we must add, represents for Kant the only means for the civilizing of an otherwise wild humanity. For Kant, the human being achieves civilized morality only through a long process of acting:

On the whole, the more civilized human beings are, the more they are actors. They adopt the illusion of affection, of respect for others, of modesty and of unselfishness without deceiving anyone at all, because it is understood by everyone that nothing is meant sincerely by this.

(quoted in ibid, 147)

As La Rochefoucauld (1976) puts it most eloquently, "hypocrisy is the homage which vice pays to virtue". The hypocritical pretence to goodness eventually leads to "real" goodness. The waning of this dimension of sincere lies, namely politeness, is nowhere more visible than in the form that some public "debates" have taken today where few even bother to feign civility. Intellectual/political arguments are increasingly indistinguishable from the triumphalism of gangster rap battles. Debaters are increasingly proud of "destroying" the other's argument, unwilling to even fake respecting the alternative position or, at the very least, the other person.[8] Instead of the required politeness of sincere lies, public debates now resort to the subterfuge of passion which attempts to fill in the gaps in argumentation with sheer bravado. Peterson's brazen dismissal of French intellectuals, Marxists, postmodern theorists (as if they were all the same) in grand sweeping *ad hominem* statements is exemplary here (e.g. "Foucault The Reprehensible & Derrida The Trickster"). Even if Peterson's (rather paranoid) critique was "valid" it would still suffer from the fact, so lucidly observed by Hegel, that such fixation "on the antithesis of truth and falsity[9] ... does not comprehend the diversity of philosophical systems as the progressive unfolding of truth, but rather sees in it simple disagreements" (Hegel, 1977, 2). Today the increased polarization of the judgments "true" and "false" in public debates (as if we were simply dealing with facts – incidentally this last word has become another contemporary fetish, a kind of trump card that "wins" every time) has hindered the slow and patient unfolding of truth through the notion that progressively sharpens its speculative complexity. Passion is indeed veritably undialectical as it blindly rejects its identity-in-difference with its Other through fatuous claims to purity. With the obliteration of politeness – now even the rich, Jameson argues, exercise the privilege of being crass – public debates have become the site of battles of pure prestige where not only right and left are pinned against each other like wild hounds but, in an uncanny twist, men and women re-enact an infantile battle of the sexes. Today it is conviction, rather than the lie, that is slaying the dimension of truth.

The dialectical unity of truth and lies is nowhere more apparent than when observing children at play; make-believe amply testifies to the fictitious structure of truth. Indeed, nothing would attest more humorously to clumsy parenting than recourse to "hard factual truth" when introducing a child to novel truths. It would be mere folly to replace the old stories of "the birds and the bees" with actual "scientific" facts or real images. Such interventions would be more akin to transgressions of the veil of modesty that should be maintained between the generations. Old-fashioned myths around sexuality may be further from the "facts" of sexuality as regards their content, however, the very form of their expression conveys the truth of the matter more efficiently. These stories, precisely by virtue of their fictitiousness, relay to the child the message that things should here remain *unspoken* and *secret*. The fabricated nature of the tales will convey to the child something of parental *unease* and this, surprisingly, is perhaps what will be most beneficial insofar as it will establish for the child the domain of taboo. The child will thereby understand that sexuality, the quintessential domain of the subtle, involves innuendo. The sexual arises in the very gesture of its repression. This lesson in subtlety, secrecy and innuendo is precisely the most important lesson a child can learn as he/she acquires what, as aforesaid, Lacan deems the highest virtue of the sexual, namely modesty (*pudeur*).

The analogy with photography shows that truth requires the minimal *death* that the dimension of fiction casts upon the *all too real*. To Hegel's "the word is the murder of the thing" we add that the word is also "the life of the thing"; without the death cast by language, the realm of things would paradoxically remain a brute reality devoid of vitality. The symbol must embody the paradoxical identity-in-difference of the *life* and *death* of the thing: "All things human may live only if they have been first killed and later reawakened to the life of the symbol. All things human must cross death and enter into resurrection" (Lacan, 1987–1988, my translation). With this we may sharpen Legendre's (2000) distinction between *symbol* and *idol*. Where the former represents the identity-in-difference of the life and death of the thing, the latter diremprts this with the paradoxical result of words imbued with *jouissance* while lacking emotional vigour. Heidegger's view that massive changes were on their way regarding our relation to language[10] could be understood as the dominance of this diremption in late modernity. Moreover, the "all-too-living" language of fascism represents perhaps another such instance of diremption where words fuelled with the energy to mobilize masses are senseless bravado aimed at conjuring hate. Fascism thus reveals itself as a linguistic/aesthetic and political phenomenon, something Benjamin (1969) presciently understood: "The logical result of Fascism is the introduction of aesthetics into political life". In an effort to abate prevailing fears that Trump will bring fascism to America, Žižek has argued that Trump is a centrist politician. Though this statement may have some political validity at the level of policies and so on, one should not dismiss the fact that Trump's use of language, most notably as an effort to conjure intense emotions, is fascist in the linguistic–aesthetic sense. Trump's diremptive use of language has the contradictory result of at once *inflaming* the passions while *numbing* the mind.[11] Trump makes much diremptive use of idols rather than symbols; or, cast in Hegelese, his language is imbued with pure thoughts to the detriment of notional ambiguity. Following Freud and Lacan, Legendre (2000) explains that primary repression leads to the essential separation of words and things. To this we should add that primary repression leads to the successful division *and* union of words and things. Repression allows for idols to become symbols and, therefore, for pure thoughts to elevate to notions. Adding a nuance to Freud's perspicacious observations regarding the psychotic relation to language, we suggest that psychosis does not only involve the equation of words and things but also entails their radical separation, whereby words become so distant from things that the vitality of language is entirely lost.

Derrida (1987) critiques Lacan's "*a letter always arrives at its destination*" (Lacan, 2006, 30). For this teleology to be guaranteed, he argues, the letter must always crystallize into a *meaning* (Derrida, 1987). Can this critique of Lacan's thesis concerning the letter and its destination be extended to the notion of truth? Does the notion of truth require a crystallization of language into meaning? Lacan's notion of truth does not depend on a prior emergence of meaning through a process whereby the signifier leaps to reach the otherwise forbidden signified. For Lacan, truth resists such "apotheosis" of language towards fixed meanings. Truth deconstructs the narratives by which the ego establishes its empire; all who have undertaken the emotionally arduous task of analysis will attest to this. Derrida's critique fails to heed to this speculative proposition: *truth is "the very antidote for fragmentation"* (Derrida, 1987, 441) *only insofar as it is also the very vehicle of the deconstruction of meaning.* Another formulation of this paradox would state that *the letter's teleology is guaranteed only when its meaning and content are compromised by the half-saying of truth.*[12] Derrida misses the critical nuance by which every letter reaches its destination "in an inverted form". If the letter fails to reach its destination, it is because meaning has crystallized all too solidly. Such is the letter's destiny in psychosis where the fixity of meaning (the triumph of the idol) eclipses the half-said truth.

Notes

1 Laplanche (1999b) very pertinently remarks that interpretations originate from the analyst while constructions are the work of the analysand.

2 Freud's "On Negation" (1925) makes precisely this point.

3 Freud (1911) describes foreclosure (*Verwerfung*) as a "not wanting to know about castration even in the sense of repression". Foreclosure represents the *obliteration* (rather than displacement, conversion or dissociation) of an idea.

4 Truth is doubly contradictory; first, by virtue of the fact that a statement and its opposite may be both true, and second, more immanently, by virtue of the fact that a truth emerges only through its negation. Of course, we should here add that the former is merely a special case of the latter.

5 Clemens (2013) provides a twin genealogy of psychoanalysis in modern science and literature, thereby giving support to the thesis put forward here that psychoanalysis represents the paradoxical dialectical unity of the pre-modern and the modern.

6 Laurent (2012) has thus argued that Joycean sublimation takes place entirely within the dimension of knowledge.

7 In order to underscore the increasing buffoonery of political leadership, Foucault (1999) coined the term "ubuesque" after Jarry's *Ubu Roi*. The contradiction here is that the buffoonery of power has done nothing to reduce it but has even strengthened its hold through this artifice.

8 Consider the following titles of YouTube videos: "Ben Shapiro Absolutely Destroys People with Facts", "Jordan Peterson OWNS Everyone". The puerile triumphalism never fails to put a smile on my face but, alas, it is a grin that hides chagrin.

9 Consider how often, with zeal bordering on the religious, Peterson imputes to an idea the simplistic judgment that it is "PLAIN WRONG".

10 Interview retrieved on April 7, 2017 at: www.youtube.com/watch?v=9_vYz4nQUcs

11 Is it not, moreover, a delicious irony of chance that this tasteless conjuror of popular sentiment should be christened by a name evoking his triumphalist buffoonery as well as conjuring the image (as in a mirror) of a hot air–spouting brass instrument?

12 Interestingly, Poe's *The Purloined Letter* tracks the itinerary of a letter whose location is always precisely known but whose content remains an enigma.

Variation 17 Thrownness and autonomy

For the subject to have a subjectivizable relation to his/her own past, primary repression needs to be operative. To *remember* his/her past in a psychically efficacious manner, he/she must also *forget* the past. Psychosis provides a limit to this idea. Insofar as the psychotic subject has not achieved primary repression, he/she will often recall very precise childhood memories. However, the meaning he/she will draw from these remembrances may be very static as he/she will be unable to engage the past in a dialectical relation to future events that may bestow on them new meanings or important nuances. The foreclosure of the past implies an inability to assume his/her genealogy, namely the contingent cultural and familial inheritance that make up the content of what Heidegger christened "thrownness". This notion points to what predates the birth of the subject and which he/she cannot escape; it is a limit to freedom and self-determination.[1] Heidegger argues that thrownness means that *Dasein* has no power of determination over that which constitutes his/her "basis": "In being a basis – that is, in existing as thrown – Dasein constantly lags behind its possibilities. It is never existent *before* its basis, but only *from* it and *as this basis*. Thus, 'Being-a-basis' means *never* to have power over one's ownmost Being from the ground up. This *'not'* belongs to the existential meaning of 'thrownness'" (Heidegger, 1967, 329–331).

This limitation on freedom, arguably the condition for the little freedom we have, entails that the subject accept being excluded from his/her thrownness. Cast in Lacanian diction, to be dupe means to take one's *contingent* thrownness as an irreducible *necessity*. The psychotic, refusing "to be excluded from his origin" (Lacan), cannot accept thrownness. The neurotic faces challenges of his/her own in this regard – thrownness raises the indignation of even the most privileged and sagacious. Neurotic fantasy is a protest against thrownness. In neurosis, fantasy addresses the problem of thrownness as a response to a question ("where do babies come from?" and so on), while in psychosis no question is posed at all. Here, there is only certainty about an answer. Fantasy represents a less radical rejection than psychotic delusion. In paranoia, the *structural necessity* of thrownness is taken to be the *contingent* effect of the Other's will, a conspiracy planned to serve its own singular *jouissance*. The paranoid subject, unwilling to accept the paradox of limited freedom, is relegated to the contradiction of unbound sovereignty indistinguishable from subjection. When Lacan claims that "the madman is the free man" (Lacan, 1969, 17, my translation), we must add that this "freedom" is tantamount to utter servitude. In melancholia we have a subject casting all the blame of thrownness on him/herself. Paradoxically, this delusional sense of guilt absolves the possibility of subjective responsibility, leading, in the extreme, to the ghastly contradiction which Freud so elegantly christened as "criminals out of a sense of guilt" and which Nietzsche named the "pale criminals", subjects reduced to "a coil of wild serpents that are seldom at peace among themselves ... seeking prey in the world" (Nietzsche; 1969, 66). The clinic also testifies to instances where a psychotic subject rejects his/her genealogy and symbolic debt to the past in the form of identity amnesia or as a decision to change his/her identity in an effort to make a radical new start. Both instances are well attested to, respectively, in Wenders' *Paris, Texas* and Antonioni's *The Passenger*. In the former, Travis, in the grips of complete amnesia, slowly re-enters the social bond and confronts subjective historical truths regarding his failed marriage and the question of paternity. Interestingly, the transitional space (to borrow a Winnicottian term) from the no-man's land where he had been relegated back to social co-existence was a desolate oasis named "*Terlingua*", akin to the Latin for "land of language". Travis' return to society and his re-engagement with historical truth begin with an effort to relinquish the silence of foreclosure and engage again with the Other of speech. *The Passenger* recounts the story of a man in pursuit of an alternate identity/ reality, the quintessential gesture of foreclosure moving in the direction diametrically opposed to symbolic castration. In both cases, the identity-in-difference of freedom/autonomy and thrownness is dirempted, thereby relegating the subjects to the contradiction of complete social impotence co-existing with a gargantuan effort towards absolute self-sufficiency.

Thrownness is intimately connected to the irremediable debt that structures the relation to previous generations. Thrownness means that this debt cannot be effaced. Attempts to obliterate it for the sake of total self-sufficiency *à la Rousseau*[2] result in the buildup of actual (rather than symbolic) debts. As Darian Leader (2012) has convincingly argued, this tendency is most evident in the manic-depressive psychoses. In such cases, the substitution of the symbolic debt to the past for a monetary debt to a present creditor exemplifies an instance of the psychotic re-emergence in the real. Interestingly, this phenomenon lends further credence by way of psychoanalytic proof, above and beyond the already existing economic evidence, that capital is today's real (cf. Žižek). Late modernity thus testifies to subjects who, rather than acquire their dignity through a relation of reverential deference to the past, are reduced to the humiliating submissiveness to a literal creditor inspiring more fear than respect. The *religion* that is capitalism (cf. Benjamin (2004)) functions in precisely this manner. Having abolished the subject's reverential relation to his/her forefathers – the great achievement of capitalism consists of having severed us from the chains of tradition – the foreclosed *Other of thrownness* returns in the form of faith in the future, namely in one's ability to later pay one's debts to one's creditor.[3] In paranoia thrownness is reduced to a persecutory conspiracy, in melancholia it is depreciated to a delusional sense of guilt and, finally, in the manic-depressive psychoses it is transformed into an actual debt taking the form of an overwhelming sense of obligation to an idealized Other or, more literally, a financial debt to a creditor. In all cases, the subject desperately flees from the structural necessity of thrownness through an omnipotent delusion of autonomy. Each time, the subject is paradoxically doomed to fulfil his/her destiny through the very effort of trying to surmount it. Thrownness here functions as the ineradicable symptom-torsion that is, at once, the obstacle to autonomy and yet also its very *sine qua non* condition (Žižek, 2015, 69). Diremption leads to the triumph of the "lower" term such that the very effort to assert unconditional autonomy paradoxically flounders into indigent dependency. The rejection of the past – American a-historicism as Lacan (2006) had it – is a feeble and puerile attempt at "freedom" which enslaves one all the more.

The hypotheses that Lacan put forward regarding Joyce provide a very interesting and fascinating exception to the rule concerning thrownness as a condition of sanity. What Lacan shows with Joyce is a subject capable of dirempting his past (foreclosure of the name of the father) without thereby suffering the consequences of madness. According to Lacan, Joyce separates from his ancestors and thus rejects his genealogy. As Soler puts it, Joyce is "voluntarily uprooted" (Soler, 2015, 70). Joyce rejects the genealogical tree; he wants to make himself the origin (ibid, 130). Such a string of foreclosures would generally lead to madness if it were not for the very successful work of compensation Joyce achieves by way of his writing. How, according to Lacan (2005a), Joyce achieves stabilization within foreclosure goes beyond the scope of this treatise. However, what is important to note for our purposes is that Joyce, according to Lacan, was able to provide an exception to psychoanalytic theory. To this we may add that Joyce also provides an exception to dialectical thinking and speculative philosophy. He shows us how much a subject can bear diremption without going mad. In this way, Joyce could indeed provide a great example of the Deleuzian "nomad", namely the subject who, by contrast to Žižek's (generally valid) contention, does not require thrownness as a condition of his autonomy. The topology of knots that Lacan further develops in his work on Joyce takes psychoanalysis beyond its previous purview and, perhaps, beyond Hegel's speculative philosophy. Taking us well beyond the scope of this treatise, one may ask whether Hegelian dialectics consists of *a special case* of Lacan's later topological advancements.[4]

Notes

1   The concept of thrownness represents one of Heidegger's greatest weapons against what he elsewhere (1991) termed "Western subjectivism", namely the tradition of Western conceptualizations of an endogenous human striving. Erroneous interpretations of Freud may include the *sexual drive* or *Eros* under the same banner of "subjectivism". It is to Lacan's credit to have corrected such biologistic and subjectivist

misreadings of Freud by showing that human sexuality is *imposed* on the subject from the outside.

2 Soler (2012) explains that Rousseau's father blamed him for his mother's death at his birth. She argues that this nonsensical guilt led to Rousseau's total refusal of guilt henceforth. In Heideggerian parlance, Rousseau's thrownness constituted too much of a heavy debt. It could not be subjectivized and haunted him in the form of a conviction regarding a conspiracy to defame and slander his name.

3 Agamben (2019) puts forward the argument that capitalism is based on the religious faith in one's ability to later pay for what one has borrowed today. To highlight this same centrality of belief, Sloterdijk (2018) argues that capitalism should be called "creditism" insofar as the word "credit" comes from "credere" meaning *to believe*.

4 This may explain the limited interest Žižek has in Lacanian topology.

Variation 18 Life and death

The paradox in relation to time (to have a past one must accept being excluded from it, i.e. one must repress it) is intricately linked to another important paradox concerning the human being's rapport with life and death. For the subject to maintain a relation to the future and thereby sustain *desire* for eventual *projects* (and thus feel *alive*), acknowledgment of mortality must be operative. The most famous philosophical articulation of the relation between the subject's engagement with *life* and his/her assumption of *mortality* is Heidegger's notion of "being-towards-death". As with the identity-in-difference of truth and untruth, the psychotic poses an exception to "being-towards-death". The psychotic presents a subjectivity that does away with mortality. Let us consider Balmès' argument as it is paraphrased by Žižek:

> Francois Balmès makes here a perspicuous remark that it is as if Lacan's implicit clinical reproach to Heidegger's existential analytic of Dasein as "being-towards-death" is that it is appropriate only for neurotics and fails to account for psychotics: a psychotic subject occupies an existential position for which there is no place in Heidegger's mapping, the position of someone who in a way "survives his own death". Psychotics no longer fit Heidegger's description of Dasein's engaged existence, their life no longer moves in the coordinates of freely engaging in a futural project against the background of assuming one's past: their life is outside "care /Sorge/", their being is no longer directed "towards death".
>
> (Žižek, 2012b)

To have an engaged existence that is dynamically coordinated to the future as well as to the past, the subject must assume finitude and mortality. Insofar as Heideggerian "care" is based on the notion of being-towards-death it is not applicable to the psychotic who has foreclosed the dimension of mortality. The psychotic is thus excluded from a crucial feature of *Dasein* and thus falls out of the frame that constitutes the universality of being human. This is most poignantly and *literally* seen in the clinical picture of the Cotard syndrome[1] where one witnesses the horrific sight of a subject who has in fact veritably "survived his own death" as Žižek elegantly put it. The striking clinical picture of Cotard syndrome involves the contradiction of a delusional certainty of being literally dead co-existing, at times, with the idea of being immortal. The psychotic is one who, having foreclosed the dimension of being-towards-death, is paradoxically more "dead to the world" than the neurotic who lives in the horizon of mortality. Schreber died as a subject (he describes himself as a "corpse carrying another corpse" (Schreber, (2000)) but maintained certainty regarding his own immortality.

Without directly appealing to psychoanalysis or psychosis, Alain Badiou (2015a) put forward a critique of Heidegger's idea that death represents the culmination of *Dasein's* immanent "ownmost potentialities". Heidegger (1967) likens death to the ripening of a fruit; death marks for him the realization of *Dasein's* inner necessity. Badiou explains that Heidegger's notion of death is much like Hegel's absolute insofar as both orient human life from *within*. By contrast to Heidegger, Badiou insists on the radical externality of death as a contingency foreign to the subject: "Death is something that happens to you; it is not the immanent unfolding of some linear programme" (Badiou, 2015a). For Badiou, death is not immanent to the subject. Following Spinoza who claims that "nothing can be destroyed except by an external cause" (ibid), Badiou ventures to say that the human is not even mortal if "mortal" is taken to mean that the human being immanently contains the virtuality of death. Badiou also argues that the Heideggerian insistence on mortality is symptomatic of "capitalist and religious nihilisms" (ibid) which he defines as the belief that nothing is important because of death. Such nihilism, for Badiou, equalizes and thereby devalues everything. Despite agreeing with Badiou's first claim regarding the externality and contingency of death, one should think longer about the ramifications of his second claim regarding nihilism. Indeed, death is not immanent to life; it simply *intervenes*. However, to immediately dismiss Heideggerian (but also religious, as Badiou insists) being-towards-death as *nihilistic* fails to heed to an important psychoanalytic point captured by Balmès' critique of Heidegger's claim to universalize being-towards-death rather than limiting it to the neuroses. The limit case provided by psychosis offers great proof of Badiou's point regarding the externality of the death. Indeed, death is not immanent to human life; but neither are sex and paternity. Paternity is something we encounter in the symbolic order and sex is not a biological striving internal to human life, it is a *drive* thoroughly mediated and subverted by language. That death and paternity are external to the human being does not imply that there should be no endeavour to *internalize* these. Indeed, infantile sexual researches are attempts to come to grips with the externality of sex, death and paternity in order to then *subjectivize* what is initially imposed from the outside. The institution of the family constitutes a crucial *dispositif* for enabling this process.[2]

By stark contrast to Badiou's indictment against Heidegger's alleged nihilism, psychoanalysis holds that *without* death nothing is important.[3] Death must be internalized for life to have meaning and for the subject to access a sense of *future*. Paradoxically, the psychotic is not able to open the space of human temporality to include a *futural* dimension wherein the possibility for a *project* could be established precisely because his/her future is reduced to a chronological sequence devoid of a reference to death. The inability to internalize mortality, paternity and sex leads to the great impasses of subjectivity. For Schreber, the promotion to Supreme Court judge (an emblematically paternal role) led to the displacement of his non-subjectivized sexual libido on to the imaginary figure of a cruel God of *jouissance* and to the absurd contradiction of a delusion of quasi-immortality co-existing with the aforementioned conviction of being a corpse carrying another corpse. With Badiou, it must be held that death (but also sex and paternity) is not immanent to human life. However, one must not label as "nihilistic" the effort to internalize it insofar as the failure to do so risks leading us to the true nihilism of total de-subjectivization. It is curious to note how the contemporary philosopher most intent upon reviving the notion of the subject (in the face of its deconstruction in post-war French philosophy) fails to recognize that human *subjectivity* hinges on the gesture by which the externality of death is partially internalized to give life meaning and open the realm of human temporality for existential *projects* requiring *futural* engagements. By opposing life and death and thereby failing to see the coincidence of contraries, Badiou remains bound to the finite. Against Badiou's "Down with death!" – a hysteric (but not so sublime) protest against the (absolute) master if there ever was one – one must say "rise with death" as the only possible life for a human subject is a life after *resurrection*.[4] As Žižek argues, "the awareness of one's finitude immediately reverts into the experience of one's true infinity" (Žižek, 2012a, 994). In similar vein, Lebrun notes that, for Hegel, the subject can show him/herself to be free and elevate him/herself above all constraints only insofar as he/she is capable of dying (Lebrun, 1972, 29). For Hegel, "the life of Spirit is not the life that shrinks from death and keeps itself untouched by devastation, but rather the life that endures it and maintains itself in it" (Hegel, 1977, 19).[5] The defiant "Down with death!" precludes such awareness and, as a result, rather than open access to the infinite, appends the subject all the more stringently to finitude. Death is an external universality that singularizes. If we lived forever, infinite time would level all differences and singularity would be abolished. We all die and yet the awareness (symbolization-internalization) of this universality is the only thing that singularizes us. Moreover, the awareness of death is what allows the subject to separate minimally from his/her own image. Lacan makes this pivotal point in the following passage:

> Indeed, it is by means of the gap in the imaginary opened up by this prematurity, and in which the effects of the mirror stage proliferate, that the human animal is capable of imagining himself mortal – which does not mean that he could do so without his symbiosis with the symbolic, but rather that, without the gap that alienates him from his own image, this symbiosis with the symbolic, in which he constitutes himself as subject to death, could not have occurred.
>
> (Lacan, 2006)

It is only through the awareness of death that the human being is able to achieve a symbiosis with the symbolic and, therefore, some separation from his/her self-image. Interestingly, we here see the way various identities-in-difference intermingle in mutual implication. Through awareness of the dialectical unity of life and death, the subject achieves symbiosis with the symbolic (i.e. the subject-collective identity-in-difference is achieved) and can, thereby, separate from him/herself such that the I coincides with the not-I.

Badiou takes affirmation for granted without giving enough consideration to its dialectical rapport with negation (death/mortality). For Žižek too, freedom requires detachment from the body (a kind of "Down with death!"). However, this *detachment* occurs through an excessive *attachment* to an "organ without a body" (Žižek, 2012a, 992). Thus, "attachment itself becomes the form of appearance of its opposite" (ibid, 992). The subject can only be free from the body (and therefore partake in the infinite) through a paradoxical excessive affirmation of the body (a partial object):

> The paradox is thus that the zero-level of negativity is not a negative gesture, but an excess affirmation: by getting stuck on a partial object, by affirming it repetitively, the subject detaches itself from its body, enters into a negative relationship towards its body.
>
> (ibid, 992)

The "subject as actual infinity" arises insofar as "the very worthlessness of the object for which I am ready to risk everything makes it clear that what is at stake is not it but myself, my freedom" (ibid, 992).

Though death is external to life, the human subject will *necessarily* experience this exteriority. Žižek provides an overview of the different ways Lacan conceptualizes the manner in which language accounts for the death drive. At the time of the "Rome Discourse", Lacan's notion of the death drive owes much to the Hegelian idea that "*the word is a death, a murder of the thing*" (Žižek, 1989, 131). By relegating a "thing" (corporeal reality) to the status of a concept, language introduces a radical "negativity". In the period of the "Purloined Letter", the death drive is equated to language as a whole. Here the symbolic, conceived as "*a differential system of elements*" (ibid, 131), disturbs the imaginary order of homeostasis through its "*blind automatism*" (ibid, 132). The third and final stage introduces the notion of the real. Here, the symbolic is the principle of homeostasis while the real is the "traumatic core" lying beyond the grasp of the symbolic (ibid, 132). What is important to remember with respect to this third formulation of the death drive is that the real emerges only retroactively as an effect of the symbolic itself. As a result, in all three cases, it is language that introduces a radical negativity leading the sexual drive away from any kind of pre-given goal such as reproduction or harmonious union with a counterpart. The fact of *speaking* subjects the human being to a sexual drive that is always also a death drive. There is thus a parallel between death and the symbolic order; both are a necessary exteriority that the subject encounters as something foreign yet ubiquitous. The consciousness of death is encountered in lived experienced rather that acquired innately. It is absolutely necessary and certain that every subject will encounter death though each subject will do so in his/her own singular way.

Badiou reduces the relation of life and death to simple difference; they are conceived as external to each other. Death is thus a "radical exteriority". For this reason, Badiou also commends La Palice who, regarding a recently deceased person, states that "a quarter an hour before his death, he was still alive". Badiou continues, "'a quarter an hour before death' he wasn't what Heidegger sees as 'a quarter hour before death' – he wasn't 'a-being-toward-death' ever since his birth". It is indeed true, perhaps trivially true, that death is not programmed into the living. It just happens *from the outside*. If an entity can only be destroyed from the outside, it is also true that an entity can only be enriched from the outside; and what is outside need not remain outside. To die is not the only experience a subject has of death. As we have seen, the subject will encounter the *death drive* through many registers of human experience. Access to the eternal or the infinite can only arise through this first experience of the death drive. For Hegel, the encounter with death leads to the recognition of infinitude. Life and death stand in a paradoxical relation of mutual interdependence such that each comes to itself through a kenosis in the Other. Badiou is right to claim that the deceased man La Palice speaks of does not *suddenly* become "a-being-toward-death" retroactively on the basis of his *literal* physical death. That Badiou would even bother to refute such a view is, of course, intended to mock Heidegger's philosophy of death. The subject was "a-being-towards-death" prior to his actual death through other experiences where the ubiquity of the death drive made itself felt in his *living* body. Psychoanalysis claims that every subject necessarily encounters death through the particular idiosyncratic vicissitudes of his/her life. This necessary encounter with death leads to the possibility of becoming being-towards-death through subjective responsibility (the internalization/subjectivization of the externality of death). If this transpires, it opens the space of the infinite thereby freeing the subject from the cage of finitude. Badiou's passion for the infinite is something that our Hegelian inspiration celebrates and commends. However, following Žižek and Hegel, we add that this awakening to the positive dimension of the infinite occurs through the negativity of the death drive. To Montaigne's (2009) assertion, with which I agree, concerning the fact that "to study philosophy is to learn to die", I simply add that learning to die will also teach us how to live and, more importantly (and in line with Badiou), it will teach us how to live as subjects aligned with immortal aims. For life to have vigour it must accept death (the death drive) as its symptom and Other. To reject the death drive as symptom disparages life itself (the "higher" term) to lowly death; yet another instance of the triumph of the "lower" term consequent upon diremption. As aforesaid, psychosis represents the exemplary case of such diremption. The result is the massive mortification of the subject.

Interestingly, if we combine Hegel with simple biology we come to the conclusion that infinite spirit requires mortal being (i.e. beings that reproduce sexually and which are hence mortal). Creatures that reproduce through cellular division (mitosis) are by contrast literally immortal in that their genome is reproduced infinitely. For Hegel, such creatures are confined to finite spirit. The encounter with death and the ability to *tarry* with it are essential for the ascension to infinite spirit. When the "higher" term (life or infinitude) dirempts the symptomatic "lower" term (death or finitude), we get a massive separation by which the subject is doomed to the vicious dialectical unity of an *infinite life of morbidity*.

Badiou's "Down with death!" suffers from the symptomatic limitation of his work which consists of repeatedly denying the element of the death drive. The celebration of life and disdain of the *memento mori* may seem like a profanation (against death) but, above all, they are expressions of the sacredness of life. What is missed here is the dimension of a profanation against life itself. A necessary "Down with life!" should accompany Badiou's "Down with death!" The strength of psychoanalysis lies in that it dares to celebrate the profanatory-suicidal dimension under the rubric of the death drive. Badiou, by contrast, generally opts for the sacred diremptive remain, something that gives his thought an undeniably religious tenor. Could we not say that Badiou's philosophy (despite its merits) represents the contradiction of a religious thought that poses as atheist? Badiou's celebration of life and infinitude (against mortality and finitude) misses the crucial point that our conception of infinity and eternity is born out of the experience of mortality. When a loved one dies we inevitably face the fact that we will *never* see them again. The *never* becomes here the marker, albeit in negative form, of the infinite. A statement of infinitude that is utterly unwedded to the experience of the negative dwindles to the absurdity of infinitude as *never-ending*, something that lives on forever temporally and literally. This is most evident in psychosis where it is precisely the *memento mori* that is foreclosed and where, as a result, infinitude emerges in the disparaged mode of *forever-ness*. The *memento mori* is the torsion that permeates the surface of life, something Hans Holbein's artistic intuition knew well as he incorporated it in the guise of anamorphosis, a distortion that paradoxically sets the world aright.

Notes

1 The central symptoms of Cotard syndrome consist of convictions regarding the rotting (or even total disappearance) of the body and its internal organs, damnation and, most importantly, the certainty of being dead.
2 Althusser views family with an altogether negative valence as a central "ideological state apparatus" (2012) or as "conjugal obscenity" (2014b). Hegel and psychoanalysis, by contrast, view the family as a necessary bridge to civil society.
3 Lacan states that life would be intolerable if we lived with the idea that we are immortal (https://m.youtube.com/watch?v=i43rWqNwnd0).

4 This is not only the explicit meaning of Christ's example but also the very foundation of psychoanalytic treatment. If the cure involves *a child being killed* this is so that the subject may rise again on his/her ashes and finally truly *live* after having undergone a symbolic *death*.

5 Most famously, Hegel asserts, "Spirit is this power only by looking the negative [i.e. death] in the face, and tarrying with it" (Hegel, 1977, 19).

Variation 19 The force and frailty of the law

The human being's relation to law also involves a central paradox with the ensuing risks of diremption. Modern legal thought promotes an external and objective conception of the law thereby obfuscating the intrinsic tie connecting law and desire (Goodrich and Carlson, 1998, 1). By contrast, psychoanalysis reveals the "Law's unconscious, its 'other scene'", (ibid, 1998, 3). Following Lacan, Legendre underscores the fact that desire itself is at work in the law as the subject's "love of the censor" (ibid, 1998, 9). Likewise, for Žižek, "the system of Laws" is inconsistent insofar as "the Other's impenetrable desire, as well as its *jouissance*, are [therein] located" (Žižek, 2018, 16). The desire inherent to law splits it from within, thereby making it weak and inconsistent. However, psychoanalysis reveals the paradox according to which the force of law is tied to its frailty. When Lacan claims that the "symbolic father is, strictly speaking, unthinkable" (Lacan, 1994, 210, my translation) he means that no father can hold his symbolic mandate without blemishing it with a taint of personal *jouissance,* thereby partially delegitimizing his authority. The wager, however, is that without this blemish, the father's authority falls. The paradox of paternal authority is that it can sustain itself only when partly discredited from its sanctity by the father's own *jouissance*. For Lacan, "there is cause only in something that doesn't work" (Lacan, 1977, 22). The law is no exception; to have causal efficiency it must be tainted by failure. The power of the law and its weakness are one and the same but for the understanding they appear opposed. Common understanding cannot grasp this paradox and thus denies the inconsistencies of law in the hope of establishing an "objective" law. However, speculative and psychoanalytic reason tell us that the law as "objective" and "consistent" leads to a law deprived of force. Moreover, such an "impotent" law leads to more oppressive subjugation. This is the university discourse with its principle contradiction of an "objective" law "without force" that is all the more tyrannical. This leads to a contradiction at the level of the subject: the "free" and "equal" subject of liberal democracy is more than ever constrained by a "theo-technological power, which is incontrovertible [and] speechless" (Schütz, 1998, 206).

Drawing on Agamben (1998), Santner (2011) explores the contradiction by which the subject of university discourse is at once "sovereign" and "bare life". Like the medieval king, this subject has two bodies, one made sublime through symbolic investiture and the other made abject by the imminent threat of social upheaval. With the decline of paternal authority, children are today's sovereigns. The child who is the object of maternal *jouissance* has two bodies wavering from the sublime privilege of having the mother's unique attention to being haunted by a possible castration which, foreclosed from the symbolic, may vehemently return in the real thereby confirming the body's abject destitution. In Althusserian terms, we witness a decline of the "ideological apparatus" of the family. Formerly, the family was the principle ideological apparatus (with the Church and education apparatuses also having important roles) responsible for assuring symbolic castration. Today we see the child's direct and premature encounter with the ideological apparatus of psychiatry and, what is worse, the repressive police apparatus. Parents are increasingly distrustful of their own authority and rely on police and psychiatrists to discipline their child. The danger is that the child's confrontation with such apparatuses is far more terrifying than former negotiations with parents. Punishment in the hands of the police cannot claim the expiatory power it had when delivered by parents.

Insofar as the family ideological apparatus is the home of symbolic castration minimally guaranteeing subjectivity, the negative designation of "ideology" requires some elucidation. The family represents the beginnings of the encounter with the values of society. A tremendous process of internalization takes place through which social substance marks itself on the flesh. The Name-of-the-Father allows for some respite from the spell of this subjugation enabling the child to work through trauma in an on-going neurotic questioning. Repressive apparatuses, Althusser explains, leave little room for flexibility (Althusser, 2014a, 248) while ideology has a "double character"; it is a *recognition* in the form of *misrecognition* or an *allusion* in the form of an *illusion* (ibid, 259). Ideological apparatuses are founded upon fictions (ibid, 252) while repressive apparatuses appeal to force in brute reality. As fiction is the condition of truth, the loss of the family threatens the space of working through where truth may emerge in the interstice of fiction, where recognition may occur in the site of misrecognition and where an allusion to a subject is made in the midst of illusion.

Some ideological apparatuses are arguably more conducive to truth and subjectivity than others. Psychiatry, for instance, harbours a more distant relation to subjective truth than family. Here fiction, illusion and misrecognition do not readily pave the way to truth, allusion and recognition. Perhaps the older feudal apparatus of the Church provided a space commensurate with truth and subjectivity. One should not undervalue the potential for subjective truth concealed within Christianity's mystifications.[1] Much likens family and Church. Firstly, both appeal to paternal authority. As Kojève explains (2014), the authority of the father was theoretically elaborated by scholastic philosophy and theology. Secondly, the Christian religion is arguably founded on a "family romance" (the virgin mother, the immaculate conception) and, conversely, Biblical stories offer allegories for the dramas of family life (the story of Abraham and Isaac delivers an unparalleled metaphor of symbolic castration). Thirdly, faith plays a prominent role in both; the religious man must take a leap to enter the community of believers as the good son must give his "yes" to the father to partake in the privileges of family.

The constricted spaces of psychiatry and disciplinary power are not abodes for myths through which truth emerges. A young subject relegated to the apparatuses of police and psychiatric power finds reconfirmed in the Other his/her paranoid defiance against society. Family enables the ever-renewed construction of fantasies-ideologies commensurate with the growth of subjectivity. It hinges on the identity-in-difference of submitting to the law and finding refuge from it: *one must say "yes" to paternal authority in order to thereby gain some freedom from the family*. Psychotic children who refuse this affirmation are more tightly bound to the family, seldom leaving home – so much for the "nomadic" schizophrenic. Likewise, the seeming paradox of faith is that atheism is possible only for those who do not relinquish Christianity; something Žižek has argued in his effort to reveal the materialist potential of Christianity. Those who cannot grasp this remain bound to the contradiction of naïve atheism where vulgar materialism enslaves the subject more stringently to the Other. The liberating identity-in-difference through which adherence to an ideology affords respite from that ideology is less likely to operate in medical ideology where the subject faces the contradiction of increased subjugation with every effort towards freedom – the more passionately one claims sanity, the more the medical straightjacket is enforced. The scientistic space of psychiatry leaves little space for truth and the thriving of subjectivity. This is truer for the repressive apparatuses where Agamben's (2009) sinister idea of subjugation without subject is a looming threat. The emancipatory potential of a given apparatus is thus proportional to how close it remains to the coincidence of contraries (truth-fiction, recognition-misrecognition). Psychiatry and the police are, in this regard, more diremptive than the apparatuses of Church, family and education.

The decline of the family "state apparatus" is commensurate with the rise of the university discourse. In the family, law and authority could be encountered by the child in less daunting ways. In other words, in the family, the child may more readily experience and fathom the paradox of the force and frailty of law. The paternal law is more easily accepted insofar as the real father's *lack* – precisely his *lack* of power (and therefore the ground of his power) – is more visible than that of a police officer. When Hegel claims that the aim of the punishment of children is "to lift the universal into their consciousness and will" (Hegel, 2008a, 173) this implies that the law must be accompanied by force. However, we must also note that (for Hegel himself) a serious ideological operation is at work in the chastizing of children. For Hegel, a criminal act is its own punishment. To separate the two moments of *crime* and *punishment* is to suffer of the ideology of time. In short, to be a criminal is its own punishment – what need then for greater reprimand?[2] Nevertheless, this minimal ideological operation is a necessary diremptive remain without which the *realization* that one's crime is its own punishment would be impossible. When punishment is delivered *with love*, opportunity is given to the child to achieve true *concern for the other* (conscience) and realize that the pain inflicted on the *other* was *already* and in-itself pain inflicted on the self (for "no man is an island", as Donne would say). Achieving the height of this Christian wisdom requires a bit of the proverbial paternal stick but its aim is precisely to overcome the stick. The paternal stick provides its own sublation. If it hits the child *once*, it is with the aim of never having to do so again. As self-sublating, the stick is a *speculative* object, namely *a thing of love*. Finally, the pain felt by the loving father as he chastizes his child will reinforce *belief* in the goodness of the law. The encounter with paternal lack, namely the father's pain and trembling as he delivers the stick, will not reduce his authority. Our father can still have authority even after his lack is exposed: "The subject is free only when its substantial Other suffers abject humiliation without ceasing to be the expression of authority" (McGowan, 2019, 162). As speculative object, the paternal stick is, to quip Hegel, "not only as *Substance*, but equally as *Subject*" (Hegel, 1977, 10). The policeman's club is sheer loveless substance. There is no law without a *voice* of law. Lebrun speaks of a voice as the necessary median of communicative content. He adds, however, that the voice must disappear so that its message is received (Lebrun, 1972, 298–299). He makes use of Hegel's notion of *expression,* referring to a presence that is inseparable from dissolution (ibid, 298). Castration will be rejected (foreclosed) if the voice carrying it out persists beyond its message – the persistence of the voice is an instance of a psychotic *return in the real*. The voice of the father and the fear that it arouses must be flushed out so that a law remains that is less heavily tainted by the *jouissance* of the voice.

The "repressive" moment of authority is indispensable, without it one falls into university discourse. We witness this at the levels of the state, the family and the psychoanalytic setting. For Žižek (2015), the way out of the contin-gency of law is through its redoubling in the figure of the monarch. Without this, we err into the university discourse which veils the contingency of power with the false semblance of knowledge. Žižek here draws on Hegel for whom the king is closer to the universal than the Estates Assembly which is a group of private individuals fighting only for their private interests (McGowan, 2019, 79). Paradoxically, McGowan explains, the king is closer to the people than their representatives in the Estates Assembly. Althusser (1999a) argues the same concerning Machiavelli in whom he sees a proto-Marxist who seeks to strengthen the power of the prince so that the latter better protects the people from the nobility, which, insofar as it is a special interest group, cannot access a universal perspective.[3] Within the family a similar problem occurs when the redoubling of contingency fails, when the father fails to embody law while also standing outside it. The escape from the "caprice" of maternal law is not achieved by grounding her power in "scientific" necessity (endless books on parenting) but by *repeating* this contingency with the father as family "mon-arch". When the task of castration is left to the public sphere (psychiatrists and police) rather than a loving father, it is harder to reduce the persecutory tenor of the voice. The "mirror stage" takes on a peculiar form as the "clinical gaze" of psychiatry and the disciplinary measures of law replace the mother's gaze and the father's voice; pure thoughts take the place of these speculative objects. For some, the psychiatric label and the criminal record are the last vestiges of (one-sided) identity for bodies reduced to bare life. Althusser's notion of interpellation arguably represents a reformulation of the mirror stage in light of the late modern decline of family. In the past, institutions liminal to the public and the private (school or Church) provided spaces enabling symbolic castration. Today, the repressive apparatus is a veritable emergence of castration in the real resulting in Foucaultian "carceral archipelagos" (Foucault, 1975), such as Goffman's "fugitive communities" testifying to "the massive expansion of criminal justice intervention into the lives of poor Black families" (Goffman, 2014, 249) where the subject is forced into exemption from whole sectors of public life. Analogous difficulties result within the therapeutic setting when the analyst does not occupy the place of *sovereign exception*. This occurs when the analyst opts for transparency and erases any trace of difference in power.[4] The Lacanian scansion re-introduces sovereignty in the analytic session thereby opening the space of the treatment – without a sovereign exception there is no transference.[5] The cure involves the realization that the analyst is not a subject of knowledge but, rather, someone akin to the Žižekian-Hegelian "idiotic" monarch there to "dot the 'i's", namely to simply "return the analysand's own message in an inverted form".[6] When hierarchy is flattened and the place of authority abolished, the unconscious remains closed and transference cannot transpire. The transference cannot emerge without a radical dissymmetry, suspending notions of reciprocity: "The relation of the one with the other that is set up in analysis … is established on a plane that is not reciprocal, not symmetrical" (Lacan, 1977, 137).

The function of the monarch, the father and the psychoanalyst is to make apparent division/lack. By founding all three of these in the contingent will of a particular subject, it becomes evident to the people, the child and the analysand that these cannot be grounded on pure knowledge alone. The paradox consists of the fact that authority incarnated by a "sovereign" provides the means of better enabling the subject to heed to the force and frailty of law. It is, as it were, a way of creating an exit out of the university discourse for the subject. The idea that decisions are grounded, in the last instance, in the *will* of these three figures makes evident what would otherwise remain mystified, namely the fact that law can never be fully substantiated in necessity. It would be a dystopian nightmare to live in a state where every decision purported to be "scientifically" justified. Where in such a constellation would the confidence to question and subvert law and power come from? The analyst too functions to mitigate the illusion of the scientificity of the process rather than add to its prestige. By contrast, psychiatry eschews appeal to the subjectivity of the clinician perpetrating thereby the myth of scientificity. While the psychiatrist seeks refuge in the aseptic setting of the hospital where the aura of knowledge is magnified, the psychoanalyst prefers a personal space that functions as insignia of his/her subjectivity and therefore lack of (scientific) substantiality.[7]

The slave revolt in morality involves what Schmitt diagnosed as the ubiquitous "onslaught against the political" (Schmitt, 1985, 65) where endless parliamentary debates replace the political. If, as Badiou (2013) holds, Nietzsche is the thinker of the "archi-political" it is because he fought most stringently against the "democratic prejudice in science" that has obliterated authority and installed the reign of endless chatter. Psychoanalysis as "conflictual science" (Althusser, 1999b) cannot regress to dialogue. The decline of the political implies the demise of the therapeutic.[8] Kojève (2014) argues that the *political* defends the exercise of authority while the sphere of *ethics* critiques it. The contemporary late modern disparagement of the notion of authority is symptomatic of the waning of the political and, concomitantly, the obliteration of the dimension of conflict. To counter this tendency, Žižek (2012a) argues for "a political suspension of ethics" rather than the ethical deferment of the political where authority is weakened, for instance, by the nagging subterfuge of political correctness (what Kojève would call "private ethics" deployed to eradicate the political dimension of conflict). Nietzsche's critique of a "slave revolt in morality" points towards a similar discontent with the waning of authority. The neologism "politico-therapeutic" may denote the common object of Marx's critique of political economy and Freud's discovery of the unconscious and help us better appreciate that the law is at once political and intimate, political because intimate. The slave revolt in morality grounds the end of the politico-therapeutic and paves the way for the triumph of the university discourse, the antithesis to the conflictual sciences. With the decline of the politico-therapeutic, late modernity testifies to the daunting contradiction of subjugation-interpellation without subjectivity, a predicament akin to madness.

According to Hegel, the slave provides the truth of the master. If the master refuses this truth his position flounders into impotent rage thereby rendering for us that the truth of power is impotence. Concomitantly, Lacan highlights the speculative identity of freedom and servitude: "This means that, in the movement that leads man to an ever more adequate consciousness of himself, his freedom becomes bound up with the development of his servitude" (Lacan, 2006 148). Freedom that refuses its kinship with servitude risks becoming hedonistic debauchery where man is serf to aimless passion. The master's "freedom" is a pure thought that disparages into its opposite. Insofar as the master rejects–dirempts his/her dialectical unity with the slave, the latter becomes the master's truth-symptom and, unless an epiphany of wisdom terminates diremption, the slave will be experienced as an ever greater assault on the identity of the master. A master who accepts his/her identity-in-difference with the slave is no longer a master but a leader. The step taken to acknowledge this dialectical unity represents the shift from master to analyst discourse. All the ideological jargon currently surrounding "authentic leadership" may be granted greater credulity with the idea that such a leader embraces his/her identity-in-difference with his follower. In such a case the master-slave relation gives way to leader-follower; where the former involves the master as pure thought (S1 in Lacanian parlance), the latter comprises the cooperation of two agents in raising the *notion* of authority to its dignity. When Hegel claims that the "essential nature [of lordship] is the reverse of what it wants to be" (Hegel quoted in Jameson, 2010, 41), he is pointing to the master's unwillingness to recognize in the slave-symptom the secret of his/her own identity. For Hegel, the master faces the impasse of being recognized by one whom he/she does not recognize. The master, in refusing to recognize the slave, rejects-dirempts the very kernel-symptom of his/her own being. As a result, the rejection of the slave is, for the master, a repudiation of self. It is akin to a father who, in rejecting his son, denies the very heart of his own being. The parent must accept the child as his/her symptom. Only this way will the child be able to free him/herself from the position of symptom. The monarch makes evident the contradiction of the social while the psychoanalyst embodies the symptom so that the subject can eventually re-appropriate it as his/her own. When authority does not dirempt its extimate relation to the symptom it will dwindle neither into tyranny nor libertarianism. Here authority is modelled on the analyst discourse where the frailty/inconsistency of the law is revealed precisely and paradoxically to render it more integral.

Notes

1 "In the end, for Bloch, the point of religion is that, within its fables and mythologies, its inconsistencies and its dangerously irrational tendencies, it contains a kernel of truth which is about the fulfilment of the dream of Utopia" (Peter Thompson in Bloch, 2009, xxv).

2 Freud's hypothesis concerning "criminals out of a sense of guilt" and Nietzsche's "pale criminal" reverse the ideological temporality according to which crime is the cause of guilt and thereby reach the speculative wisdom that posits the identity-in-difference of crime and guilt/punishment.

3 In all his lunacy and lies, Trump helps us see (albeit in the modality of deception) the secret kinship between monarch and people. He got elected on the (false) rhetoric that he is for the people and not the elite. Sanders would represent the authentic version of the same promise of a paradoxical kinship between the highest and the lowest.

4 The comparison with the therapeutic and family settings shows that the redoubling of the contingency of power need not absolutely take the form of a monarch even in the case of the state. Means more appropriate to our times may be devised.

5 Could not Lacan's eccentric clinical style (digging into purses, pulling hair, throwing a flower pot, caress of the face while saying *geste à peau* and so on), scandalous to our squeamish ears, be understood as practices intended to establish the position of sovereign exception and thereby facilitate access to the unconscious?

6 Strangely, the obliteration of the sovereign position is today accompanied by the rise of despots.

7 McGowan put what is at stake very accurately:

> Hegel's political philosophy includes the monarch as the mark of the state's insubstantiality. It is the point at which individuality manifests itself in the

universality of the state, the point at which the state expresses its own self-division. The monarch lays bare the state's absence of any self-identity. It is thus a moment of failure within the successful state.

(McGowan, 2019, 208)

The argument could be extended to the respective roles of the father and the psychoanalyst in the family and the clinical setting.

8 An imposition is also at work in psychoanalytic treatment; it goes by the euphemism of *interpretation*.

Variation 20 Madness and sanity

At times, Lacan deems madness to be the kernel of inhumanity, the classic insignia of the death of the subject (Lacan, 2006, 473), while elsewhere he holds that "Not only can man's being not be understood without madness, but it would not be man's being if it did not bear madness within itself as the limit of his freedom" (ibid, 176). An abyss seemingly separates the early "Not just anyone can go mad just by wanting it" (ibid, 176) from the later "We are all mad, that is to say, we are all delusional" (Lacan, 1979, 278). A stringent divide between neurosis and psychosis thus paradoxically co-exists with the dissolution of the barrier separating madness from normality. How to do justice to the claim positing the continuity of madness and sanity while also acknowledging the clinical and theoretical acuity of the strict boundary Lacan rightfully maintains between neurosis and psychosis? As with all other identities-in-difference, the self-reflection of madness and sanity leads each term to its respective Other. To proudly proclaim one's untarnished sanity is the quintessential pretence of madness itself. Likewise, to humbly confess one's madness is the sign of sanity. Thus, Lacan posits the identity of insanity and being human stating that "men are so necessarily mad that it would be another twist of madness not to be mad" (Lacan, 2006, 283). It is precisely this paradoxical logic that is not operative in psychosis. The psychotic subject cannot fathom that the absence of madness is insanity itself. Psychosis is more diremptive of the sanity-madness identity-in-difference. The division of subjective structures (neurosis/perversion vs. psychosis) takes the identity-in-difference of madness and sanity into account. It posits that the neurotic symptom is a madness, which is, paradoxically, the condition of our only modicum of sanity. The diremption of this paradox leads to the contradiction of the *ordinariness* of madness marked by the striking lack of a symptom. We must thus first posit the identity-in-difference of madness and sanity so that we may then starkly distinguish neurosis from psychosis in terms of how each relates to this paradox. Where neurosis can better fathom this paradoxical identity, psychosis displays a greater tendency towards diremption. Modern American psychiatry has relinquished the division of structures and posits instead a salad ontology marked by an ever-increasing plethora of novel diagnostic categories such as the downright ridiculous "dyscalculia" and "trichotillomania". Foucault (1972) famously revealed the falsity of the madness–sanity division. His error was to claim that psychoanalysis is guilty of this division. He could not appreciate that the Freudo-Lacanian division between psychosis and neurosis-perversion does not overlap with the Cartesian error of excluding madness. The division of structures hinges precisely on the firm affirmation of the dialectical unity of madness and sanity. The prevalent continuum hypothesis in the American psychiatric model is diremptive of this identity-in-difference and thus leads to the contradiction by which the vague idea that we are all somewhere on a mental health continuum (this is its "democracy prejudice") is accompanied by the most inhuman treatment of the mad. The mad are here seen to lie outside the realm of what is treatable by speech while, for Lacan, all structures are within the purview of what is amenable to speech and language.[1] Sadly, the prevalence of the developmental model in post-Freudian thought (most notably due to the influence of Karl Abraham) has led to the idea that the neurotic is more "mature" than his/her psychotic counterpart more prone to "primitive" libidinal fixations. Regarding the use of the word "primitive" in non-Lacanian psychoanalysis (it is a remarkably popular – indeed "fetishized" – word in the International Psychoanalytic Association), all one can say is that a little familiarity with Lévi-Strauss' (1991) critique of this notion would liberate discourse from this rather – dare I say – "primitive" diction. The intervention of language into the human organism means that we are all forever separated (dirempted) from the primitive. We must recall that psychosis, in general, is marked by an overinvestment of words, and paranoia, more specifically, involves an intricate theoretical system which, moreover, Freud saw as akin to his own libido theory. Even the most "primitive" mind could see that there is little here of the primitive. What are missed are the *advantages* and *disadvantages* of each structure. For instance, the psychotic subject (due to a less stringent alienation) is a keener observer of his/her social world as he/she is less duped by the social semblances that rivet the naïve neurotic eye to false paradises (see variation 22).

Intimately tied to the dialectical unity of madness and sanity are the diremptive remains of the *symptom* and the *sinthome*. We all secretly claim, even if minimally, our untainted sanity which means, paradoxically, that we are all mad. Alternatively, my claim that I am mad does not immediately and completely exempt me from madness. Likewise, the claim that I am sane does not immediately make me mad. An obstacle resists full sublation in both directions. In the first case, it is the *symptom* that prevents the full assertion of my untainted sanity. In the second case, it is the *sinthome* that prevents the psychotic's plea to sanity to be reduced to utter madness. No matter how "insane" the pretence to sanity may sound, there is a kernel of truth that it hides (even the wildest delusion is an attempt at a cure). Formulaically, we may argue that *the symptom is the neurotic diremptive remain of the self-reflection of madness to sanity* while *the sinthome is the psychotic diremptive remain of the self-reflection of sanity to madness*. These two diremptive remains, through which the psychotic can have his/her share of sanity and the neurotic/pervert his/her share of madness, are arguably the reason for the persistence of the continuum hypothesis in psychology and modern American psychiatry. Psychiatry has taken a diremptive *remain* (i.e. a *surplus*) and, by the power of its prodigious ignorance, elevated it to the status of a full blown diremption of thought resulting in the abolition of the notion of distinct and separate psychic *structures* (neurosis, perversion and psychosis). The aim of my speculative rendition of the difference between structures is to provide an immanent *boundary without a limit* separating the clinical structures without recourse to an externally imposed border susceptible to the aforementioned vicious dialectical reversals.[2]

Notes

1 Lacan's doctoral dissertation (1975) revealed the aetiology of paranoia in the "personality" rather than some mythical biology.
2 The gesture of delimiting an externally imposed frontier between madness and reason is itself the very essence of madness: "what is the mere madness caused by the loss of reason compared to the madness of reason itself" (Žižek, 2012a).

Variation 21 The diremptions
of fantasy

Love entails the crossing of fantasy through which the paradoxes of castration
can be fathomed. At the level of the subject, castration involves the idea that
lack coincides with phallic power. At the level of the Other, castration involves
the recognition of the identity of the force and weakness of law. My contention
is that once these are recognized, castration ceases to be a fantasy and becomes,
instead, an acknowledgment of the impossible-real. This occurs if the identity-
in-difference of the structural *manque-à-être* and the phallic function is firmly
posited. The fantasies of origin, isolated by Laplanche and Pontalis, also move
in the direction opposed to the impossible-real. Here too, crossing the fantasy
entails unveiling the identities-in-difference hidden by fantasy. If the fantasy of
castration hides the identity-in-difference of lack and phallic power, the seduction fantasy obfuscates the fact that passivity alone provides the basis of any
possible activity. The primal scene fantasy hinders the subject from agreeing to
be excluded from his/her own origin in order to minimally partake in social
co-existence. Traversing the fantasy entails giving up the myths of origin by
which the subject stages an Other that deprives, assaults and excludes. This
marks the transition from *ressentiment* to loss understood as an effect of structure
rather than the ill will of an Other. Fantasy always stages a dominator set against
a victim, a strong subject vis-à-vis a weak counterpart. In fantasy there are only
winners and losers. Fantasy cannot fathom that the greatest loss lies precisely
in the folly of triumph and, conversely, that the greatest victory consists of
defeat[1] – hence Leclaire's claim that the aim of analysis is *to kill the child within*.
Indeed, only a thin threshold separates the guillotine's blade from the piercing
edge of interpretation. For humanity not to perish under violence, a symbolic
death is needed (Legendre, 2000). Nasio (2005) perspicaciously remarks that
fantasy stages the Other's annihilation and murder – something removing us
far from the apprehension of the Other's non-existence. Crossing the fantasy,
by contrast, entails recognizing that there is no big Other; something which
paradoxically allows for relations to otherness. Through it the subject can also
acknowledge that "the Woman does not exist"; something which, oddly, makes
possible some symbolization of feminine difference. Finally, traversing the fantasy means that the subject acknowledges that there is no sexual rapport; a realization ironically central to the possibility of sexual intimacy.

The "me too" movement – though a laudable and necessary effort to lessen abuses of male power – may degenerate into an attempt to make the Woman exist as "victim" and create a semblance of the sexual rapport on the rudimentary "predator-victim" model. Such praise-worthy and courageous movements need to remain attentive to the dangers of diremptions. Here the reign of fantasy may block precisely the advent of *love and reparation,* replacing it with the vengeful spirit to win, a desire that leads to the contradiction of triumphant despondency. Just as the tendency to blame the Other hinges on the belief in an Other, the prevalence of misogyny in male paranoia pivots on the fact that the non-existence of the Woman has not been registered in psychosis. Against superficial feminist critiques of Lacan, it may be suggested that the thesis concerning Woman's non-existence is a first step towards the abolition of misogyny. Indeed, once men fully recognize that the Woman does not exist they will assume responsibility for the impasses of *jouissance* and sexuality. The realization that the Woman does not exist brings about trust and faith in women; it is akin to the paradox of faith and atheism where true belief leads to the realization that the Other does not exist. As anathema as this may sound to the shallow ears of the understanding, *Woman does not exist* may be the only viable motto of a future feminism.

Contrasting Sophocles' tragedy with Shakespeare's *Hamlet,* Lacan claims that we Moderns, unlike our Ancient counterparts, cannot *act* insofar as we are held firmly in the grips of fantasy. Moderns have more deeply fallen prey to the understanding's inability to fathom the paradoxes hidden by fantasy. Each fantasy of origin corresponds to the misrecognition of an identity-in-difference. In turn, each of these misrecognitions results in a specific contradiction plaguing our contemporary situation. The castration fantasy's misrecognition of the identity-in-difference of lack and phallic power has led to the modern contradiction of heightened narcissism accompanied by increased self-abjection – an incongruity poignantly captured by Agamben. Moreover, the misrecognition of the identity of the castrated and the potent father has led to the aforementioned contemporary crisis of paternity (see variation 9 where I speak of the simultaneous rise of "humiliated" fathers and perverse seductive fathers). The misrecognition of castration has resulted in the contradiction by which the radical repudiation of femininity has led to the push-to-Woman. Thus, beyond Eric Santner's splendid reading of Schreber's *Memoirs* as testament to modernity's "crisis of investiture", this confession is also a harbinger of the contemporary rise of transsexualist discourse with its at times contradictory blend of the postmodern denial of sexual difference and the quasi-essentialist reference to "nature's error". Seduction fantasy's obfuscation of the concomitance of passivity and activity has led to the contradiction of hyper-masculinity co-existing with impotence. Moreover, subjects held in the grips of this fantasy ceaselessly rail against the alleged seducer in manic paroxysms of hate with the uncanny result that their petulant cries (often going viral in epidemics of hysteric mimicry) only fortify their sense of passivity and inability to achieve empowerment. At a theoretical level, we have the contradiction by which the denunciation of the so-called assault *on* truth (Masson, 1984) is itself nothing more than the cowardly retreat in the face of the inevitable assault *of* truth. Finally, the primal scene fantasy's rage against exclusion results in the contemporary craze of social media where, in the vain effort to partake in the lives of all, the subject paradoxically increases her sense of marginalization as she enviously watches a fabricated display of artificial paradises. Fantasy's degradation of identity-in-difference represents the transition from *impossibility* to *impotence* – in lieu of dynamic paradoxes we have the deadlock of contradictions.[2] Heirs to Hamlet, we moderns are afflicted with the contradiction of inhibition coinciding with *jouissance*. The modern superego does not simply say "Enjoy" by contrast to the pre-modern interdiction. More subtly, it is a contradictory incitement to enjoy one's inhibition paving the way to morbid political inertia.

When Lacan claims that the Oedipus complex is a "dream of Freud's" he urges us to traverse Freud's fantasy. Žižek follows Lacan's abandonment of the patricidal theme in order to discredit the myth of a "crime" at the basis of power. To Joseph de Maistre's "anti-Enlightenment axiom" concerning the "mysterious laws which ... should be covered by a religious silence and revered as a *mystery*" (Žižek; 2012a, 971), Žižek adds that "we should resist the false fascination: what the law ultimately hides is that *there is nothing to hide*, that there is no terrifying mystery sustaining it ... that the law is grounded only in its own tautology" (ibid: 971–972). The diremption of the paradox by which what "the law ultimately hides is that *there is nothing to hide*" leads to conspiracy theories (fantasies) and the contradiction by which a subject's over-vigilance regarding a malevolent Other subjugates him/her all the more. Žižek (1998a) elsewhere elaborates on this same theme by a consideration of the distinction between synchrony and diachrony. While the former is connected to the everyday experience of the force/weakness of law, the latter denotes the narrativization of this experience as a myth of origin concerning a primal crime. The synchronically experienced inconsistency of the law leads to the narrativization of a diachronic myth of origin: "this diachronous process, the story of the 'original crime', is the narrativization of the necessary, structural, synchronous incoherence of the Law" (Žižek, 1998a, 90). The law's inherent violence does not *repeat* that of the original crime. Rather, the so-called original crime *repeats*[3] the incoherence of the law (its "everyday" superegoic violence). The result of the repetition is the never-ending constant (re)-narrativization of the "original crime". The idea that the law is "violent" involves a form of diachronic revision of the fact that synchronically the force/violence of law is, in fact, tied to its frailty/weakness. As Hegel puts it best, "we say that tyranny is overthrown because it is execrable, odious and so on. In reality, it is simply because it is superfluous" (Hegel quoted in Lebrun, 2004, 214 my translation).

Notes

1 Psychoanalysis is wary of the diremptions of triumph: "psychoanalysis does not seek to convince/triumph" (Lacan, 1998). He is here playing on the homonymy between "*convaincre*" (convince) and "*vaincre*" (to triumph).

2 Fantasy's attempt to avoid paradox thus leads to the return of the latter as contradiction insofar as the latter is, for Hegel, inescapable. As McGowan explains, "One never escapes contradiction for good through the neurotic fantasy because this fantasy nourishes itself on contradiction. It stages what it avoids" (2019, 152).

3 According to Deleuze (1968), a temporally earlier event "repeats" a later one. We may shed light on this counterintuitive logic through the psychoanalytic idea of the *après coup*. The later synchronically lived experience gives rise to an urge to build the fantasy of an earlier "experience" that would constitute the basis of the later. Deleuze's theory of repetition and the psychoanalytic notion of *après coup* thus provide the greatest bulwark against myths of origin.

Variation 22 The untimely-contemporary

Agamben (2009) introduces his notion of "the contemporary", an idea which, following Barthes, he likens to the Nietzschean idea of the "untimely". For Agamben, those

> who are truly contemporary, who truly belong to their time, are those who neither perfectly coincide with it nor adjust themselves to its demands. They are thus in this sense irrelevant. But precisely because of this condition, precisely through this disconnection and this anachronism, they are more capable than others of perceiving and grasping their own time.

From a Lacanian perspective such subjects are often the psychotics and perverts, namely individuals whose paranoid distrust and aversion of the social Other puts them at odds with their time and society. Indeed, a passage Agamben quotes from Nietzsche's *Untimely Meditations* poignantly captures his will to impeach the *jouissance* of his epoch:

> This meditation is itself untimely because it seeks to understand as an illness, a disability and a defect something which this epoch is quite rightly proud of, that is to say, its historical culture, because I believe that we are all consumed by the fever of history and we should at least realize it.
> (Nietzsche quoted in Agamben, 2009)

In psychosis, we may attest, at times, to the paradox of a subject at once *contemporary* and yet *out of joint with the present moment*. In light of this we may have to gamble the conjecture that the psychotic is the paradigmatic untimely-contemporary; with this we will also have achieved much in the way of forsaking the deficit-model of psychosis that plagues much of modern psychiatry. Here we attest to psychosis as a more apt realization of identity-in-difference, one that a neurotic is more likely to dirempt.

Quoting Marx regarding the great achievements of capitalism – most notably its central role in eliminating the semblances of feudalism – Badiou (2011) argues that philosophy should measure itself against the heights of capital's demystifications. In the same vein, I argue that philosophy should not shy from the challenges that psychosis poses to thought. Much like capital, psychosis is an indispensable source for the deconstruction of the artifices that hold psychic life in place. Though at times psychosis testifies to a thinking limited by the perspective of the understanding, in other ways it opens new pathways of thought challenging the primacy accorded to neurosis and freeing the space for the advent of philosophical reason's better attunement to identity-in-difference. When Thomas Mann exclaims "And I say to you that I am weary to death of depicting humanity without partaking of humanity" (quoted in Fassbinder, 1979), he gives expression (be it in the form of a desperate cry) to the aforementioned paradox by which deeper immersion into reality may involve a greater degree of alienation from that reality.

We know from Kojève's (1980) Hegel that desire follows fashions; subjects *identify* with each other's desires. This philosophically isolated phenomenon is not, however, generalizable. The neurotic is prone to this epidemic of desires which comes at the cost of real bodily enjoyment. In some extreme cases, "there are empty desires or mad desires that are based on nothing more than the fact that the thing in question has been forbidden you" (Lacan, 1977, 243). Here the Other's verdict on an object has absolute primacy over the subject's own gratification. The psychotic, by contrast, shuns the domain of the epidemic of desires. He/she is not duped by this particular irrationality and remains closer to the *jouissance* of the body. The neurotic prefers to forget the drives and *jouissance* insofar as these escape the clutches of the symbolic Other. *Jouissance* violates what is holiest to a community of people; it breaks their ideals, transgresses their interdictions and ignores their imperatives. For the neurotic who has taken the leap of faith that *belief* in the sanctity of the Other entails, *jouissance* is inadmissible. It causes anxiety and shame, the insignia of our recognition of the Other's gaze. The pervert is not afraid of the transgressive nature of *jouissance*. If the neurotic's faith in the Other leads him/her to deny *jouissance* (not necessarily to give it all up but cover it with a cloak of shame), the pervert's incredulity makes for greater fidelity to the *jouissance* of the body. Apollon (2005) has ventured to speak of the pervert's *passion for truth*. Is it not to this passion that we owe de Sade and Pasolini's explorations of the limits of desire and *jouissance*? Žižek's opposition of transgression and subversion is somewhat one-sided. Though, one should not confuse transgressions against the law with veritable subversions, one should also not dismiss the aforementioned *passion of truth*. One here notes an excessive prejudice in favor of neurosis in Žižek's work where, for instance, Hegel is praised (following Lacan) as "the most sublime hysteric" (Žižek, 1989). This privileging of neurosis is also seen in Žižek's critique of Deleuze and Guattari's (1972) celebration of the "schizophrenic on a walk" by contrast to the paltry "neurotic on the couch".

Much thought has taken philosophical interest in madness. Beyond the aforementioned *Anti-Oedipus*, we have Foucault's effort to re-introduce the "sovereign speech of madness" (1972) after Descartes' alleged eradication of it from philosophical reason. Kristeva's (1984) schizophrenic "khora" concerning a *revolution* in poetic language is also notable. Deleuze's *Coldness and Cruelty* (Deleuze and Sacher-Masoch, 1991) sees in masochistic perversion a great resource for subverting power. Perhaps Žižek's effort to re-establish neurosis as the truly subversive structure is a reaction to this trend. Žižek's return to neurosis is arguably predicated on a one-sided conflation of neurosis with non-diremptive thought. Though the neurosis-perversion-psychosis distinction is clinically invaluable, drawing philosophical consequences from it concerning possibilities of subversion is unjustified. My contention throughout this enquiry has always been that the distinction (perhaps I should say distinction and equation) between the recognition and the diremption of identity-in-difference is where we have the highest hope of truly "carving nature by its joints" (Plato, 2015), something which, I believe, is the crucial theoretical labor that *must* precede any praxis aiming to subvert.

The psychotic, unconcerned with shame and profoundly skeptical of the Other, is more attuned to the palpitations of the body's *jouissance*; the pervert and the psychotic never lose sight of the fact that a body is what enjoys itself. The paranoid's hypochondria, the schizophrenic's "organ speech" and the sadist's heedfulness to the tremors of the other's body all attest to this greater familiarity with *jouissance*. Can this attunement to *jouissance* (Lacan (1998) speaks of the pervert's supplementary knowledge in the field of sexuality) evince a more refined adjustment to the stipulations of reason?[1] The psychotic's snubbing of the follies of the circuitry of desire takes us far from the deficit models of psychiatry. He/she has an advantage consisting of not succumbing to "falling prey" and losing him/herself in "Das man" ("the they") (Heidegger, 1967). This immersion into *jouissance* further attunes the psychotic to the Other. The captivation by the Other (Lacan speaks of the psychotic as a "martyr of language", the Other *par excellence*) is precisely what may allow him/her an easier path to being a contemporary, namely one who can better perceive the follies of his/her time. Psychotic grandiosity (see variation 7) has nothing to do with "too much" ego but, rather, with the excess of *jouissance* resulting from a deficient cathexis of self. When one evinces snobbery from the psychotic this is disdain for the neurotic's puerile attachment to epidemic desires. If this, at the very least, allows the neurotic to question his/her falling prey, then such condescension should be welcome. Indeed, could Lacan's enigmatic notion of "metempsychosis" ("*metempsychose*") (quoted in Massat, 2007), written as a kind of imperative enjoining us to "put into psychosis" ("*mettre en psychose*"), consist of counsel urging the neurotic to follow psychosis in the direction opposed to the diremption responsible for his/her falling prey?

Once again, the psychotic poses a challenge to Heideggerian philosophy insofar as he/she reveals to us a subject immune to a pivotal feature of Dasein. Unlike the other central features isolated by Heidegger (e.g. thrownness), falling prey is the result of a diremption rather than the site of an identity-in-difference. In this case the psychotic is more attuned to reason and less at the mercy of the understanding. Social media attests most widely to the diremption of desire keeping the modern subject riveted to the field of *Das Man*, attached to his/her own alienation and thus hindered from joining the epoch as its contemporary.

As Lebrun notes, "man does not reach his truth by joining the public thing" (Lebrun, 1972, 99, my translation). This loss of self in the "public thing" is what the untimely-contemporary refuses. The prevalence of suicide in the psychoses attests precisely to the assertion of such a refusal: "Rather to die than live among *Das Man*". Žižek (1996), inspired by Schelling, speaks of a "contraction of being" by which the subject severs from the social (an act diremptive of the subject-collective identity-in-difference) in order to connect to the deepest kernel of his/her *jouissance*.[2] Through this reconnection, one may say that subjectivity is in fact lost for the sake of accessing a kind of *hyper-subjectivity*, the genius within. Popular consciousness rightly asserts the link between genius and madness. The madman is not held in the grips of alienating *Das Man*. This allows him/her to more fully embrace the richness of the inner world. The pathos apposite to philosophical reflection cannot do without self-diremptive severance.

All philosophy, insofar as it makes a claim to *love* and *wisdom*, must hold itself at the height of the psychotic decision to walk against the grain of the times in order, paradoxically, to grasp the times more profoundly. History has no shortage of such untimely-contemporary subjects (some perhaps psychotic and others neurotics who knew how to "put into psychosis" in order to subvert falling prey) playing a pivotal role in the critique of the modes of *jouissance* of their time. To the aforementioned Nietzsche, we may cursorily add Rousseau and La Rochefoucauld. The latter is of particular psychoanalytic interest insofar as he lucidly critiqued the *jouissance* of narcissism endemic of his time (a quintessentially neurotic *jouissance*). A "thinking" that is diremptive in this regard can make no veritable claim to thought; here we are in the realm of ideology and the doxa of the understanding. Insofar as ideology is a diremption of authentic thought, it may involve (as with other diremptions) the impasse of a vicious contradiction. This is indeed the case insofar as the most effective ideology, according to Žižek, takes the form of the phenomenon of "cynical distance". Johnston (2004) lucidly summarizes the contradiction involved in such a position: "the individual consciously professes disbelief in relation to the status quo system while nonetheless behaving 'as if' he/she really accepts the authority of this system".

Ego-psychology, with its mandate on adaptation, is far from authentic thought.[3] The symptom, by contrast, is the expression of the subject's fidelity to what keeps him/her *out-of-joint*. As such, the symptom is testament to the budding philosopher within. I expressly note that the symptom points to a *budding* philosopher because, as we clinicians know all too well, it is also "the embodiment of ignorance" (Žižek, 2006, 217). Could this take us to a new way of formulating the *neurotic compromise* – a *healthy* way worthy of the Nietzschean *gay science* – as the self-reflection of ignorance (rather than its adaptive obliteration) into its Other, namely philosophical wisdom?

Strictly speaking, Lacan's claim that the ego is the privileged symptom of mankind is not correct. Insofar as it claims unity and mastery, the ego is a diremption of the symptom. The ego is, moreover, the site of a central contradiction and impasse; the more stringently it insists on its autonomy the more fragile it becomes. This contradiction is indubitably the source of all the ills and pains of narcissism. Where the symptom attests to the feminine and the infantile, the ego has pretence to the "higher" terms, namely the masculine and adult. However, insofar as the "lower" term triumphs under diremption, the ego then becomes, indeed, symptom through a dialectical reversal. When the symptom is dirempted from the ego's pretence to normalcy, the ego (as the "higher" term) dwindles precisely into what it sought to shun. Only by taking account of this complex dialectical reversal do we reach Lacan's claim that the ego is the privileged symptom of humankind. To this we must add the proviso, however, that the ego is symptom in the sense of a hyper-symptom disparaged to pure thought.

The identities-in-difference explored in this treatise reveal two contrasting aspects of the real. We have what I name the *paradoxical real*, namely the site of the dialectical unity of two terms, which, from the perspective of common understanding, stand in rigid opposition. We also have what I designate as the *diremptive real,* namely the locus of a contradiction and impasse resulting from the failure to recognize the paradoxical real.[4] The last of the paradoxes discussed and its accompanying diremptive contradiction has a special place insofar as it represents at once an identity-in-difference (between the untimely-contemporary and the maladjusted) and a diremption (of the subject-collective unity). To put it formulaically, we may say that it stands for *the hyper-paradoxical dialectical unity of the paradoxical and the diremptive real.* Philosophy, I claim, occupies this hyper-anxious place of the hyper-paradoxical identity-in-difference of paradox and contradiction. The philosopher gives expression to the identity-in-difference of the subject and the collective and to the diremption of this very dialectical unity. Žižek, following Badiou, claims that "thought as such is communist" (Žižek, 2018, 374). However, he also argues (Žižek, 1996) for a view linking philosophy and the *contraction of being.* Does the communist utopian dream not precisely consist of giving body to a paradoxical community of subjects free to indulge in the conceit of their singular contractive self-diremptions? The genius of Nietzsche's *nostrils* sniffed out the hidden desire of philosophy, namely the wish for an absolute diremptive severing from the world: *Pereat mundus, fiat philosophia, fiat philosophus, fiam* (Nietzsche, 1998).[5] The philosophical passion is, for Nietzsche, an extension of the noble *pathos of distance* that unabashedly asserts egoism as "the very essence of a noble soul" (Nietzsche, 2000a). Philosophy's impossible task is to minimally reconcile this diremptive ascetic ideal – for Nietzsche (1998) self-diremption is the hidden meaning of the ascetic ideal in the case of philosophers – with the communist motto: "We are nothing, let us be all". Philosophy is the paradoxical unity of the highest self-conceit, the most arrogant assertion of self *against* the world and the humblest self-effacement faced with the universal.[6]

All authentically philosophical thought rests on a diremptive gesture by which the subject relinquishes his/her participation in the collective. As *love of wisdom*, philosophy has perhaps no other choice than to *hate the masses.* We must thus posit the paradoxical dialectical unity of diremption and self-reflection. The human (philosophical) subject is the *diremptive being* embodying the contradiction of *divine bestiality*. The philosopher can only reach him/herself (self-reflection) through the paradoxical effort of striving away from him/herself (diremption). In the flight away from self and kin, the human being finds again a forgotten part of him/herself lost in the hustle and bustle of fallen everydayness. It is no wonder that Zarathustra's rise to mountainous *heights* required the company of *lowly* beasts, his eagle and his serpent. The choice of animals replicates the dialectical tension – the soaring bird and the slithering snake.

Notes

1 Could this explain Lacan's enigmatic claim regarding the "rigour" of the psychotic (cf. Massat, 2007)?
2 In this regard, the understanding immediately (without separating moments) achieves the work of speculative reason, namely that of sustaining paradox. Through the work of *separation*, the understanding *joins* the subject to its truth. Throughout I have set the common understanding against speculative reason. We now see that this too is diremptive.
3 If Freudian-Lacanian psychoanalysis is founded upon the gesture by which truth is said to speak (cf. *The Freudian Thing*) then ego-psychology marks the moment in the history of psychoanalysis where the ego, site of irremediable alienation, spoke and, regrettably, was heard. The result was the deplorable notion of the ego as a "conflict-free zone" granting theoretical sanction to the delusional pretence of autonomy. To speak of a conflict-free zone in the ego is as contradictory as to speak of a torsion-free zone in the Moebius strip. Conflict (symptom) is the kink in the Moebius strip that is nowhere and everywhere at once.
4 This opposition coincides with Hegel's distinction between "contradiction" (internal division) and "difference" (external opposition). The diremptive real is akin to the specular imaginary and its battle of pure prestige. It thus represents a disparagement of the real to the imaginary.
5 "Let the world perish, but let there be philosophy, the philosopher, me".
6 Žižek (2015, 182) counts Plato, Descartes and Hegel among the great philosophers of madness and self-withdrawal. Alas, he omits Nietzsche, the thinker who took self-diremptive severance to the height of divine madness.

Variation 23 Religion and atheism

Symbolic castration is a matter of faith. One must, like Tertullian, believe in the absurdity of a law contradicted by its enunciation. One must be duped by the paternal law so that one may, in turn, kill the father (dupe him) and emerge as a subject. One must *die* to the law in order to *live* for God. In the psychoses, where this mutual duping is lacking, the subject is confronted with a monstrous Other. Unlike this nightmare of the real, "in religion proper", Žižek argues, "one does not know God, but risks trusting in him" (Žižek, 2012a, 865). The psychotic, by contrast, *knows* God but does not *trust* Him.[1] He/she has absolute certitude regarding the voices he/she hears but does not trust them as he takes them for evil. He/she sees and hears evil in the voice and gaze-objects that surround him/her to the extent that his own position of defiance is one of radical evil. The subject is witness to the *literal* evil of the Other (paranoia, mania) as well as that of the self (melancholia, schizophrenia). In the constitutive lie at the basis of truth and in his/her own gestures of defiance, the psychotic sees an Other that deceives and a self that is polluted with sin. The literalness of radical evil in the psychoses, by contrast to hysteric protest, submits the subject to an Other that remains indifferent to her suffering, a Schreberian God marked "by a peculiar ignorance about living human beings" (Santner, 1996, 62). The dimension of religiosity is targeted in psychosis; do Schreber's memoirs not testify to the most thoroughgoing perversion of religion fathomable? Atheism proper is also abolished here insofar as true atheism and religiosity belong together. Faith and atheism involve symbolic castration. Religion and atheism without castration correspond, respectively, to fanaticism and scientistic/dogmatic materialism. The escalation of religious fanaticism and new religiosities as well as the rise of vulgar materialism (e.g. Dawkins' (1989) claim that intelligent life emerges only when an organism has discovered evolution – i.e. when it reduces itself to a mere living creature trapped in finitude)[2] represent, according to Žižek, two sides of the same coin. The atheist's rage against religion (e.g. Hitchens' (2007) puerile "God is not great") and the fundamentalist's fury at heathen faithlessness are manifestations of narcissistic suicidal aggression where the subject blindly strikes at the *kakon* of his own being in the other.[3] The plethora of new religions on the rise in our contemporary situation attests to an ontology of juxtaposition where everything loses its specificity. The diremption of the identity-in-difference of faith and atheism leads to the contemporary contradiction inherent to the trendy Western appropriation of Eastern faiths (e.g. Buddhism/Hinduism/Sufism). This contradiction is evidenced in the phenomenon of the "millionaire yogi" politely christened as "Zorba the Buddha", a most ghastly name for the incongruous wedding of the height of materialist expenditure and the hypocritical pretence to humility. Here a strictly "privatized eschatology" (Rudolph Bultmann quoted in Bloch, 2009) unabashedly put to the service of material gain (e.g. techniques of visualizing a wish, referred to as "manifesting", in the hope of having it realized) is sold to the naïve as the height of spiritual attainment.

Lacan rejects Nietzsche's infamous "God is dead" as "a shelter against the threat of castration" (Lacan, 1977, 27) as well as Dostoevsky's idea that the inexistence of God would lead to everything being permitted (Lacan, 2007). Dostoevsky fears that the loss of God targets civil society while Nietzsche sees in this loss the possibility of the overman. We have Nietzsche the atheist and Dostoevsky the theist; both miss the proper dimension of religiosity-atheism. By contrast, Lacan makes many interesting statements attesting to the dialectical unity of faith and atheism. For instance, the idea that "a thinking that is rigorously atheist" is situated at "the frontiers of the *ex nihilo*" or "in the perspective of creationism" (Lacan, 1986, 303, my translation) will surely shock the common understanding insofar as the categories of *ex nihilo* and *creationism* are decidedly religious. Ordinary doxa opposes these to scientistic atheism where the category of causality reigns. Lacan makes the further paradoxical claims that "theologians are the only atheists" and that the proofs of the existence of God are the means by which He has been killed (1998). Lacan's "God is unconscious" (1977, 59) may provide the formula for this atheism as religiosity and, concomitantly, pave the way towards symbolic castration. Only through symbolic castration can the subject achieve the paradox by which faith in the Other (religiosity) coincides with its barring (atheism). Incidentally, the failure to recognize the identity-in-difference of atheism and religiosity explains the blaring contradictions of Dostoevsky and Nietzsche's personal lives, a pious sinner on the one hand and an impious saint on the other.[4]

Earlier (variation 5), the dialectical relation between religion and reason occupied our attention. We also lengthily considered the opposition between good and evil (variation 15) where the religious thematic is present such that the two terms could be replaced with religiosity (piety, the sacred) and ir-religiosity (impiety, the profane). Finally, we contemplated the opposition between religiosity and atheism where each term accedes to itself through a self-reflection taking it to its Other. I would here venture to introduce a fourth opposite to religion (alongside reason, profanation and atheism). If the word religion comes from the Latin *ligare*, meaning to join together, could one not venture the bold claim that faith should be denoted by another word capturing not only the aspect of union but also that of separation? Such a word would better render the idea that true religiosity does not simply consist of union with God but, more precisely, of a union-in-separation. As Žižek argues in light of Hegel, "it is our very separation from the Thing that joins us to it". If we were to coin such a new word, we would have to look for a Latin term denoting separation or cut which would take us incidentally to "seco", namely the origin of the word "sex". Sex and religion are thus etymologically opposed as "separation" and "union". In light of the Hegelian frame of our study, could we not argue for the identity-in-difference of sex and religion as constituting the veritable "essence" of both such that one without the other would constitute a disparagement of both? Sex without the raptures of religion would be but a pale placid imitation, a mere tomfoolery of the senses rather than veritable eroticism while religion without sex would be an empty fascination with the divine akin to idolatrous narcissistic captivation.

Lacan's teaching is essentially deconstructive, pointing to *impossibilities* and *negations* rather than positive terms. Three principal statements of inexistence emerge from his thought: 1) there is no Other of the Other, 2) Woman does not exist, 3) there is no rapport between the sexes. These are inoperative for the uncastrated subject. For Schreber, the Other did indeed exist in the guise of a cruel God demanding endless sacrifice for the sake of his own *jouissance*. Also, it was bestowed upon him to embody Woman in order to submit to the dismal God. Finally, Schreber's vision puts on stage a veritable sexual rapport between the insatiable God and himself – a rapport which, unlike neurotic sexual relations marked by points of impossibility, leaves space for neither frustration nor dissatisfaction. Schreber's delusion marks the twilight of the symbol and the advent of the idols of the Other, the Woman and the sexual rapport. Each of these fills in a gap in the symbolic order, while the symbol holds the place of the gap without trying to make up for the lacuna.

Madness (neurotic, perverse or psychotic) attests to the incomplete self-reflection of religiosity into its four Others, namely reason, evil, atheism and sex. The failed passing into atheism leads to a diremptive religiosity where the Other wavers from utter non-existence to concrete persecutory presence. What fails to ensue is the instance of a non-existent Other which, paradoxically, assures a minimal relation to social otherness. The failed passing into sex results in either a total/literal impossibility that flounders into impotence or a mad effort to sustain the impossible dream of sexual harmony. Here we also have the erection of the false idol of "The Woman", a concrete and literal embodiment of femininity, which, paradoxically, forbids the subject's access to the feminine. We may here take our cue from the other two opposites of religiosity (namely, reason and evil) in order to generate, in the spirit of Lacan, two new propositions of impossibility. With respect to the opposition between good (piety) and evil (impiety), we may say that *there is no tablet of the good*. Paradoxically, it is the recognition of the absence of "Commandments" that allows for a minimal guarantee of moral conduct; wild resurgences of depravity are seldom separate from pretences to moral rectitude. Finally, we may argue that *there is no measure of reason*. Paradoxically, it is the realization of the lack of such a common measure that allows for a modicum of reason. If the phallic signifier provides a semblance of sanity for the speaking being it is precisely because it is an empty signifier without a signified. The mark of insanity is more the presence (rather than the absence) of a standard by which the world could be measured. Paranoia is a knowledge system that proclaims itself as the very measure of all things. Paranoia is not the lack of rhyme and reason but the testament to a reason that rhymes all too well; so well, indeed, that it must be the doing of the gods.

The contemporary triumph of the common understanding has led to the misrecognition of the identity-in-difference of religion with its alleged contraries, namely reason, atheism, evil and sex. Thus, instead of the paradoxical unity in opposition through which each term accedes to its Other and itself through self-reflection, we testify to a regression to a pre-Kantian "salad ontology" marked by an endless proliferation of falsely novel elements celebrated under the banner of diversity. The realms of love, ethics and psychoanalysis have been thereby disparaged to disciplines of management. Instead of love acceding to its rightful dignity by joining its opposite, we have the management of love, "love without the fall", with its dialectical correlate of the "fall without the love". Instead of a good achieved through its courageous self-reflection into evil, we have the mediocre ethical stances of what Cortés christened the "discussing class" (the liberal bourgeoisie), where the lofty realm of ethics is reduced to a petty calculus of utility. Good unwedded to the added spirituality of evil is a mere utilitarian negotiation. Jesus' summoning us to the good cannot be separated from his call to betray our kin. Finally, instead of the daring exploration of the unconscious through which humankind's delirious madness may self-reflexively sublate into wisdom, we have the abandonment of psychoanalysis in favour of "anger management" and "life coaching". If Žižek (2012a) locates our only hope in the intersection of reason and drive, it is because reason is the self-reflection of madness. If "men are so necessarily mad that it would be another twist of madness not to be mad" then we live today in the times of "ordinary madness", where the divine insanity of love, ethics and psychoanalysis are replaced by the petty idiocies of management.

Notes

1 With respect to the relation between faith and psychosis, Maleval argues that "the delusional certainty of the paranoid subject reveals the absence of the term that founds the doubt that always inheres to faith" (Maleval, 2000, 111, my translation).

2 For Bloch, what is missed by vulgar materialism is that the way out of superstition into atheism is offered by Christianity: "the counter-blow against the oppressor is biblical, too, and that is why it has always been suppressed or distorted, from the serpent on" (Bloch, 2009, xv). For Bloch, Thompson argues, "We seem to be trapped in a dualistic [specular we may say] but essentially static way of thinking about the relationship between religion and science" (ibid, x).

3 Thompson (in Bloch, 2009, x) puts it well:

In the forum of religious belief, therefore, theists and atheists battle it out, each convinced they are on the back foot, each fighting against what they see as a combined tide of muddle-headedness, dogmatism and irrationality, threatening to overwhelm us with theocracies, technocracies, sterile democracies, faithless scientism, value-free liberality and fundamentalist regimes and movements.

Indeed, religion has become today one of the feistiest battlegrounds for the imaginary mirror relation.

4 Consider the following two remarkable speculative propositions: "Only an atheist can be a good Christian; only a Christian can be a good atheist" (Bloch, 2009, xxi) and, more scandalously-profanely, "The best thing about religion is that it makes for heretics" (ibid, xxv).

Variation 24 The death of God

Hegel is undoubtedly the philosopher of the paradox of God:

> God has died, God is dead – this is the most frightful of all thoughts, that everything eternal and true is not, that negation itself is found in God. The deepest anguish, the feeling of complete irretrievablity, the annulling of everything that is elevated, are bound up with this thought. However, the process does not come to a halt at this point; rather a reversal takes place: God that is to say, maintains himself in this process and the latter is only the death of death. God rises to life again and things are reversed... the death of Christ is the death of this death itself, the negation of negation.
>
> (Hegel, 2008b, 323–324)

By contrast, Nietzsche is the philosopher of the diremptive remain. Against Hegel, Nietzsche insists that something of God's death remains:

> God is dead. God remains dead. And we have killed him. How shall we comfort ourselves, the murderers of all murderers? What was holiest and mightiest of all that the world has yet owned has bled to death under our knives: who will wipe this blood off us? What water is there for us to clean ourselves? What festivals of atonement, what sacred games shall we have to invent? Is not the greatness of this deed too great for us? Must we ourselves not become gods simply to appear worthy of it?
>
> (Nietzsche, 1974, 181)

Following Lacan, we dismissed Nietzsche's "God is dead" as testament to failed atheism consequent upon diremption. We may now reconsider that Nietzsche may be giving voice to the profanatory diremptive remain without which atheism would dwindle to the insufficiency of the merely secular. If Hegel is, for Lacan and Žižek, the *sublime hysteric subject*, Nietzsche is for us, the *abject psychotic hyper-subject*, a necessary *surplus* to the latter if we are to break from the chains of the late modern slave revolt in morality. This is why Nietzsche is the thinker of the "archi-political" (Badiou, 2013), the hyper-revolt against "against everything that had been believed, demanded, hallowed so far" (Nietzsche,

2000b). The hyper-melancholic apathy of his late-life aphanisis is the essential correlate to his hyper-subjectivity. Nietzsche's fall into madness is the fruition of his wisdom, the necessary Other of the lucidity of his archi-political hyper-revolt. His profanations are indispensable weapons towards the desacralization of theological modernity. Hegelian-Žižekian Christianity provided the first death of God, while Nietzsche's profanation (too easily dismissed by Lacan as a shelter against castration)[1] grants a necessary second death. Our emancipation from theological modernity requires the convergence of speculative reason and its partial diremption. It is not sufficient to rise beyond the ontology of juxtaposition to Kantian opposition and finally to Hegelian self-reflection. The latter step must be supplemented with a profanatory thought that heeds to the diremptive remains. Psychoanalysis has a twin genealogy in Hegelian dialectics and Nietzschean diremptive profanation. Žižek is the thinker who has most rigorously and thoroughly argued for the dialectical genealogy of psychoanalysis while Henry (2003) was a stringent advocate of its Nietzschean heritage. For us, psychoanalysis is, at once, dialectical-Hegelian and diremptive-Nietzschean. Psychoanalysis is, at once, philosophy and its subversion. It is the hyper-paradoxical place where diremption (i.e. separation) separates from itself. Here philosophy — also the dwelling place of a hyper-paradox — meets itself by separating from itself. Psychoanalysis completes philosophy precisely by dividing it from within. Without its Hegelian heritage psychoanalysis flounders into the perversity of a quasi-Sadian *jouissance* and without its Nietzschean legacy it is reduced to a mere game of shadows.

The evolution of Žižek's theory of humour is noteworthy. Žižek initially believed that all humour, to be effective, relies on minimal cruelty. Later, he abandoned this view in favour of the idea that laughter can be caused by a simple unexpected dialectical shift. However, the force of Žižek's jokes consists of the fact that both levels remain operative throughout. Without the profanatory supplement of Nietzschean *Schadenfreude* humour loses its *sting*. We may win a smile with a playful dialectical reversal, but *Schadenfreude* is indispensable if we are to achieve *Olympian* laughter and kill the *spirit of gravity* haunting theological modernity. To Lacan's speculative "God is unconscious" one must add Nietzsche's diremptive-profanatory "God is dead" as the necessary supplement to complete desacralization.

If God is the name of the paradoxical coincidence of contraries, such that His death coincides with His resurrection, God is also the appellation christening the diremptive remains testifying to partial sublation. We may baptise the former as the God of speculative reason and the latter as the God of psychoanalysis or the God of diremptive remains. This is the God of profanation, the atheist God, the dead God, the evil God and the voluptuous God of *Jouissance*. This God is symptom of man; He is a Woman-God, a child-God and a psychoanalyst (plague-bestowing) God. He is an egotistical God, a narcissistic God, a mad God, a lying and humiliated God. The primordial God is the God of self-contracting diremption. The creative God is the God of speculative reason submitting to self-evacuating kenosis to realize Himself in spirit. Heine poetically captures these two moments in the History of God: "Illness is no doubt the final cause of the whole urge to create. By creating I could recover. By creating I became healthy" (Heine quoted in Freud, 1914).The ill God is the God of nihilistic self-diremption caged in the sorrow and self-laceration of divine cabin fever.The valetudinary God is the creative God of paradoxical self-realizing kenosis.To these we add a third God of the diremptive remain, namely the psychoanalytic God, the profane remainder of the incomplete sublation of the primordial self-contracting God into the God of reason.

Correlative to the identity-in-difference of religiosity and atheism we have the dialectical unity of sacralization and profanation: there is "a zero-level at which profanation cannot be distinguished from sacralisation" (Žižek, 2012a, 987). For Žižek, profanation is not the same as secularization, only the former "is the true materialist undermining of the Sacred" (ibid, 987).[2] The thorough way out of the sacred requires profanation which, as we have seen, stands in dialectical unity with the sacred. Paradoxically, sacralization alone leads the way out of the sacred. In a similar vein, Nietzsche argues that atheism is born out of Christianity's will to truth (Nietzsche, 1998). He speaks of "the law of the self-overcoming of all great things" (ibid) according to which to overcome something one has to push it to its extreme. Evil is overcome through the radicalization of evil.The sacred is overcome through its escalation in the profane (the profane is not the opposite of the sacred, it is its radicalization). Nietzsche's profanities (titling a book as "The Antichrist", mocking Socrates' ugliness (*monstrum in fronte monstrum in animo*), calling Christ a "fool" to name a few) function as inflated sacralizations through which alone humankind may finally free itself from the sacred. The style of Nietzsche's prose is undeniably sacred-profane (Dionysian dithyrambs, the Biblical style of *Zarathustra*). If Nietzsche sought at all to disenchant the world ("sounding out idols" (Nietzsche, 2005, 155)), his preferred means was always that of an excessive and exorbitant enchantment.

The diremption of this paradoxical identity-in-difference (sacralization is the way out of the sacred) leads to the daunting contradiction by which the sacred re-emerges in the very field from which it was excluded by the effort of secularization. As Žižek has shown, "secularization always relies on its disavowed sacred foundation, which survives either as an exception or as a formal structure" (Žižek, 2012a, 987). We find the resurgence of the sacred within the secular world in both forms isolated by Žižek, namely as *exception* and as *formal structure* (these correspond, of course, to the masculine and the feminine).With respect to the first, Žižek isolates the vastly repeated motif of the "spiritual" in counterpoint to the dominance of the otherwise largely scientistic paradigm. We may say that the post-secular and the secular are one and the same, in a logic mirroring the return of the repressed on the ashes of the repressed. As for the resurgence of the sacred within the form of capitalism, we have the functioning of capital as a mystical real for which the subject is willing to sacrifice him/herself.[3]

According to Žižek, capitalism *secularizes* rather than profanes the world. The result of this is that the religious principle is re-introduced in the capitalist economy itself. Agamben's *The Kingdom and the Glory* is a testament to the failed atheism of modernity. For Agamben, modernity "maintains the theological model of the government of the world" (Agamben, 2011, 285). Interestingly much of what Agamben says pushes us to the conclusion that it is a diremption that leads to the contradiction of a *theological modernity*. More specifically, it is the diremption of the atheism-religiosity paradox that is responsible. It is modernity's (liberalism, to be precise) emphatic denial of transcendence and God ("kingdom" as Agamben calls it) that leads to failed atheism:

> Liberalism represents a tendency that pushes to an extreme the supremacy of the pole of the "immanent order-government-stomach" to the point that it almost eliminates the pole "transcendent God-kingdom-brain" … And when modernity abolishes the divine pole, the economy that is derived from it will not thereby have emancipated itself from its providential paradigm. In the same way, in modern Christian theology, there are forces that cast Christology into a near a-theological drift; but in this case as well, the theological model is not overcome.
>
> (ibid, 284–285)

The contradiction of modernity is that secularization, rather than lead to atheism, reinforced instead the theological paradigm: "Modernity, removing God from the world, has not only failed to leave theology behind, but in some ways has done nothing other than to lead the project of the providential *oikonomia* to completion" (ibid, 287).

Zarathustra incarnates the three aforementioned moments of the divine with the aim of achieving Nietzsche's singular vocation to free modernity from the clutches of the theological. We have, firstly, the resolution to live on the mountaintop, namely the moment of diremptive self-contraction. Secondly, there is a resolve to return from the mountain. Zarathustra now chooses self-realizing kenosis as the tension of self-contracting diremption becomes unbearable:

> I am weary of my wisdom, like the bee that has gathered too much honey; I need hands outstretched to take it from me. I wish to spread it and bestow it, until the wise have once more become joyous in their folly, and the poor happy in their riches.
>
> (Nietzsche, 1969)

Noteworthy here are the dialectical reversals from poverty to wealth and from foolish wisdom to joyous folly, attesting to the fact that the moment of *joining* is the moment reason. The need for kenosis, spilling oneself into the Other, is further poetically rendered by Zarathustra's proclamation to the sun: "O great star what would become your happiness if you did not have those for whom you shine" (ibid). The sun here functions as the prophet's *alter ego*; what he addresses to the star is counsel to himself, a reminder of what his joy owes to those who *receive* his joy. The third Zarathustra is attested to by Nietzsche's *style*, the scriptural writing that is, at once, sacred and profane and which, as such, eschews the pitfalls of the merely secular as it heralds the coming of the overman beyond the entrapments of theological modernity.

Notes

1 Lacan's dismissal of the Oedipus as a "dream of Freud" is another refusal of profane patricide.
2 Žižek's own forays into the profane (e.g. "Heidegger is 'great' not in spite of, but because of his Nazi engagement" (Žižek, 2017), "crazy, tasteless even, as it may sound, the problem with Hitler was that *he was not violent enough*, that his violence was not 'essential' enough" (ibid), occasional pornographic remarks and so on) can, in this light, be understood as necessary steps on the path of de-sacralization.
3 For a compelling argument regarding the constitutive religiosity of capitalism see Benjamin (2004) and Agamben (2019).

Variation 25 The symptom as human notion

I have christened that which subsists beyond self-reflection as the *diremptive remains*. I group these here into the following categories: 1) ignorance, 2) *jouissance*, 3) narcissism, 4) difference, 5) fantasy, 6) subject and 7) structure.

Let us begin with those diremptive remains which I connect to ineradicable *ignorance*. Age-old speculations regarding otherworldly realms belong here. The presupposition of "noumenon" can never be entirely eliminated, as there is no full sublation to phenomenon without remainder. The idea of transcendence will always remain for the speaking being. As Lacan has noted, "the God hypothesis" (Lacan, 1998, 45) will always persist. Lacan (2005b) thus speaks of the inevitable *triumph of religion*. Theological modernity may be a structural necessity that has taken a particularly virulent form in our epoch.[1] Self-reflection may lessen the force of this theological remnant but the hope for total *disenchantment* is as naïve as the prospect of complete sublation. The move from difference (external opposition) to contradiction (internal division) requires recognizing that "depth" or "transcendence" is an immanent illusion of the surface. The surface has a *symptom* (torsion) that renders the illusion of depth or otherworldliness. The surface's self-reflection renders it a twisted surface with a kink. Concomitantly, faith-emotion and reason-knowledge will not fully reconcile. The hypothesis of modes of thinking beyond reason will always remain. Meillassoux (2008) unfairly blames Kant for the advent of modalities of thought other than reason. He holds Kant accountable for a structural problem. A world of mathematical reason alone may be nothing more than a "dream of Meillassoux". Succinctly put, there will always be *faith in faith*. Atheism and religion will retain a minimal difference and a degree of fanaticism, however small, will persist in both. There is always a *leap of faith* in one direction. This dimension of the leap is the *surplus* that resists sublation. Even the most temperate religiosity and the wisest atheism posit a minimal *split* in relation to their respective Other.[2] Faith (the "irrational" in general) and dogmatism are the inexorably *human all too human* faces of ignorance. The spectre of ignorance will retaliate with dialectical vehemence insofar as there will always be a diremptive resistance to psychoanalysis. The dream will always tempt towards scientistic rationalization and mystical lucubration. Freud discovered a realm of thought where pre-modern mysticism and modern science reconcile in a new paradoxical dialectical unity. Psychoanalysis is solidary with the paradigm of modern science (cf. Lacan (2006) and Milner (1995)) and yet it has given voice again to long forgotten objects of pre-modern fascination (dream, fantasy, hallucination). As Derrida aptly puts it, psychoanalysis veritably believes in ghosts.[3] It also believes in the miracle, namely the magical process of *changing one's past* through mere speech. Psychoanalysis has achieved the paradoxical task of re-enchanting the world without regressing to pre-modern superstition. Paradoxically, this is why it alone achieved the most thorough disenchantment (materialism). Finally, another facet of human ignorance is *falling prey* where we attest to a diremptive remain produced by the self-reflection of untimely lucidity and social maladjustment. Even the most luminescent are not immune to the estranging effects of alienation.

Jouissance is arguably tied to the impossible complete dialectical unity of sex and religion. Religion will always maintain its *intrinsic* resolute link to the ascetic ideal, while sex will preserve an unwavering wish to remain an earthly delight. The ethics of psychoanalysis institutes a third between the two insufficient alternatives of *asceticism* and *hedonism*. The latter are facets of the superegoic injunction to *jouissance,* while their dialectical unity gives an idea of the desire that psychoanalytic treatment aims to recover for the subject. If Sade represents *jouissance* in the form of sexual depravity and Kant stands for the ascetic obedience to moral law – two sides of the same coin according to Lacan (2006), Adorno and Horkheimer (1997) and Nietzsche (1998) – Freud stands for the singularity of desire. Though "the unconscious is structured like a language", reason cannot entirely account for it as a kernel of indecipherable *jouissance* forever plagues the human body. The proper handling of the signifier will not eliminate the unpredictable joys and torments of affective life.

Under the rubric of *narcissism*, I isolate the diremptive remains tied to the paradox of identity. There can never be a perfectly non-diremptive mirror stage as the dis-identifications concomitant with identification are partial. Narcissism remains a fundamental (self-diremptive) passion of the human soul. The subject's mortal relation to his/her image is ineradicable. All human identity harbours a stubborn diremptive, I = I, a conceited assertion of self-identity. Humiliation will thus forever haunt the fragile precincts of the imaginary. For Levinas (2003, 64), what "appears in shame is thus precisely the fact of being riveted to oneself, the radical impossibility of fleeing oneself to hide from oneself". Humiliation represents the radical impasse of self-diremption, namely the vain passion to flee from oneself that paradoxically confines one to greater narcissistic incarceration. With respect to object loss, all mourning harbours a pathological core. The object casts an indelible shadow on the mourner plagued with the spectre of manic-melancholic despair. With this, I partially reconcile with Butler as the shadow of the object accounts for a diremptive remain that marks sexual identity as *constitutively* melancholic.

With respect to the three fundamental differences isolated by psychoanalysis, there are remnants testifying to partial sublation. The parent's envy of the child's youth and the child's jealousy of the parental couple remain insurmountable obstacles to self-reflection. Something of the hoped for re-appropriation of knowledge, through which transference love/"paranoia" is brought to an end, is curtailed. The subject never fully wakes from the transference dream. Correlatively, the analyst can never observe entirely "without memory and without desire" (Bion, 1967). Counter-transference will always taint the ideal of analytic objectivity. Finally, anatomical difference forbids the full self-reflection of each sex to its Other. Lacan's logical formulation of sexual difference cannot entirely ignore Freud's "anatomy is destiny" (Freud, 1924, 178). The dialectical shifts between *having* and *not-having* or between *having* and *being* lose much fluidity when faced with the anatomical obstacle. There is real sexual difference prior to *the real of* sexual difference.[4] Regardless of sexuation, men and women have concerns that the other sex cannot fathom. A man cannot know of pregnancy, labour and menstruation. Likewise, a woman will not know the anxiety of impregnating someone accidentally and of having less decision power regarding abortion. This is not a biological argument. Every subject has to come to terms with an *externally imposed* anatomy; one is never quite at home with one's body which always retains a quantum of foreignness. One is not born knowing what to do with one's anatomy. Anatomy is destiny that must be reckoned with. By positing an unsurpassable "rock of castration" Freud (1937) heeds to the bodily diremptive remain.

Fantasy can never be entirely traversed, as the yearning for phallic power will always defy castration. The seduction fantasy cannot be entirely crossed insofar as the thirst for activity (mastery) is insuperable. The primal scene fantasy too, cannot be traversed to completion as no subject will ever fully agree to be excluded from his/her origin. Myths of origin will remain an ideological temptation. The idols of Woman, the Other and the (harmonious) sexual relation will continue to seduce subjects. Finally, the fantasy superegoic underside of the law can never be fully sublated through self-reflection.

Sixth, we have the diremptive remains tied to the category of the subject. The good cannot sublate evil insofar as an exorbitant evil will only partially pass into the good. Something of evil will remain and be felt as evil. There is thus no revolution without some "terror".[5] Likewise, one's symbolic suicide never suffices to eliminate the patricidal wish.[6] What here remains is the Oedipus complex, which will never be reducible to a mere "dream of Freud".[7] We must here recall that the force of law is not entirely "false fascination" (as Žižek calls it (Žižek, 2012a, 971)) hiding an ultimate weakness. There is a power of the law that is irreducible to fantasy – belief to the contrary leads to the mystifications of the university discourse.[8] Evil, terror and patricide are arguably counter measures to the diremptive violence of law which is itself evil and terror; they are the *Verwerfung* that accompanies every *Ausstossung*. Political engagements always risk regressing into the private use of reason. A self-diremptive kernel remains seeking refuge in self-contracting egotism away from the collective. The profane and the sacred too will not fully reconcile. A degree of offensive affront will forever divide them. Lies cannot completely sublate to truth as an enduring element of mischievous deceit will not be sanitized by the self-reflexive process. Even the most sagacious relation to one's heritage includes rejection of thrownness. Concomitantly, there is always a minimal denial of death and mortality. Badiou's "Down with death!" is part and parcel of a necessary profanation against finitude; what it lacks, however, is profanation against life (death drive) that founds the basis of all true passion. Even the most serene interiority (resulting from adjustment to the social) harbours a paranoid kernel. These are testament to the fact that the subject is primarily a *hyper-subject*. Self-assertion, faced with the ponderous weight of the pre-existing symbolic order, requires the extravagant forms of evil, patricide, obstinate prejudice, egotism, profanity, deceit, rejection of the past, defiance of mortality and self-diremptive paranoia. Today, the violence constitutive of subjectivity fails to assert itself sufficiently. This may be the real meaning of the "death of man".[9]

Finally, the diremptive remain of structure concerns the university discourse, the realm of abstract universality and formalism. Our relation to the symptom is not immediately psychoanalytic-speculative. Looking at the world from the perspective of the university discourse is a structural necessity, an unavoidable diremptive remain. The transition to analyst discourse is not immediately given and, therefore, resistance to psychoanalysis (and Hegel) will always remain. Freud and Hegel are not merely ahead of *their* time; they are ahead of *all time,* as no epoch will ever be wholly aligned with psychoanalysis and German idealism (they are the universal symptoms of humankind). The university discourse is a necessity that cannot be fully overcome. Adam's decision to bite the apple of knowledge attests to the great temptation of the university discourse. The university discourse is as elemental as the fall. The *jouissance* of the body compels the subject towards an explanation in the modality of formal abstract knowledge.[10] The child's epistemophilic drive wants to know in the mode of the university discourse. Children are veritable researchers with regard to the enigma of sexuality. And if children can also be the psychoanalysts of their *jouissance* (a bold claim indeed), such an alleged analyst's discourse would not be untainted by university discourse. The fantasies of neurotic children are inextricably linked to this human tendency towards formalism. They are responses to the enigma of *jouissance* in the form of knowledge. Analytic intervention could unveil the "holes" of truth obfuscated therein.[11] God's command to *not bite the apple of knowledge* is a prohibition against this fundamental human tendency (a passion for ignorance) towards formal knowledge.

Hegel's thinking, insofar as it champions concrete universality against formalism, continues "God's work" by beckoning us to abandon empty formalism. Hegel is opposed to "monochromatic" formalism that applies abstract principles from above. For Hegel, formalism is "cognition naively reduced to vacuity" (Hegel, 1977, 9). He thus asserts, against Kant, that formalism "imagines that it comprehended and expressed the nature and life of a form when it has endowed it with some determination of the schema as a predicate" (ibid, 29). At the level of infinite spirit, the inadequacy of formalism is most obvious. By extension, Hegel rejects formalism even in the case of finite spirit. The laws of finite nature are also only "valid" by approximation. Nature, much like human spirit, is irreducible to law – or to cast it in Žižek's favourite Lacanian idiom, nature is *not-all* reducible to law. All theoretical models are doomed to fall, as finite and infinite spirit resists formalism. Scientific theories as well as personal life narratives need constant replacement, though the former enjoy greater longevity. When Hegel claims that "everything turns on grasping and expressing the True, not only as *Substance*, but equally as *Subject*" (ibid, 10), he expresses the limitation of abstract formalism. Subject is the name of that aspect of substance that will not allow substance to be *all* substance. This recalcitrance to abstract universality is most evident in the human being, that entity that most rigorously defies its definition.[12] Lacan's topology is a paradoxical formalization without meta-language or generalization. That all of spirit is irreducible to law can also help finally put an end to the false idea, repeatedly put forward by biologically uniformed Lacanians, that animal behaviour obeys predictable laws. Žižek's return to an ontological Hegel informs us that *all* of spirit is *not-all*. For Žižek, all nature is mad and wildly contingent (something that Darwin already knew). Infinite human spirit only represents the peak and high point of that madness; it is the point at which the *semblance* of order is hardest to maintain.[13]

More specifically, the symptom – the marker of discomfort *par excellence* – testifies to this highest madness that contests most explicitly all formalism. Freud's discovery owes everything to the hysteric symptom's obstinate insubordination to medicine. The symptom provides *the notion of human*. As any notion, the symptom is the antidote to abstract universality. The subject is the symptom, namely that which he/she is not. In this regard, McGowan remarks that *absolute knowing* involves "identification with the subject's foundational symptom" (McGowan, 2019, 47).[14] Such an achievement would be the height of the speculative and highly recalcitrant paradox by which the human and the inhuman stand in identity-in-difference. In Lacanese, the subject would here achieve the move from i(*a*) (the specular image or ego) to *a* (the kernel of surplus enjoyment that is the symptom and which resists inclusion in the image). This consists of nothing other than *subjective destitution*.[15]

The diremptive remains are as necessary as human suffering. De Boer explains that

> *the positive turns out to suffer from the contradiction between what it is in itself* (the unity of its contrary moments) *and what it has actually become* (a determination opposed to its contrary), and the same is true of the negative.
>
> (de Boer, 2010, 362)

Suffering exists insofar as there is a diremptive remain ("a determination opposed to its contrary"). Despite an entity's speculative unity with its Other, it harbours a kernel of resistance to that identity-in-difference and thereby causes suffering. Man contradicts himself when he dirempts his speculative identity with woman. This self-contradiction leads to man's suffering even though, and, indeed precisely because this diremption was motivated by a will to avoid suffering. The diremptive remain brings suffering and therefore *jouissance*.

Correctly perceiving the *jouissance* within the suffering (what we owe to Freud's interpretive genius) allows one to mitigate the force of the diremption. Man's suffering, consequent upon his diremptive denial of femininity, will reduce once he recognizes suffering as the expression of an unconscious enjoyment that contradicts his claim to pure masculinity. The Freudian-Lacanian discovery of *jouissance* (the contradiction of *enjoyed suffering*) is one of history's greatest feats of speculative thought countering diremption. Melancholia is an inevitable diremptive remain plaguing mourning from within. The recognition of the *jouissance* hidden within the pain will help finally overcome the last hurdle before the acceptance of loss.

Two points need to be highlighted at this moment. Firstly, the diremptive remain is, at once, an obstacle to and condition of full sublation. Secondly, the psychoanalytic notion of symptom entails all seven diremptive remains. The symptom is, more than all else, that which makes speculation possible precisely by offering an obstacle to it. Let us now consider the symptom in light of the aforementioned diremptive remains. The symptom is "embodied ignorance" (Žižek, 2006, 217) and yet, as we will see, it is also the locus of (self-)consciousness. The symptom is suffering-*jouissance* and yet it allows the mitigation of suffering by recognizing *jouissance*. Freud discovered the *jouissance* in suffering through his self-analysis (mediated, as Lacan reminds us, by his transference to Fliess). The discovery of psychoanalysis was thus his symptom.[16] It was born of his suffering and yet it mitigated that suffering by introducing it to the field of the Other. Thirdly, the symptom breaks narcissism and is, for that reason, what prompts the subject to erect an ego based on the narcissistic will to deny the symptom. Without the challenge posed by the symptom to the self, there would be no will to *hoist* oneself above it. The symptom abolishes (through identity-in-difference) sexual, generational and power difference and yet it is the only way of maintaining these differences with the required integrity that only a boundary without a limit can achieve. Fifthly, the symptom crosses the fantasy and yet provides the kernel around which fantasy knits its narrative. The symptom is the marker of the subject's singularity; it is what is most "me" despite and by virtue of being also what "feels least me". Finally, the symptom is the basis of the university discourse (the Diagnostic and Statistical Manual of Mental Disorders is a list of symptoms in isolation). It beckons the subject to seek an answer in knowledge. Yet it is also that which contests the university discourse most rigorously, thereby paving the way, for those who have ears to hear, for a shift to the discourse of the analyst.[17]

The symptom as human notion implies that the human being's conduit to itself (or, in Hegelese, the absolute) has to take recourse to an ego-dystonic path of despair. The symptom, as speculative notion, is at once 1) a symbol, namely that which unites (*symbolein*) and 2) that which separates and dirempts (*diabolein*).[18] As uniting force, the symptom moves the subject to present it to the Other (e.g. psychoanalyst). The symptom paves the way towards the absolute, if one lets it speak (free association). It is the diremptive remain testifying to our separation from the absolute and thereby paradoxically also uniting us

with it. The symptom is *the fragrance of the absolute*[19] because it summons the subject to consider the whole rather than speculate on the local (a contradiction
indeed). The DSM represents the epitome of the abstract scientistic formalism.
Its constant changes and revisions testify to the symptom's recalcitrance in the
face of this inane indexing. In its *diabolein* aspect, the symptom is suffering
that separates one from others; it is an *idiotic* autoerotic *jouissance*. Also, and
most crucially, the diabolical aspect of the symptom most rigorously accounts
for its resistance to formalism and its subversion of pre-existing doxa.[20] The
opposition of the symptom's two moments (*symbolein* and *diabolein*) unite in
psychoanalysis. The symptom's mutiny *separates* from psychiatry in order to *join*
psychoanalysis.

The symptom signals the lack of a human "nature". Some subjects try to sub-
sume their being under the rubric of a pure thought. This leads to the contradiction of *fragile rigidity*. The symptom provides the form for the notion insofar
as it marks the failure of any formal definition of human being. Earlier, however,
we saw that for Hegel love provided the model for the notion. We now see that
the symptom has usurped love's privileged position. Indeed, Žižek (2019) even
holds that love is a mask cast upon the trauma of the real (i.e. the trauma of the
symptom). How, if it all, can these two views be reconciled? Can both love and
the symptom provide the model of the logical notion and thereby of human
infinite spirit? This would mean that love and the symptom share the same
basic structure, namely that of giving expression to the same highly recalcitrant paradoxes. Let us now verify this hypothesis concerning the isomorphism
of love and the symptom by testing whether the paradoxes of the former are
applicable to the latter. Love represents, firstly, the identity-in-difference of triumph and defeat. The same can be said of the symptom insofar as it marks
the subject's defeat (it is radically ego-dystonic) and from there its triumph (it
testifies to the "true" self). Secondly, like love, the symptom testifies to the dialectical unity of lack and plenitude insofar as it depletes the subject (through
jouissance) and yet it is the only thing that can replenish him/her and grant a
modicum of meaning to existence. With respect to the love-hate opposition,
the symptom is the human notion only insofar as it stands for *the inhuman in the
human*. The symptom occupies, as such, the place of *das Ding*, namely of hate-
jouissance. The symptom is the *neighbour* within. As with love, which is, at once,
communism and egotism, the symptom separates the subject in self-diremption
and yet also joins him/her to the community of sufferers. Without the suffering
induced by the symptom, the subject would remain closed upon him/herself
unable to relate to another.[21] Again, in strict parallel with love, the symptom is
both atheism and piety. It marks the fact that there is no Other of the Other
insofar as we have to find our own way of dealing with it. The symptom breaks
with abstract universality. And yet, it connects us with the divine; it is a feminine *jouissance* seeking its God/witness. In *Encore*, Lacan argued that *jouissance*
seeks a divine witness to sustain itself.[22] The psychoanalytic treatment begins
by creating a "God" through the artifice of the transference. For this it makes
use of the symptom's need to make itself heard. In this initial phase, the subject

seeks an answer in the form of abstract universality to the enigma posed by his/her symptom. Where, in psychosis, the symptom is foreclosed, this first "pious" moment does not occur. This is most evident in the schizophrenias, namely the structure most impervious to transference. As a result of this foreclosure, the second atheistic moment, tied to the undoing of transference, also cannot occur. The symptom is thus instrumental in both erecting the God (the deity that will hear my pain) and eventually dismantling Him. As aforesaid, love must be addressed to the person not "right" for us so that this person, by virtue of this inappropriateness, will raise us to the heights of philosophy. The symptom is likewise not "right" for us. And yet through this discomfort it raises us to philosophy and to the dignity of our notion. Finally, true love requires overcoming the *feeling* of love; it is neither a pleasure nor a source of happiness. Likewise, the symptom is quintessentially ego–dystonic. To love it requires the challenge of neighbourly love.

Love and the symptom provide the structure of the concept. While Hegel insisted on love as the key to the notion, psychoanalysis underlines the symptom. Like the symptom, true love represents, within the realm of infinite human spirit, the point of highest chaos. The human subject in love is more impervious to formalism than one unmotivated by this striving. For Hegel, the notion is inherently "mad" insofar as it stands in paradoxical unity with its opposite. Formalism refuses the inherent madness of the concept. Love provides Hegel with the model for the concept insofar as it is marked by intense dialectical tensions. Love and Hegel's conception of the notion are quintessentially opposed to the principle of identity.[23] Love marks the moment of the subject's self-differentiation; like the notion, love transpires in dialectical unity with its Other(s). The love which heeds to the aforementioned paradoxes is a *speculative love*, it is a love of the neighbour-Thing-symptom addressed to the real Other rather than the imaginary counterpart (the latter love is mere *specular* (pseudo)-love). This is the most difficult and paradoxical love and yet the only love worthy of its name. That is why there is no true love at the start of an encounter. There we only have love as a "pure thought", rather than *notional love*. As a result, the early stages of an amorous encounter between two subjects often attest to massive dialectical swings between the dread of the fear of loss and the bliss of the encounter. Online dating aggravates this problem insofar as two complete strangers test out their compatibility for intimacy. The massive dialectical shift involved in the transition from strangers to lovers reduces love from its privileged status as *notion of all notions* to pure thought. For many, the dating app itself is the partner where the notifications of messages, the number of matches made, short meaningless dialogues, "ghosting", "textlationships", "slow fade" and so on become the Other more than an actual other person. The Other is thus reduced to the *promise* of a *potential* rather than actual partner. The *promised* Other repeats the dynamics of the Oedipal configuration where the toddler relinquishes the desired parent for the sake of a *future* partner. Dating apps capitalize on the store of unresolved infantile tendency in order to maintain subjects within a libidinal economy where virtual potentiality is valued higher than real actuality. This is the general libidinal economy of capitalism where belief in a better future (recall that credit comes from the Latin "*credere*" meaning "to believe") outweighs concern for the present – the quintessential religious idea. Capitalism here makes use of the kinship, highlighted by Lacan (1988, 197), between the field of love and that of the promise as symbolic pact. Our late modern predicament thus reveals us as the dupes of a "broken promise" and the fools of unrequited love.

The (pseudo-)lover denies the symptom and therefore the dimension of the human notion. Unlike veritable lovers, they refuse, in the case of women, to be symptom of man and, in the case of men, to elect a woman as their symptom. This refusal is tantamount to a denial of the fall. Adam bit the apple with the hope of ascension. However, it led instead to his descent. Genesis attests to a vicious dialectical shift consequent upon Adam and Eve's conceit to defy God. Paradoxically, newfound mortality made them possibly truly immortal. The fall is a dialectical notion insofar as *the fall is nothing but our refusal to accept the fall*. To speak is to fall and to fall is the only grace available to the human being. The ideological error, which I christen the *pre-lapsarian fallacy*, is the veritably non-dialectical idea that falsely opposes fall and grace. The return to Eden (the refusal to fall) is the biggest fall of all. What is the fall from Eden in comparison to the fall that is Eden? The symptom is our fall from grace and, precisely through this fall, our only paradoxical means of achieving grace. In his seminal piece on the marionette theatre, Kleist's (1972) interlocutor-companion admirably renders this paradox:

> We can see the degree to which contemplation becomes darker and weaker in the organic world, so that the grace that is there emerges all the more shining and triumphant. Just as the intersection of two lines from the same side of a point after passing through the infinite suddenly finds itself again on the other side – or as the image from a concave mirror, after having gone off into the infinite, suddenly appears before us again – so grace returns after knowledge has gone through the world of the infinite, in that it appears to best advantage in that human bodily structure that has no consciousness at all – or has infinite consciousness – that is, in the mechanical puppet, or in the God.
>
> (Kleist, 1972)

Kleist then asks whether "we would have to eat again of the tree of knowledge in order to return to the state of innocence?" (ibid). His friend answers thus: "Most certainly… That is the last chapter in the history of the world". (ibid). The symptom marks that paradoxical point at infinity where grace is finally regained, not through the false ideology of a forced *return*, but through a second biting of the apple. As Nietzsche puts it most eloquently, "Everyone who has ever built anywhere a 'new heaven' first found the power thereto in his own hell" (1998). The symptom is the inner hell from which alone a heaven may emerge.

Sin is diremptive of the paradoxes of love and the symptom. In sin, the diremptive subject fails the speculative notion and thus regresses to the principle of identity. Hegel (2008b) believes it was unnecessary to make Adam a lone sinner (rather than invoke humanity at large). By contrast, I argue that the idea of a first lone sinner is crucial as it portrays for us the very structure of sin, namely its self-diremptive aspect.[24] One is always alone in sin. At most one is with a woman. In sin the human becomes a manic non-concept, something well attested to in plays that stage characters reduced to the one-sidedness of pure thoughts (e.g. Molière's *L'avare* or his *Don Juan*[25] representing for us the sins of avarice and lust respectively). The diremptive sin of Don Juan consists of rejecting the woman-symptom. He leaves them before they stabilize to such notional dignity. The consequence, brought about by the triumph of the "lower" term, is that he becomes symptom himself, the symptom of all women. Not to mention the angry return of women as hyper-symptom. The infamous fiery hell of woman's rage is that of the hyper-symptom scorned.

Sin leads to the demise and loss of the human. Yet sin is as constitutive as the fall. Sins are a lonely idiotic *jouissance*. They are ways of avoiding love, the concept and the symptom insofar as these disturb identity. More specifically, sin – diremptive of notional love and the symptom – rejects a "lower" term and paradoxically reduces itself (by the logic of the triumph of the "lower" term) to its lowest instance. Greed hides that wealth (the "higher" term) is the highest paucity ("lowest" term): what is the poverty of the loss of wealth in comparison to the poverty that is wealth? Wrath hides the fact that power is the greatest impotence: what is the impotence of the loss of power in comparison to the impotence that is power? Vanity hides that superficial beauty is the height of ugliness: what is the ugly in opposition to beauty in comparison to the ugliness that is shallow beauty? Gluttony hides the fact that satiety is the highest form of hunger (not to be hungry, to lack hunger, is the greatest hunger of all): what is the hunger of lost satiety in comparison to the hunger that is over-satiety? Envy hides the fact that to triumph is the greatest defeat of all: what is the defeat of lost triumph in comparison to the defeat that is triumph? Lust hides the fact that phallic sex is empty *jouissance*, truncated as it is by orgasm: what is the renunciation of lost lust in comparison to the renunciation that is lust? Finally, sloth (the master's sin *par excellence*) hides the fact that to not work is greater alienation than labour: what is the alienation of labour in comparison to the alienation of the refusal to work.[26] In sin, the human remains a pure thought and thereby avoids, at once, the anxiety of the concept and, to quip Kierkegaard, *the concept of anxiety*. Only love, not law, is the antidote to sin.[27] If sin is defined as the triumph of the "lower" term resulting from the "higher" term's diremptive will, then we may say that sin is commensurate with the Christian slave revolt in morality. In the spirit of Nietzsche – the greatest moral philosopher that ever was – we may ask and thereby revive his gargantuan *revaluation of all values*: what is a sin against Christianity in comparison to the sin that is Christianity?

If, as Schelling (quoted in Žižek, 2009b) holds, "man is nature's way of looking at itself" it is because the human being is endowed with a symptom. The symptom undoes repression[28] and subjects us to the pain of self-awareness. The human invented repression to eschew the task of being nature's self-observer. The symptom is a profanation against repression. It aligns humankind, once again, with the task of self-reflection. Kleist's (1972) interlocutor argues that the boy dancer falls from grace precisely with the advent of consciousness. The dancer's grace, by contrast to the marionette's awkwardness, is an index of non-consciousness rather than the opposite. The fall from grace occurs when the light of consciousness robs us from the innocence of ignorance. Where Plato's (2000) allegory highlights freedom from the clutches of illusion, *Genesis* highlights the dark side of the light. What, to quip Brecht again, is the darkness before the light in comparison to the darkness that is the light? The symptom is that kink in the Moebius strip which embodies the self-reflexive turn by which humanity falls from grace into the pain of a veritable bite of (self)-consciousness.[29] And yet, through a dialectical turn, the symptom is the only viable grace after the fall. Only a heightened consciousness, rather than a dive into darkness, can constitute our grace.

That the symptom is the human notion means neither more nor less than that the notion itself, in its logical structure, is the human notion. With a flash of flare, one may say that the *notion of love* is the *love of the notion*[30] – philosophy is where they meet. We thus come to the unexpected identity-in-difference, hitherto falsely opposed by common understanding, of the *speculative* and *tautological* propositions in the following statement: *the notion is the human notion* or, conversely, *the human notion is the notion.*[31] This tautological-speculative proposition should ring to the dialectically well-trained ear as at once self-evident and paradoxical. The recurrence of *notion* as subject and as predicate renders its self-evidence while the constitutive inner division of the notion[32] decrees it as paradoxical.[33]

Notes

1 The contradiction of a theological modernity is mostly apparent in America where the discourse of (pseudo)-atheism co-exists with the on-going growth of new segregated religious groups.

2 When Freud (1938) decided to generalize the phenomenon of splitting to a universal mechanism, he was in a sense giving voice to the diremptive remain by which the setting of antipodes is a universal human tendency. The Kleinian School took this idea and aptly made it the basis of its metapsychology.

3 Interview: https://m.youtube.com/watch?v=0nmu3uwqzbI

4 Gherovici (forthcoming) has written of *realness* with respect to the actual factors that influence desire (e.g. penis size rather than symbolic phallus).

5 This may contradict my earlier argument against Žižek. However, my view regarding a *speculative* revolution, rather than a wildly *dialectical* revolution, is that adequate self-reflection will only leave behind a diremptive *remain* rather than a full-blown diremption such as 20th century communism.

6 For Pommier (2013), the patricidal wish/fantasy is the only means at a subject's disposal for putting an end to incest. Unable to symbolically kill the Other of seduction, the psychotic becomes its object.

7 If Oedipus is Freud's dream, this dream is a *particularity* that has *universal* import. A veritable (concrete) universality finds its support and source only in the singular.

8 As the Latin saying goes, *auctoritas non veritas facit legem*. Agamben (2005) debunks the mystifications of university discourse by showing that Western democracy is sustained by the always-imminent threat of explicit force.

9 Today, Žižek argues, violence functions as "an implicit admission of impotence" (2012a, 998). Where "the Paris *banlieue* or British riots were a 'zero-level' protest, violent outbursts which wanted nothing, terrorist attacks act on behalf of that *absolute* Meaning provided by religion" (ibid). In both cases, "violence and counter-violence are caught up in a deadly vicious cycle, each generating the very forces it tries to combat" (ibid).

10 Lacan (2007) spoke of knowledge as "means of *jouissance*".

11 For Lacan, truth is a hole in knowledge.

12 Neuroscience and genetics argue that the human being is genetically programmed to defy its genetic programming (cf. Ansermet and Magistretti (2004)).

13 And yet for centuries the dogma of human superiority, "crown of creatures", persisted unchallenged.

14 Jameson (2010, 4) argues that we must "read Absolute Spirit as a symptom".

15 *Disgrace* tells the story of a white South African woman who was raped while her father was held captive. Her decision to keep the child, despite her father's admonishments, attests to the courage of admitting the unconscious. It testifies to the realization that true freedom and enslavement are only opposed from the limited perspective of diremption. This is a mother who accepts the child as her symptom – indeed as the symptom of the complexities of her world. The daughter (raped) stands for universality, while the father (urging her to abort) remains fixated to cowardly particularity.

16 That the Oedipus is a "dream of Freud" should thus not be taken only as critique.

17 In abandoning neurology for the sake of founding the pillars of psychoanalysis, Freud achieved that subtle yet gargantuan shift of perspective. He was aided by *love*, which, as Lacan (1998) showed, makes possible all change of discourse. Love of? Love of the hysteric-symptom-neighbor of course, namely the very love that he later (mistakenly) denied his own capacity to achieve.

18 For the distinction between *symbolein* and *diabolein* see (Han, 2018).

19 I am playing on the aforementioned formulation from *The Philosophy of Right* where Hegel speaks of "the fragrance of world-spirit". A slip of the tongue, a hysteric conversion symptom, an unconscious formation in speech and a dream are all fragrances insofar as they call out minimally to the Other. They are the budding expression of transference to come. The transference neurosis, by contrast, is no longer a mere fragrance; it is a full-blown *stench* that will dazzle even the insipid nostrils of the least weathered clinician.

20 Bion's (1959) "attacks on linking" are the symptom's diabolical-diremptive aspect. They constitute the subject's foundational "no" to all pre-existing schemas. We owe psychoanalysis to this diabolical striving.

21 A clinician learns the art of healing precisely through his/her own suffering, his/her symptom. Is every case study not also an intimate memoir of the clinician him/herself?

22 Nietzsche (1998) also argued that humans created gods in order to assure that no suffering would go un-witnessed.

23 Jameson (2010) agrees that one cannot impute the principle of identity to Hegel. However, he argues that "Narcissism [is] a better way of identifying what may sometimes be felt to be repulsive in the Hegelian system as such" (ibid, 130). This is a strange imputation to make to the philosopher who made love/kenosis the basis of his whole speculative philosophy.

24 Hegel also finds that the idea of the inheritance of sin is superfluous. For him, it is only there to correct the idea of a lone sinner. However, we know that this idea has great psychoanalytic merit (cf. Freud, 1909 – "The Rat Man").

25 On the impasses of Don Juan see (Zupančič, 1996).

26 According to Jean-Claude Milner (1995), the great achievement of psychoanalysis (specifically its Lacanian rewriting) consists of the fact of stripping the subject ($) of all substance (soul etc.) in the same way that Galilean science (according to Koyré (2016)) stripped the object of all substance (Platonic forms etc.) by introducing measurement (henceforth the substantives "hot", "cold", "tall" and "short" would be substituted, respectively, by the measurements of degree (Celsius) and height (metres)). By defining sin as diremptive of the *notions* of love and symptom (love of the symptom, one could say), I hope to further the extraction of substance inaugurated by modern science (cf. Milner, 1995). However, this task should in no way reduce the ethical weight psychoanalysis re-introduces into the subject's life. The modern de-substantialization of the subject will heighten responsibility by removing the various figures-idols of the Other. We may here speak of *disenchantment* necessary to the ascension to humanity's newly found adulthood.

27 Freud's position in this regard is trepidatious and ambiguous as he dismisses the love of the neighbour as "an excellent example of the unpsychological [expectations] of the cultural super-ego" (Freud, 1930) and yet urges elsewhere that "we must begin to love in order not to fall ill" (Freud, 1914).

28 More accurately, the symptom is the marker of repression as well as its undoing. If the *repressed* is nothing other than *the return of the repressed*; the symptom is the name and locus of this paradoxical co-existence.

29 When Lacan (2006) claims that the ego is the privileged symptom of humankind, ego must not be understood as "self-image" but, rather, as locus of (self)-consciousness, namely the marker of the fall from grace into paranoid awkwardness.

30 For Lacan (1998), *to speak of love* is the same as *to make love*.

31 Thus, Hegel treats concepts like human beings and Lacan treats human beings as concepts.

32 For Hegel every proposition is synthetic no matter how seemingly analytic/tautological. Speculative reason, McGowan (2019, 26) argues, shows the minimal synthetic nature of every statement of identity. Psychoanalytic work consists of the same.

33 Could Heidegger's late reflections on tautological thinking reveal an unexpected kinship with speculative philosophy?

Conclusion

From *via dolorosa* to *gaya scienza*

The aim of this treatise has been to free thinking from one-sidedness and recognize, as Hegel put, "the reciprocally necessary moments that take shape as a conflict and seeming incompatibility" (Hegel, 1977, 2). The inability to apprehend contradiction consists of a denial of the *subject within substance*. This is tantamount to reducing all to the level of things[1] or finite nature (for Hegel even the latter is also subject – something that quantum mechanics has confirmed in the most uncanny way). The failure to grasp the contradiction in identity leads to *reification* of the object considered and of ourselves as perceiving subjects. We are becoming more akin to finite spirit in modernity and our self-understanding reflects this reification. Scientistic theories concerning the innate predisposition to autism provide an autistic aetiology of autism. They consider the autist in isolation, thereby perpetuating his/her segregation, rather than heed to the dynamic relationships that contributed to foreclosure. The absurdity of treating psychosis through "faecal microbiota transplantation" (stool transplant) is a psychotic "remedy" insofar as the anal object is taken in its concrete literality, rather than in the complex intersubjective relation of demand in which it is exchanged while potty training. This procedure fails to grasp the anal object "not only as *Substance*, but equally as *Subject*" (Hegel, 1977, 10).

Reification is the result of the aforementioned seven diremptions. In *narcissism*, we bear witness to the triumph of his majesty the ego, that most rigid "false self" lacking verve and spontaneity. *Jouissance* marks the moment where the subject is beside him/herself, overwhelmed to the point of fading. What we christened as *ignorance* is the triumph of religiosity where the subject surrenders sovereignty to the deity. In *fantasy*, the rich complications of intersubjectivity are reduced to the determinations of triumph and defeat. The disparagement of *power differential* has made of therapy, leadership and pedagogy rule-ridden enterprises, while *sexuality* has become a matter of (rigid) *identity* rather than *difference*. Parenting has lost confidence in itself insofar as the naturalness of filial love has given way to rule-obsessed education. The university discourse (what we placed under the rubric of *structure*) has invaded all walks of life. It denotes the triumph of biologistic essentialism that seeks to find a "definition" (pure thought) for the human. Finally, and surprisingly, the category of *subject* too has its de-subjectifying aspects testified by the rise of bravado, namely the over-exalted attempt at self-assertion which, by virtue of its one-sidedness, flounders into vacuity and despondency.[2]

However, total reification is impossible. The universal can never be abolished and subjectivity can never be entirely lost and truth totally eradicated. Topologically speaking, the torsion on the Mobius strip can never be fully ironed out. These *real traces of subjectivity* will resist reification. Indeed, it is on the ashes of reification's seven diremptions that the subject will rise again as the phoenix. The erasure of the torsion on the surface is the torsion itself – the kink will thus never be expunged. The impotence-rendering contradictions of our time will themselves pave the path to impossibility. The solution is immanent to the problem; to find it one must simply *look awry*.[3] For Bloch (2009), even suicide bombers aim to bring paradise on earth. Even such an extreme case of *the impotent one-sidedness of a pure thought*[4] carries the torsion that could lead to *the openness of notional impossibility*. Such psychoanalytic and Hegelian optimism requires the courage to see the world from the standpoint of the absolute. The Hegelian-Lacanian, and indeed Freudian, topology here put forward advocates (against the rarity of Badiou's "event") *the utopia of everyday life*. Every slip of the tongue, amnesia, lapsus and dream is the index of paradoxical *freedom through lost sovereignty*. The thinness of the eyelid separates "common man" (Badiou's ill-christened "individual")[5] from the great artist; in dream even the illiterate make claim to creative genius. We all live in a post-evental[6] world where language's encounter with the living gives birth to the divine madness of the human. Badiou misses the fact that the "pre-evental individual" does not live in happy ignorance but that he/she lives in *sickness,* and that it is this very sickness itself that attests most passionately to humanity. "The sickness of the animal is the birth of spirit" (Hegel quoted in McGowan, 2019, 36). The exigency of speculative thought requires that we abolish Badiou's false individual/ subject dichotomy and assert proudly that all humanity is subject of truth.

There is no event other than the *human* and yet the birth of *each and every* human subject repeats this event anew in a thoroughly singular way. All humans are *subjects*. While some bathe in the graces afforded by art, sex, love, laughter and music, others bear the curse of illness. However, these are essentially the same, separated by an invisible torsion on the plane. More accurately, every human is at once graced and cursed by the human; the human event is the symptom. Badiou misses the speculative-tautological proposition: the human is the human. The only condition of philosophy is the love of the symptom, namely the pain and sickness of the animal. The *universal* forced choice, imposed on all, is that of accepting the *singular* symptom. True freedom involves the forced choice of choosing the symptom rather than maintaining self-conceit for the sake of a false freedom, which, by virtue of the triumph of the "lower" term, would dwindle to servile enslavement. The rejection of the symptom leads to the paranoia of being persecuted by the symptom. Hegel beckons us to

> recognize reason as the rose in the cross of the present and thereby to enjoy the present, this is the rational insight which *reconciles* us with actuality – the

reconciliation which philosophy affords to those in whom there has once arisen an inner voice bidding them to *comprehend*.

(Hegel, 2008a, 15)

Philosophy affords respite to those willing to comprehend. It allows them to recognize the symptom as the rose in the cross they must bear. Indeed, philosophy (the notion) is the symptom itself, with its two faces that are one, the rose and the cross. Speculative philosophy, like the symptom, is the locus of a speculative paradox; it is at once "the great way of despair" ("*via dolorosa*") and the "*gaya scienza*". Non-psychoanalytic treatments do not grasp the paradox of the symptom. The symptom achieves the diremptive work of the understanding. It separates the subject from his/her community in the way that *jouissance* and suffering separate. But, if the subject overcomes moral cowardice, the symptom allows him/her to consider the larger network of interrelations that constitute the totality of which that symptom is part. The symptom is not an irrational oddity, blemishing the purity of an otherwise rational being. By contrast to this anti-psychoanalytic and anti-dialectical commonplace of the understanding, the symptom is *hyper-rational*. Hegel's (in)-famous "What is rational is actual; and what is actual is rational" (Hegel, 2008a) could be translated thus: *what is rational is the symptom* and, conversely, *that which is a symptom is rational*. The hyper-rationality of the symptom becomes increasingly evident as we look at the world from *the standpoint of eternity* (the absolute) rather than narrow conceit. The symptom, viewed *locally*, is sheer madness. Viewed *globally*, it is the height of rationality, as it condenses in one intense paradoxical point the obfuscated complications of the whole. American psychiatry's will to pathologize the symptom is itself *symptom* of its inability to consider the whole by letting the symptom speak. Psychoanalysis, by contrast, recognizes that the symptom is *the spectre of the absolute*. The symptomatic torsion on the Mobius strip is not the insignia of unreason but, rather, the sign of reason's hyper-presence. As "voice of the intellect", the symptom "does not rest until it has gained a hearing" (Freud, 1927, 53).[7]

Lacan (1977) argues that the voice has the privilege of being the object whose presence is the most permanent. Unlike the gaze, which vanishes in a moment, the voice can retain its presence indefinitely: "the invocatory drive … has … the privilege of not being able to close" (Lacan, 1998, 200). The superego functions as a privileged partial object insofar as it is vehicled by the voice, the form of the object *a* that is the least transient and that hence poses the least enigma. It is the form of the object *a* which thus resembles most a master signifier. The superego is a pure thought rather than a notion.[8] It is quintessentially one-sided and de-humanizing.[9] It represents the disparagement of the human and divine notions[10] to pure thoughts. God becomes "alive" again as "Punisher" and the subject becomes pure "sinner".[11] For Lacan (1977), the relation to an other mitigates the pain of castration. As a result, the loss of the other brings the subject back to the condition of being castrated.

The one-sided veiling over of castration is temporally "corrected" by a subsequent one-sided re-emergence of castration. Something similar happens, according to Freud, with respect to ambivalence. During the relation, ambivalence (notional love-hate) was veiled over for the sake of maintaining the pure thought of pure love. However, with the onset of loss, the other side of the ambivalence (hate – a "pure culture of the death drives") rises to consciousness. Finally, one must recall the importance Freud granted to the narcissistic factor in the aetiology of melancholia. There too, the one-sidedness of narcissistic self-conceit (prior to loss) takes its vengeance in the form of melancholic self-disparagement (after the loss). This narcissistic one-sidedness testifies to the foreclosure of the torsion in the Mobius strip, which may explain the infamous loss of libido and interest in the external world in melancholia. Such a topological outlook allows us to abandon biologistic models. Libido is not an "organic substance"; it is simply the kink which gives life and movement to the surface. Freud's (1913) myth of the primal murder in *Totem and Taboo* stages a similar temporal lag dubbed "deferred obedience". By contrast to melancholia, here it is the pure thought of hate that is on the forefront. After the primal murder, the suppressed love emerges to the fore in the form of pure guilt. In all these cases, we have two pure thoughts separated in time such that the appearance of the second functions as a correction to the one-sidedness of the first in a violent and persecutory operation that may be felt as "vengeful" ("karma", the "evil eye"). Pure thoughts are notions, the two moments of which emerge separated by a temporal interval thus perpetuating the ideological falsity of their distinctness. The diphasic nature of trauma, i.e. that it is experienced as trauma only *après coup* in a second temporal moment, may be understood with the idea that trauma is a pure thought. Trauma's moments necessarily split into two. The psychoanalytic cure consists of transforming trauma into a notion. Likewise, the human philosophical vocation consists of the arduous labour of joining moments slowly together. Was this not precisely the aim of Hegel's *Phenomenology*, to gradually bring together the falsely opposed moments of a pure thought in ever more recalcitrant paradoxes testifying to the patient advent of the notion? Sexuality is, at first, one-sidedly imposed on the subject in infancy. As such, metabolization-subjectivation (taking responsibility for and re-appropriating the drive as one's own) must occur at a second time, which will "correct" *a posteriori* the one-sided passivity of infancy. Lacan's *identification with the symptom* may entail precisely this operation, by which the two moments are brought together in such a way that trauma becomes its own convalescence.

A peculiar ambiguity exists in Freud's discussion of melancholia. Melancholia is presented as an *error* insofar as the subject disparages him/herself instead of the actual object of ambivalence. However, Freud also claims that melancholic self-complaints actually hit the mark, that the subject has caught sight of something accurate about himself. At one level, "the shadow of the object fell upon the ego" (Freud, 1917) and yet, at another level, the subject has gained lucidity. In light of the latter vicissitude, the *spectre (shadow) of the absolute* has fallen on the ego. In melancholia, the absolute shines a glimmer and opens the way to self-knowledge. The (melancholic) voice of conscience is a voice of reason and unreason. As one turns one's ear away from it, it morphs into the persecutory voice of punitive unreason. If one grants it a hearing, it reveals its kernel of rationality. Through the arduous work of analysis, the superegoic voice may regain its notional status as *reason*.[12] Psychoanalytic treatment combines the *via dolorosa* and the *gaya scienza*, two sides of the Mobius strip that stand in dialectical unity. Marx's "first as tragedy then as farce" should not be read as the separation in time of two temporal moments (tragic and comic). Likewise, the "from" and the "to" of the title of the conclusion – appearing to separate the *via dolorosa* from the *gaya scienza* – should be read topologically as a near-instantaneous transition between moments of *one* speculatively unified phenomenon. The psychoanalytic treatment is a procedure of ideological correction. It aims to reduce the obfuscations of temporality by bringing together the separated pure thoughts in an effort to constitute anew the notion in its philosophical dignity. When ignored and left to insist incessantly, the symptom is the haunting *spectre of madness*. However, when it gains the hearing of a receptive ear, it reveals itself as *birth of the absolute*, namely the locally isolated bit of singular *jouissance* that paradoxically grants a glimpse of the universal.[13]

Diremption involves the imaginary degradation of the symptom–notion. The neurotic psychical diremption, known as repression–denial, leads to the phenomenalization of the object *a* aimed at obfuscating the horror of castration. Eventually, castration triumphs as neurotic guilt, where the subject is persecuted by this very same object *a* returning as a menacing internal voice. Perverse diremption involves the erection of a fetish in the service of disavowal. In a commentary on a boy whose disavowal was immediately followed by the creation of a symptomatic fear concerning his toes being touched, Freud elegantly announces the implacable triumph of castration: "in all the to and fro between disavowal and acknowledgment, it was nevertheless castration that found the clearer expression" (Freud, 1938, 278). Finally, psychotic diremption (foreclosure) leads to castration in the real where the subject is confronted with an "unbarred" and persecutory Other. In all three cases the identity-in-difference of symptom as *spectre of madness* and *advent of the absolute* is dirempted, leading to three contradictions defining each structure. The contradiction central to neurosis is that of a subject who refuses "to sacrifice his castration" (assuming that the Other demands it of him/her (Lacan, 2006, 700)) but who, for that very reason, remains all the more bound to his/her castration. In perversion, we have a desire that puts on the aura of subverting the law while functioning as the very support of that law (Lacan, 2004, 176). The pervert does not know for whose *jouissance* his activity is exercised. What is sure is that "it is not, in any case, in the service of his own" (ibid, 177). This subject may indeed use the Other but, in so doing, he/she paradoxically instrumentalizes him/herself for this same Other's *jouissance*. Finally, in psychosis we have a subject sheltering him/herself from the Other for fear of becoming its object. Yet this effort to wall him/herself off reifies him/her all the more. In all three cases we witness the triumph of the "lower" term. In denying the symptom, all become *hyper-symptom* and pure thought.[14]

Just as all truth emerges through misrecognition and is thus only a *"mi-dit"* (half-said), all error is also only partially error. The isomorphic relation of thought and being[15] has the consequence that no thought, irrespective of the degree of its fallaciousness, can ever be completely divorced from the truth. There will, of course, be degrees of truth and error but even the wildest bull-shit retains some kinship, however infinitesimal, to universality. Just as humanity will never free itself from the clutches of error, it will also never free itself from truth. We must, however, take this with a grain of salt insofar as the specula-tive identity-in-difference of truth and lies or even truth and bullshit cannot entirely do away with their opposition in actuality. To *achieve* speculative iden-tity will require a stringent effort on the part of the analyst or the thinker; the modicum of truth that resides as a kernel within falsehood will not easily sur-render itself.[16] Without the decision to engage on this path, speculative identity is an empty hypothesis akin to abstract universality. It is likewise with Lacan's early distinction between full and empty speech. To divide the analysand's speech into what is worthy and full, rather than empty and negligible, regresses from the radicality of psychoanalytic discourse to pre-psychoanalytic notions of truth. However, to reach this speculative identity one requires the analyst's right interpretation as well as the analysand's capacity to hear it productively. Otherwise, empty speech will remain as vacuous as abstract universality. Full speech is *produced* in the psychoanalytic relation as the transition from abstract to concrete universality or, in Lacanese, from university to analyst discourse. Everything turns, to quip Hegel, on recognizing that all that is said is *not only as empty speech, but equally as full speech.*

The modern patient, as Žižek has argued, comes to the session with an already rather thorough understanding regarding his/her symptoms. This previ-ously acquired knowledge may even come as an obstacle to building trust and faith in the analyst. The proper manner of conducting the clinical treatment is to neither reject the analysand's knowledge nor to endorse it but, more artfully, to consider the *form* of the exposition and decipher therein the kernel of the *half-said* truth that will begin the unfolding of concrete universality.[17] Left alone, a dream represents the quintessential domain of the mirages of the imaginary and the symptom is mere idiotic *jouissance*. However, once brought into trans-ference and subject to analytic interpretation the dream may become the "royal road to the unconscious" (Freud, 1900). The transference, which includes the interpretation and its reception and metabolization, is where the abstract uni-versality of empty speech meets the concrete universality of full speech. In our transference-phobic times, the diremption of the identity-in-difference of the dream as what wakes us from our slumber ("royal road") and that which keeps us asleep has led to the contradiction by which today's cultural climate wavers between the irreconcilable extremes of the scientistic relegation of the dream to meaningless non-sense and its obscurantist elevation to oracle or divination (the growth of New Ageism and the renewed interest in Jung). In the first case, the dream is reduced to nothing, while in the second it is celebrated as abstract universality.[18] Both miss the *process* by which, through the patient labour of the analytic work, concrete universality slowly unfolds in the transference. What Žižek christens as the understanding "in its productive aspect" (2016, 45) thus finds its noblest exemplar in the analytic process. Its effects will only be known in *retrospect,* as one listens to whether and how the analysand takes up an interpretation; only then will the path to full speech (concrete universality) have been opened. The "owl of Minerva begins its flight only with the falling of dusk" (Hegel, 2008a 16).

Žižek (2012a) argues that we live today in a world dominated by "paraconsistent" logic that rejects the principle of non-contradiction while adhering to the principle of the excluded middle term. We also live in times that reject the paraconsistent and are therefore subject to the vengeance of the paraconsistent – the return in the real of the foreclosed Other of pure thoughts. Nietzsche has never been more of a contemporary; today he truly weeps as we enter the reign of the slave revolt, namely the triumph of vengeful hyper-symptomatic "lower" terms. Under the slavish revaluation of values, the slave is master and defeat is victory, as the meek and downtrodden are the new bearers of the emblems of pride and honour.[19] For Badiou (2007), change has to be sought in "classical" logic endowed with the highest potency of negation, as it endorses both the principle of non-contradiction and that of the excluded middle term. However, Žižek has shown that our solution cannot consist of classical negation since, under the auspices of the paraconsistent logic, "negation gets caught up in the game" (Žižek, 2012a, 1010). Where the slave revolt dominates, negating it will only result in its inexorable triumph. In a paraconsistent world, we must opt instead, Žižek argues, for the logic that rejects both the principle of non-contradiction and that of the excluded middle term – this is the road of the weakest negation. We may link this to Žižek's defence of monarchy; a veritable middle term that breaks the paraconsistent logic by which slave morality co-opts every defeat into a reconfirmation of its hegemony and that also rejects the principle of non-contradiction as this "monarchy" is self-annihilating such that the king is an "idiot" that "dots the 'i's'" (Žižek, 2015), the father a "dead" and "humiliated" figure and, finally, the analyst but a "dummy" echoing one's message. Rather than stark negation, our paraconsistent world requires repetition. Badiou (2007) bemoans the paraconsistent where "everything is identical". Moreover, he fails to think of the affirmation of repetition; something Nietzsche (1969) ardently celebrates as the "marriage ring of rings", namely the eternal return of the same. If "the wound can be healed only by the spear which smote it" (Žižek, 2004) then perhaps nothing is more opportune than repeating the paraconsistent. Against Badiou, we must here hold that the paraconsistent does not posit a drab identity between all things. Rather, it posits the specific identity of opposites through which the said non-self-identities may be better apprehended. As such, a genuinely paraconsistent thought will take us in the direction opposed to diremption where seeming contraries are set against each other. Deleuze (1968) does not lament the state where all is the same since the repetition of the actual is the condition of true change at the level of the virtual. If, according to Žižek (2009a), the superegoic underside of the law is our only prospect of emancipation then the repetition of the paraconsistent logic – which recognizes the hidden identity between Benjamin's (2007) "mythic Lawmaking" and "divine Law-destroying" violence – is our only hope today of breaking the spell of the slave revolt in morality. Through repetition, the paraconsistent logic – heir to the Hegelian dialectic – sublates into the desired logic that rejects both aforementioned principles and thereby opens a third way beyond the endless chatter of the "discussing class" and Nietzsche's nostalgia for antique lands, two options we must rigidly discard lest we wish to keep on weeping. Our only hope today is to will the eternal return and start anew with the speculative courage that recognizes in every ending a mere fading away into the …

Notes

1 Milner (2011) argues that today the idea of *evaluation* reduces humans to things. This is tantamount to obliterating the symptom (the most spiritual part of human-kind). This neglect will not remain without consequence, as the vexed symptom will vengefully return as hyper-spiritual symptom. *Fight Club* provides a great elucidation of the modern tendency towards becoming finite spirit in the narrator's (an unnamed character played by Edward Norton) desire to mould himself to the desire of the Other as his symptom seethes with the vengeance of a neglected "lower" term. Tyler Durden's violence represents the return of the symptom as vengeful hyper-symptom demanding to be reckoned with.

2 One should here speak of *subjectivism* (Heidegger, 1991) as opposed to subjectivity. The former involves the self-celebrating conceit by which the latter is made to fall. Such boastful swagger is attested to in rap and hip hop (veritable exercises in tri-umphalism) as well as in the intellectual sphere that is becoming increasingly akin to a boxing ring. Is it not emblematic of our times that a UFC commentator is also a prominent public intellectual?

3 For Bloch, according to Thomson, "the contradictions within a situation carry within them the potential solution of that situation" (Bloch, 2009, x). Jameson (2010, 72) also notes the immanence of change to the situation: "the future is already present within the present of time: the present is already immanently the future it 'ought' to have".

4 For what is rage other than one-sided impotence?

5 For Badiou, the "subject" has seen the grace of the event while the "individual" lives in a numb and dumb world outside of "truth process". Badiou cannot see that everyone is *not only as Individual but also as Subject*.

6 The word "post-evental" is a neologism commonly used by Badiou and his followers as an adjective denoting the state after the event.

7 Denis Lortie entered the National Assembly of Quebec intent on murdering the gov-ernment. Legendre (1989, 36–37) explains that this act was a patricide with a *corrective* aim, namely that of killing an incestuous primal father. Even the wildest *passage à l'acte* attests to the speculative identity-in-difference of madness and hyper-rationality.

8 Klein's laudable aim of directing the treatment towards the constitution of the *whole object* (with its contradictory traits) reveals a clinical will to transition from a fixation to pure thought towards greater receptivity to the notion.

9　By contrast, Kleinian *concern*, insofar as it is the mark of the depressive position, is a notion. True concern is notional; the care, love and intimacy it gives the other are concomitant with *separation*. Superegoic diremption leads to the contradiction of guilt heightened by every renunciation.

10　The gods of the ancient Greek and Roman pantheons were veritable pure thoughts standing for magnified one-sided human traits, emotions, capacities, tendencies and so on. Christianity marks a gradual *becoming-notion* of God. And, needless to add, this paved the way for atheism.

11　The same kind of stringent dichotomy exists in paranoia where the subject is "innocent" while the Other is "guilty". The Hegelian beautiful soul (like Freud's (1915a) "pure pleasure ego") is the exemplary pure thought, relegating guilt to others while preserving an untarnished self-image.

12　Seneca too hastily claims that "Time heals what reason cannot". Where it seems that time has healed a wound, reason has surely been secretly at work.

13　The Persian poet Hafez stages an exchange between lover and beloved where the former says, "The fragrance of your locks has made me lost to the world". To this the wise beloved replies, "If you only knew that this itself [the fragrance of the locks] will be your guide" (Hafez, 2010). The symptom is akin to this fragrance; we lose ourselves in it and yet that self-oblivion is our greatest guide.

14　The symptom is indeed the spectral-spiritual-materialist antidote to reification.

15　Following Parmenides, Hegel holds that thought and being are isomorphic.

16　Incidentally, this is why Hegel is not a pantheist. Not all is the expression of the absolute or the unconscious (though, pardon the pun, *not-all* may be). The moment of interpretation and its reception or, more generally, the moment of thinking is crucial in making possible the movement towards half-truth.

17　Sometimes a merely well-timed scansion can wake the subject from the "dogmatic slumber" of obsessive musing and reveal the hole in abstract universality from where the movement towards concrete universality begins.

18　Jung's insistence, against Freud, on the universal meaning of symbols is the very quintessence of an abstract universality that eschews the strenuous work of concrete universality.

19　The most comical and distressing of today's contradictions is undoubtedly the fact that toddler-sized hands control the world's greatest nuclear arsenal. Heidegger's "There-Being" (*Da-sein*) – the reflective being "which in its Being has this very Being as an issue" (Heidegger, 1967, 68) – morphs into Hal Ashby's *Being There* (Peter Sellers), a veritable "diremptor-in-chief" granting concrete historical face to the late modern triumph of the common understanding.

References

Adorno, T. W. (1973) *Negative Dialectics*. Translated by Ashton, E. B. Continuum.

Adorno, T. W. (2009) *In Search of Wagner*. Translated by Livingstone, R. Foreword by Žižek, S. Verso Books. Radical Thinkers.

Adorno, T. and Horkheimer, M. (1997). *Dialectic of Enlightenment*. Verso Classics.

Agamben, G. (1998) *Homo Sacer. Sovereign Power and Bare Life*. Translated by Heller-Roazen, D. Stanford University Press.

Agamben, G. (2005) *State of Exception*. Translated by Attell, K. The University of Chicago Press.

Agamben, G. (2009) *What Is an Apparatus? and Other Essays*. Translated by Kishik. D. and Pedatelio, S. Stanford University Press.

Agamben, G. (2011) *The Kingdom and the Glory: For a Theological Genealogy of Economy and Government*. Translated by Chiesa, L. Stanford University Press.

Agamben, G. (2019) *Creation and Anarchy. The Work of Art and the Religion of Capitalism*. Translated by Kotsko, A. Stanford University Press. Meridian.

Allouch, J. (2004) *Ombre de ton chien. Discours psychanalytique, discours lesbien*. Epel.

Allouch, J. (2015) "Psychotic Transference". In Gherovici, P. and Steinkholer, M. (eds.) *Lacan on Madness: Madness, Yes You Can't*. Routledge.

Althusser, L. and Matheron, F. (1999a) *Machiavelli and Us*. Verso.

Althusser, L. (1999b) *Writings on Psychoanalysis: Freud and Lacan*. Columbia University Press.

Althusser, L. (2006) *For Marx*. Translated by Brewster, B. Verso.

Althusser, L. (2012) "Ideology and Ideological State Apparatuses (Notes towards an Investigation)". In Žižek, S. (ed.), *Mapping Ideology*. Verso.

Althusser, L. (2014a) *Initiation à la philosophie pour les non-philosophes*. Texte établi et annoté par Goshgarian, G. M. Presses Universitaires de France.

Althusser, L. (2014b) *The Spectre of Hegel. Early Writings*. Edited with an introduction by Matheron, F. Translated by Goshgarian, G. M. Verso. Radical Thinkers.

Ansermet, F. and Magistretti, P. (2004) *À chacun son cerveau: plasticité neuronale et inconscient*. Odile Jacob.

Antonioni, M. (1975) (director) *The Passenger*.

Apollon, W. (1997) *La différence sexuelle au risqué de la parenté. Conférences et écrits*. Collection le Savoir analytique. Gifric.

Apollon, W. (2005) *La Passion de la vérité*. Gifric.

Ashby, H. (1979) (director) *Being There*.

Attar, F. (1984) *The Conference of Birds*. Penguin Classics.

Badiou, A. (2000) "What Is Love?" In Salecl, R. (ed.), *Sexuation*. Duke University Press.

Badiou, A. (2003a) "The Scene of the Two".Translated by Fulks, B. *Lacanian Ink*. Vol. 21.

Badiou, A. (2003b) "Philosophy and Truth." In *Infinite Thought. Truth and the Return to Philosophy*. Edited and translated by Feltham, O. and Clemens, J. Continuum Books.

Badiou, A. (2007) "The Three Negations". *Cardozo Law Review.* Vol. 29.

Badiou, A. and Truong, N. (2009) *L'Éloge de l'amour*. Flammarion.

Badiou, A. (2010) *Five Lessons on Wagner.* With an afterword by Žižek, S. Translated by Spitzer, S. Verso.

Badiou, A. (2011) *Second Manifesto for Philosophy*. Polity.

Badiou, A. (2013) *"Le Séminaire Lacan". L'Antiphilosophie (1994–1995).* Textes établi par Pienau, V. Ouvertures. Fayard.

Badiou, A. (2015a) "Down with Death". Verso. www.versobooks.com/blogs/2176-badiou-down-with-death

Badiou, A. and Nancy, J. L. (2018) *German Philosophy: A Dialogue*. Edited and with an afterword by Völker, J. Translated by Lambert, R. The MIT Press.

Balmès, F. (2007) *Dieu, le sexe et la vérité*. Éditions érès.

Bell, S. (2010) *Fast Feminism.* Autonomedia.

Benjamin, W. (1969) "The Work of Art in the Age of Mechanical Reproduction". Translated by Zohn, H. from the 1935 essay. In *Illuminations*. Edited by Arendt, H. Schocken Books.

Benjamin, W. (2004) "Capitalism as Religion". In Mendieta, E. (ed.). *The Frankfurt School's Critique of Religion*. Routledge.

Benjamin, W. (2007) "On Violence". In *Reflections: Essays, Aphorisms, Autobiographical Writings*. Edited by Demetz, P. Translated by Jephcott, E. Preface by Wieseltier, L. Schocken Books.

Benvenuto, S. (2016) *What Are Perversions? Sexuality, Ethics, Psychoanalysis*. Karnac.

Bergman, I. (1966) (director) *Persona*.

Bernstein, R. (2002) *Radical Evil: A Philosophical Interrogation*. Polity.

Bion, W. R. (1959) "Attacks on Linking". *The International Journal of Psychoanalysis*. Vol. 40.

Bion, W. R. (1967) "Notes on Memory and Desire". *The Psychoanalytic Forum*. Vol. 2, No. 3.

Bloch, E. (2009) *Atheism in Christianity*. Introduced by Peter Thompson. Verso Books.

Bowie, M. (1991) *Lacan*. Fontana Press.

Bruno, P. (2010) *Lacan, passeur de Marx. L'invention du symptom*. Éditions érès. Point Hors Ligne.

Buber, M. (1971) *I and Thou*. Free Press.

Butler, J. (1997) *The Psychic Life of Power. Theories in Subjection*. Stanford University Press.

Butler, J., Laclau, E. and Žižek, S. (2000) *Contingency, Hegemony, Universality. Contemporary Dialogues on the Left.* Verso.

Chiesa, L. (2016) *The Not-Two: Logic and God in Lacan.* The MIT Press.

Clemens, J. (2013) *Psychoanalysis Is an Antiphilosophy*. Edinburgh University Press.

Coetzee, J. M. (1999) *Disgrace.* Vintage Books.

Copjec, J. (1996) "Evil in the Time of the Finitude World". In Copjec, J. (ed.), *Radical Evil*. Verso Books.

Copjec, J. (2006) "The Object-Gaze: Shame, *Hejab*, Cinema". www.enl.auth.gr/gramma/gramma06/copjec.pdf

Dana, G. (2010) *Quelle politique pour la folie: Le suspense de Freud*. Stock.

Dawkins, R. (1989) *The Selfish Gene*. Oxford University Press.

De Boer, K. (2010) "Hegel's Account of Contradiction in the Science of Logic Reconsidered". *Journal of The History of Philosophy*. Vol. 48.

Deleuze, G. (1968) *Différence et répétition*. Presses Universitaires de France.

Deleuze, G. and Guattari, F. (1972) *L'anti-Oedipe: Capitalisme et schizophrénie*. Les Editions de minuit.

Deleuze, G. and von Sacher-Masoch, L. (1991) *Masochism: Coldness and Cruelty & Venus in Furs*. Zone Books.

De Man, P. (1979) *Allegories of Reading: Figural Language in Rousseau, Nietzsche, Rilke, and Proust*. Yale University Press.

Demoulin, C. (2002) "L'Oedipe, Rêve de Freud". *Psychoanalytische Perspectieven*, Vol. 20, No. 3.

Derrida, J. (1987) *The Post Card. From Socrates to Freud and Beyond*. Translated by Baas, A. The University of Chicago Press.

Derrida, J. (1990) "Difference sexuelle, difference ontologique." In Derrida, J. *Heidegger et la question*. Flammarion.

Derrida, J. (1996) *Archive Fever*. University of Chicago Press.

Derrida, J. (2014) *L'écriture et la Différence*. Points.

Duras, M. (1983) *La Maladie de la mort*. Editions de Minuit.

Fassbinder, R. M. (1979) (director) *The Marriage of Maria Braun*.

Ferenczi, S. (1949) "Confusion of the Tongues Between the Adults and the Child – (The language of Tenderness and of Passion)" *International Journal of Psycho-Analysis*, Vol. 30.

Fincher, D. (1995) (director) *Seven*.

Fincher, D. (1999) (director) *Fight Club*.

Foucault, M. (1972) *Histoire de la folie à l'age classique*. Gallimard.

Foucault, M. (1975) *Surveiller et punir. Naissance de la prison*. Gallimard.

Foucault, M. (1999) *Les Anormaux. Cours au Collège de France (1974–1975)*. Le Seuil.

Frankfurt, H. G. (2005) *On Bullshit*. Princeton University Press.

Freud, S. and Breuer, J. (1893–1895) *Studies on Hysteria. The Standard Edition of the Complete Psychological Works of Sigmund Freud*. Translated by Strachey, J. Vintage, the Hogarth Press. S.E. 2.

Freud, S. (1900) *The Interpretation of Dreams. The Standard Edition of the Complete Psychological Works of Sigmund Freud*. Translated by Strachey, J. Vintage, the Hogarth Press. S.E. 4.

Freud, S. (1905) *Three Essays on the Theory of Sexuality. The Standard Edition of the Complete Psychological Works of Sigmund Freud*. Translated by Strachey, J. Vintage, the Hogarth Press. S.E. 7.

Freud, S. (1909) *Notes Upon A Case of Obsessional Neurosis. The Standard Edition of the Complete Psychological Works of Sigmund Freud*. Translated by Strachey, J. Vintage, the Hogarth Press. S.E. 10.

Freud, S. (1911) *Psychoanalytic Notes on an Autobiographical Account of a Case of Paranoia (Dementia Paranoides). The Standard Edition of the Complete Psychological Works of Sigmund Freud*. Translated by Strachey, J. Vintage, the Hogarth Press. S.E. 12.

Freud, S. (1913) *Totem and Taboo. The Standard Edition of the Complete Psychological Works of Sigmund Freud*. Translated by Strachey, J. Vintage, the Hogarth Press. S.E. 13.

Freud, S. (1914) *On Narcissism; An Introduction. The Standard Edition of the Complete Psychological Works of Sigmund Freud*. Translated by Strachey, J. Vintage, the Hogarth Press. S.E. 14.

Freud, S. (1915a) *Instincts and their Vicissitudes. The Standard Edition of the Complete Psychological Works of Sigmund Freud.* Translated by Strachey, J. Vintage, the Hogarth Press. S.E. 14.

Freud, S. (1915b) *The Unconscious. The Standard Edition of the Complete Psychological Works of Sigmund Freud.* Translated by Strachey, J. Vintage, the Hogarth Press. S.E. 14.

Freud, S. (1916–1917) *Introductory Lectures on Psycho-analysis. The Standard Edition of the Complete Psychological Works of Sigmund Freud.* Translated by Strachey, J. Vintage, the Hogarth Press. S.E. 16.

Freud, S. (1917) *Mourning and Melancholia. The Standard Edition of the Complete Psychological Works of Sigmund Freud.* Translated by Strachey, J. Vintage, the Hogarth Press. S.E. 14.

Freud, S. (1920) *The Psychogenesis of a Case of Homosexuality in a Woman. The Standard Edition of the Complete Psychological Works of Sigmund Freud.* Translated by Strachey, J. Vintage, the Hogarth Press. S.E. 18.

Freud, S. (1924) *The Dissolution of the Oedipus Complex. The Standard Edition of the Complete Psychological Works of Sigmund Freud.* Translated by Strachey, J. Vintage, the Hogarth Press. S.E. 19.

Freud, S. (1925) *On Negation. The Standard Edition of the Complete Psychological Works of Sigmund Freud.* Translated by Strachey, J. Vintage, the Hogarth Press. S.E. 19.

Freud, S. (1927) *The Future of An Illusion. The Standard Edition of the Complete Psychological Works of Sigmund Freud.* Translated by Strachey, J. Vintage, the Hogarth Press. S.E. 21.

Freud, S. (1930) *Civilization and its Discontents. The Standard Edition of the Complete Psychological Works of Sigmund Freud.* Translated by Strachey, J. Vintage, the Hogarth Press. S.E. 21.

Freud, S. (1937) *Analysis Terminable and Interminable. The Standard Edition of the Complete Psychological Works of Sigmund Freud.* Translated by Strachey, J. Vintage, the Hogarth Press. S.E. 23.

Freud, S. (1938) *Splitting of the Ego in the Process of Defense. The Standard Edition of the Complete Psychological Works of Sigmund Freud.* Translated by Strachey, J. Vintage, the Hogarth Press. S.E. 23.

Gherovici, P. (2010) *Please Select Your Gender. From the Invention of Hysteria to the Democratizing of Transgenderism.* Routledge. Taylor and Francis Group.

Gherovici, P. (forthcoming) "Authenticity and Truth in Clinical Psychoanalytic Practice". *Psychoanalytic Discourse.* Vol. 5, No. 1.

Goddard, J. L. (2014) (director and writer, produced by Alain Sarde) *Adieu au langage.*

Goffman, A. (2014) *On the Run: Fugitive Life in an American City.* University of Chicago Press.

Goodrich, P. and Carlson, D. G. (eds.) (1998) *Law and the Postmodern Mind. Essays on Psychoanalysis and Jurisprudence.* The University of Michigan Press.

Green, A. (2007) *Narcissisme de vie Narcissisme de mort.* Les Editions de Minuit.

Grigg, R. (2015) "Melancholia and the Unabandoned Object". In Gherovici, P. and Steinkholer, M. (eds.) (2015) *Lacan on Madness: Madness, Yes You Can't.* Routledge.

Guyomard, P. (1992) *La jouissance du tragique. Antigone, Lacan et le désir de l'analyste.* La psychoanalyse prise au mot. Aubier.

Hafez, S. M. (2010) *The Divan of Hafez.* Fekre Rooz.

Han, B. C. (2018) *Topology of Violence.* Translated by Demarco, A. The MIT Press.

Hegel, G. W. F. (1969) *Science of Logic.* Translated by Miller, A. V. Foreword by Findlay, J. N. Humanity Books, an imprint of Prometheus Books.

Hegel, G. W. F. (1970) *On Art, Religion, Philosophy. Introductory Lectures to the Realm of Absolute Spirit.* Edited with an Introduction by Gray, J. G. Harper Touchbooks. Harper and Row.

Hegel, G. W. F. (1975) *Lectures on the Philosophy of World History.* Translated by Nisbet, H. B. With an Introduction by Forbes, D. Cambridge University Press.

Hegel, G. W. F. (1977) *Phenomenology of Spirit.* Translated by Miller, A. V. With analysis of the text and foreword by Findlay, J. N. Oxford University Press.

Hegel, G. W. F. (1991) *The Encyclopaedia Logic.* A new translation with Introduction and notes by Geraets, T. F., Suchting, W. A. and Harris, H. S. Hackett Publishing Company, Inc.

Hegel, G. W. F. (2008a) *Outlines of the Philosophy of Right.* Oxford University Press.

Hegel, G. W. F. (2008b) *Hegel: Lectures on the Philosophy of Religion: Volume III: The Consummate Religion.* Oxford University Press.

Heidegger, M. (1967) *Being and Time.* Translated by Macquarrie, J. and Robinson, E. Basil Blackwell.

Heidegger, M. (1991) *Nietzsche. Volumes 1 and 2. The Will to Power as Art. The Eternal Recurrence of the Same.* Translated by Krell, D. F. Harper San Francisco. A Division of Harper Collins Publishers.

Heidegger, M. (2015) *Hegel.* Translated by Arel, J. and Feuerhahn, N. Indiana University Press.

Henry, M. (2003) *Généalogie de la psychanalyse.* Presses Universitaires France.

Hitchens, C. (2007) *God Is Not Great.* Hachette Book Group.

Jameson, F. (2007) *Late Marxism: Adorno, Or, the Persistence of the Dialectic.* Verso Books. Radical Thinkers.

Jameson, F. (2010) *The Hegel Variations: On the Phenomenology of Spirit.* Verso.

Johnston, A. (2004) "The Cynic's Fetish: Slavoj Žižek and the Dynamics of Belief". *Psychoanalysis, Culture & Society.* Vol. 9.

Joyce, J. (2012) *Finnegans Wake.* Oxford University Press.

Kant, I. (1929) *Critique of Pure Reason.* Translated by Smith, N. K. Macmillan (reissue St. Martin's Press, 1965).

Kleist, H. (1972) "On the Marionette Theatre". Translated by Neumiller, T. G. *The Drama Review: TDR.* Vol. 16, No. 3, The "Puppet" Issue. The MIT Press.

Kojève, A. (1980) *Introduction à la lecture de Hegel.* Gallimard.

Kojève, A. (2014) *The Notion of Authority (A Brief Presentation).* Edited and introduced by Terré, F. Translated by Weslati, H. Verso.

Koyré, A. (2016) *From the Closed World to the Infinite Universe.* Angelico Press.

Kristeva, J. (1984) *Revolution in Poetic Language.* Columbia University Press.

Lacan, J. (1969) "Petit discours aux psychiatres". Conférence au cercle d'étude dirigé par Ey, H., inédit.

Lacan, J. (1970) "Of Structure as the Inmixing of an Otherness Prerequisite to Any Subject Whatever." www.lacan.com/hotel.htm

Lacan, J., (1974) "Les non-dupes errent". Unpublished.

Lacan, J. (1975) *De la psychose paranoïaque: Dans ses rapports avec la personnalité.* Éditions du Seuil.

Lacan, J. (1977) *The Seminar of Jacques Lacan. Book XI. The Four Fundamental Concepts of Psychoanalysis* (1963–64). Edited by Allain-Miller, J. Translated by Sheridan, A. W. W. Norton & Company.

Lacan J. (1979) "Lacan pour Vincennes!". *Ornicar ?*, n°17/18, printemps 1979.

Lacan, J. (1981) *Les psychoses. Séminaire III.* Texte établi par Miller, J.-A. Éditions du Seuil.

Lacan, J. (1986) *Le séminaire. Livre VII. L'éthique de la psychanalyse.* Le Seuil.

Lacan, J. (1987–1988) "Notes en allemand préparatoires à la conference sur la chose freudienne". Translated from German to French by Morel, G. and Kaltenbeck, F. Ornicar? No. 42.

Lacan, J. (1988) *The Seminar of Jacques Lacan. Book II. The Ego in Freud's Theory and in the Technique of Psychoanalysis* (1954–1955). Edited by Allain-Miller, J. Translated by Tomaselli, S. with notes by Forrester, J. Cambridge University Press.

Lacan, J. (1992) *The Seminar of Jacques Lacan. Book VII. The Ethics of Psychoanalysis* (1959–1960). Edited by Allain-Miller, J. Translated by Porter, D. Routledge.

Lacan, J. (1994) *Le séminaire. Livre IV. La relation d'objet.* Le Seuil.

Lacan, J. (1998) *The Seminar of Jacques Lacan. Book XX. Encore* (1972–1973). Translated with notes by Fink, B. W.W Norton & Company.

Lacan, J. (2001a) *Autres Écrits.* Éditions du Seuil.

Lacan, J. (2001b) *Le Séminaire de Jacques Lacan. Livre VIII. Le transfert* (1960–1961). Texte établi par Allain-Miller, J. Éditions du Seuil.

Lacan, J. (2002) *The Seminar of Jacques Lacan. Book XIV. The Logic of Phantasy.* Translated by Gallagher, C. from unedited French manuscripts. Karnac.

Lacan, J. (2004) *Le séminaire. Livre X. L'angoisse.* Le Seuil.

Lacan, J. (2005a) *Le Séminaire. Livre 23. Le Sinthome* (1975–1976). Le Seuil.

Lacan, J. (2005b) *Triomphe de la religion. Précédé de discours aux catholiques.* Le Seuil.

Lacan, J. (2006) *Écrits.* Translated by Fink, B. In collaboration with Fink, H. and Grigg, R. W. W. Norton and Company. *Page numbers refer to the French original displayed on the margin of the text.*

Lacan, J. (2007). *The Seminar, Book XVII. The Other Side of Psychoanalysis,* 1969–1970. Edited by Miller, J.-A. Translated by Grigg, R. W. W. Norton.

Laplanche, J. (1999a) "Masochism and the General Theory of Seduction". Translated by Thurston, L. In Laplanche. J., *Essays on Otherness.* Edited by Fletcher, J. Routledge.

Laplanche, J. (1999b) "Interpretation between Determinism and Hermeneutics: A Restatement of the Problem". Translated by Thurston, L. In Laplanche, J., *Essays on Otherness.* Edited by Fletcher, J. Routledge.

La Rochefoucauld, F. (1976) *Maximes et réflexions diverses: Suivi de Réflexions diverses et Maximes.* Flammarion.

Laurent, E. (2012) "Presentation of the Theme for the Eleventh Congress of the NLS, Athens 2012", delivered in French at the NLS Congress in Tel Aviv, 17 June 2012.

Leader, D. (2012) *Strictly Bipolar.* Penguin Books Ltd.

Lebrun, G. (1972) *La Patience du concept: Essai sur le discours hégélien.* Gallimard.

Lebrun, G. (2004) *L'Envers de la Dialectique: Hegel à la lumière de Nietzsche.* Éditions du Seuil. L'Ordre philosophique.

Leclaire, S. (1968) *Psychanalyser: Un essai sur l'ordre de l'inconscient et la pratique de la lettre.* Éditions du Seuil.

Leclaire, S. (1975) *On tue un enfant.* Éditions du Seuil.

Legendre, P. (1989) *Le crime du caporal Lortie. Traité sur le père. Leçons VIII.* Champs Flammarion. Librairie Arthème Fayard.

Legendre, P. (1998) "The Other Dimension of Law". In Goodrich, P. and Carlson, D. G. (eds.) (1998).

Legendre, P. (2000) *La fabrique de l'homme occidentale.* Éditions Arte. Mille et une nuits.

Levinas, E. (2003) *On Escape*. Translated by B. Bergo. Stanford University Press.

Lévi-Strauss, C. (1991) *La pensée sauvage*. Pocket.

Maleval, J-C. (2000) *La Forclusion du nom-du-père. Le concept et sa clinique*. Éditions du Seuil.

Maleval, J-C. (2015) "Treatment of the Psychoses and Contemporary Psychoanalysis". In Gherovici, P. and Steinkholer, M. (eds.) *Lacan on Madness: Madness, Yes You Can't*. Routledge.

Massat, G. (2007) "D'Oreste à Lacan". Texte de l'intervention au Cercle Psychanalytique de Paris. http://psychanalyse-paris.com/1017-D-Oreste-a-Lacan.html

McGowan, T. (2019) *Emancipation After Hegel: Achieving a Contradictory Revolution*. Columbia University Press.

Meillassoux, Q. (2008). *After Finitude: An Essay on the Necessity of Contingency*. With a preface by Badiou, A. Translated by Brassier, R. Continuum Books.

Milner, J-C. (1995) *L'oeuvre claire. Lacan, la science, la philosophie*. Éditions du Seuil.

Milner, J-C. (2011) *La Politique des choses*. Verdier. Court traité politique 1.

Moncayo, R. (2014) *The Emptiness of Oedipus: Identification and Non-Identification in Lacanian Psychoanalysis*. Routledge.

Montaigne, M. (2009) *Les essais*. Pocket.

Morel, G. (2010) "Psychoanalytic Anatomy". In Salecl, R. (ed.) *Sexuation*. Duke University Press.

Masson, J.M. (1984) *Assault on Truth: Freud's Suppression of the Seduction Theory*. Farrar Straus & Giroux.

Nasio, J-D. (2005) *Le Fantasme: Le plaisir de lire Lacan*. Payot.

Nietzsche, F. (1969) *Thus Spoke Zarathustra. A Book for Everyone and No One*. Translated by Hollingdale, R. J. Penguin Books.

Nietzsche, F. (1974) *The Gay Science*. Vintage Books. A Division of Random House.

Nietzsche, F. (1996) *Human All Too Human. A Book for Free Spirits*. Translated by Hollingdale, R. J. Cambridge University Press.

Nietzsche, F. (1998) *On the Genealogy of Morality*. Translated by Clarke, M. and Swensen, A. Hacket Publishing Company.

Nietzsche, F. (1999) *The Birth of Tragedy and Other Writings*. Edited by Geuss, R. and Speirs, R. Cambridge University Press.

Nietzsche, F. (2000a) *Beyond Good and Evil*. Translated and edited by Kaufmann, W. *Basic Writings of Nietzsche*. The Modern Library.

Nietzsche, F. (2000b) *Ecce Homo. Basic Writings of Nietzsche*. Translated and edited by Kaufmann, W. The Modern Library.

Nietzsche, F. (2005) *Twilight of the Idols or How to Philosophize with a Hammer*. Translated by Norman, J. In *The Anti-Christ, Ecce Homo, Twilight of the Idols and Other Writings*. Edited by Ridley, A. and Norman, J. Cambridge University Press.

Pagès, C. (2015) *Qu'est-ce que la dialectique?* Vrin –Chemins Philosophiques.

Papageorgiou-Legendre, A. (1990). *Filiation: Fondement généalogique de la psychanalyse*. Fayard.

Phillips, A. (1997). "Keeping it Moving". In Butler, J. (1997).

Phillips, A. (2012). "Judas' Gift". *London Review of Books*, 05 January 2012.

Plato (2000) *The Republic*. Dover Publications.

Plato (2015) *Phaedrus*. Cambridge University Press.

Pommier, G. (2013) *Le nom propre. Fonctions logiques et inconscientes*. Presses Universitaires de France.

Radiguet, R. (2004) *Le diable au corps*. J'ai lu.

Reinhardt, K., Žižek, S. and Santner, E. (2006) *The Neighbor: Three Inquiries in Political*. University of Chicago Press.

Rosolato, G. (2002) *Le Sacrifice: Repères psychanalytiques*. Presses Universitaires de France.

Safouan, M. (2004) *Four Lessons of Psychoanalysis*. Other Press.

Salecl, R. (2000) "Introduction". In Salecl, R. (ed.), *Sexuation*. Duke University Press.

Santner, E. (1996) *My Own Private Germany: Daniel Paul Schreber's Secret History of Modernity*. Princeton University Press.

Santner, E. (2011) *The Royal Remains: The People's Two Bodies and the Endgames of Sovereignty*. University of Chicago Press.

Schmitt, C. (1985) *Political Theology. Four Chapters on the Concept of Sovereignty*. Translated and with an introduction by Schwab, G. With a new foreword by Strong, B. The University of Chicago Press.

Schopenhauer, A. (1966) *The World as Will and Representation*. Volume 1. Dover Publications.

Schreber, D-P. (2000) *Memoirs of My Nervous Illness*. Introduction by Rosemary Dinnage. NYRB Classics.

Schütz, A. (1998) "Sons of the Writ, Sons of Wrath: Pierre Legendre's Critique of Rational Law-Giving". In Goodrich, P. and Carlson, D. G. (eds.) (1998).

Seneca, L-A. (2016) *Moral Letters to Lucilius*. Translated by Gummere, R. M. CreateSpace Independent Publishing Platform.

Sloterdijk, P. (2018) *What Happened in the Twentieth Century?: Towards a Critique of Extremist Reason*. Polity.

Soler, C. (2000) "The Curse on Sex". In Salecl, R. (ed.), *Sexuation*. Duke University Press.

Soler, C. (2011) *Les affects lacaniens*. Presses Universitaires de France.

Soler, C. (2012) *L'inconscient à ciel ouvert de la psychose*. Presses Universitaires du Mirail.

Soler, C. (2015) *Lacan, Lecteur de Joyce*. Presses Universitaires de France.

Verhaeghe, P. (1999). *Love in a Time of Loneliness. Three Essays on Drive and Desire*. Translated by Peters, P. and Langham, T. Karnac.

Van Haute, P. and Geyskens, T. (2012) *A Non-Oedipal Psychoanalysis? A Clinical Anthropology of Hysteria in the Works of Freud and Lacan*. Leuven University Press.

Wegener, M. (2016) "Psychoanalysis and Topology – Four Vignettes". In *Psychoanalysis: Topological Perspectives: New Conceptions of Geometry and Space in Freud and Lacan*. Transcript Verlag.

Wenders, W. (1984) (director) *Paris, Texas*.

Winnicott, D. W. (1971) *Playing and Reality*. Routledge.

Winnicott, D. W. (1969) "The Use of an Object". *The International Journal of Psychoanalysis*. Vol. 50.

Zenoni, A. (2013) "Orienting Oneself in Transference" in "Psychosis Today". *Psychoanalytic Notebooks*. Issue 26. The London Society of the New Lacanian School.

Žižek, S. (1989) *The Sublime Object of Ideology*. Verso.

Žižek, S. (1992) *Looking Awry*. The MIT Press.

Žižek, S. (1996) "Selfhood as Such Is Spirit: F. W. J Schelling on the Origins of Evil". In Copjec, J. (ed.), *Radical Evil*. Verso.

Žižek, S. (1998a) "Why Does the Law Need an Obscene Supplement?" In Goodrich, P. and Carlson, D. G. (eds.) (1998).

Žižek, S. (1998b) "For a Leftist Appropriation of the European Legacy". *Journal of Political Ideologies*. Vol., 3, No. 1.

Žižek, S. (1999) *The Ticklish Subject. The Absent Centre of Political Ontology.* Verso.

Žižek, S. (2003) *The Puppet and the Dwarf.* The MIT Press.

Žižek, S. (2004) "The Politics of Redemption. Why is Wagner Worth Saving?" *Journal of Philosophy and Scripture.*

Žižek, S. (2006) *The Parallax View.* The MIT Press.

Žižek, S. (2007) *The Indivisible Remainder. Schelling and Related Matters.* Verso Books.

Žižek, S. (2009a) "De la démocratie à la violence divine". In *Démocratie, dans quel état?* La Fabrique.

Žižek, S. (2009b) *Organs Without Bodies. On Deleuze and Consequences.* Routledge.

Žižek, S. (2012a) *Less Than Nothing: Hegel and the Shadow of Dialectical Materialism.* Verso Books.

Žižek, S. (2012b) "Hegel Versus Heidegger: Heidegger's Critique of Hegel". E-flux. Journal #32 – February 2012.

Žižek, S. (2015) *Absolute Recoil: Towards a New Foundation of Dialectical Materialism.* Verso Books.

Žižek, S. (2016) *Disparities.* Bloomsbury Academic.

Žižek, S. (2017) *In Defense of Lost Causes.* Verso.

Žižek, S. (2018) *Living in the End Times.* Verso Books.

Žižek, S. (2019) *Sex and the Failed Absolute.* Bloomsbury Academic.

Zupančič, A. (1996) "Kant with Don Juan and Sade". In Copjec, J. (ed.), *Radical Evil.* Verso Books.

Zupančič, A. (2000) "The Case of the Perforated Sheet". In Salecl, R. (ed.) *Sexuation.* Duke University Press.

Zupančič, A. (2017) *What Is Sex?* MIT Press. Short Circuits series.

Index

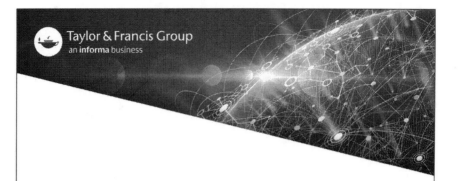